DOCUMENTS IN CANADIAN WOMEN'S HISTORY

VOLUME II

CANADIAN WOMEN
ON
THE MOVE
1867-1920

Edited by
Beth Light
and
Joy Parr

A co-publication of
New Hogtown Press
and
The Ontario Institute for Studies
in Education

New Hogtown Press
12 Hart House Circle
University of Toronto
Toronto, Ontario
M4S 1A1

The Ontario Institute for Studies in Education
252 Bloor Street West
Toronto
Ontario
M5S 1V6

Canadian Cataloguing in Publication Data

Main entry under title:
Canadian women on the move, 1867-1920

(Documents in Canadian women's history ; 2)
Bibliography: p.
Includes index.
ISBN 0-919940-18-8

1. Women - Canada - Social conditions - 19th century. 2. Women - Canada - Social conditions - 20th century. 3. Women - Canada - History - 19th century. 4. Women - Canada - History - 20th century. I. Light, Beth, 1952- II. Parr, Joy, 1949- III. Series.

HQ1453.C36 1983   305.4'2'0971   C83-098870-X

Cover: Girls learning to type, Montreal, Quebec, Pointe-aux-Trembles School, The United Church of Canada Archives.

Special thanks to New Hogtown Press volunteers John Crossley, Marta Danylewycz, Missy Powell, Alison Prentice, Pat Schulz, and Pat Staton.

New Hogtown Press would like to acknowledge the support of the Students' Administrative Council of the University of Toronto.

ISBN 0-919940-18-8

Printed in Canada

1   2   3   4   5   78   68   58   48   38

Contents *whole book*

INTRODUCTION TO THE SERIES

Women "have no past, no history...." Although historians of women tried to remedy this lack long before Simone de Beauvoir pointed it out in 1949 in *The Second Sex*, her statement nevertheless revealed a basic truth. History has been largely a male preserve with the result that women have indeed been denied a sense of their own past. The Women in Canadian History Documentary Series is part of an effort by contemporary feminist historians to end, once and for all, that denial. One of our goals is to retrieve and make accessible, for a larger public as well as for students and teachers, records of the past as the women of Canada experienced it. Beyond this, we hope also to add something to the interpretation and understanding of that past. The ultimate goal is the creation of a Canadian women's history, one that speaks both to women about the sources of their present lives and to everyone about history seen from women's point of view.

Approaching women's history through documents has its rewards and its frustrations. The primary frustration is the very difficulty of finding documents, for women's records have not been carefully preserved. The use of those documents that have been preserved is made difficult by the biases inherent in the creation, preservation, and accessibility of the documents. Upper-class women had the leisure and education necessary to write letters and keep diaries; lower-class women did not. Fortunately, rewards far outweigh the difficulties, because the sources for women's history are richly varied. There are letters and diaries of literate women, and the records of their multitudinous associations. There are apprenticeship indentures, court records, or the records of schools, as well as those of a variety of other institutions catering in whole or in part to women or children, which give some insight into the lives of illiterate or very young women. In the decorative, fine, and commercial arts, historians have another type of source: samplers, portraits, drawings, and advertisments tell a great deal about the women who created them or the women who, more often, were their subjects or intended audience. Even popular song may have something to say about the lives of women. And there are travellers' descriptions and newspaper stories. As some of the items on this list suggest, documents about women are not always written by women. The writings of missionaries, fur traders, literary men, and the keepers of church and government records, as well as the writings of fathers, sons, brothers, and husbands are important sources in women's history. Where the women themselves have been totally silent, such records in fact are often our only sources and, it must be said, are usually as fascinating for what can be read between the lines as for what is explicit. Whatever the nature of the documents, and whether they are by women or by men, they produce a sense of immediacy not otherwise available to the student of the past—a sense that one is dealing with the reality of historical lives.

The series is designed to focus on several themes. A prominent one is the life cycle—the passage of women through the various stages of life from childhood to old age. A second theme is the tension between public and domestic life, especially since this tension appears to increase over time. Finally there is the theme of women's needs and concerns juxtaposed against a variety of demands: the demands of changing economic conditions, of governments, of churchmen, and of advertisers—indeed, of a whole host of people, both male and female, who expressed views, exerted pressure, made requests, or issued ultimata concerning what women should be or do. Introductions to each volume and to individual chapters alert readers to these themes, to recent interpretations of Canadian women's history, and to some of the questions that current research poses.

The questions perhaps loom largest. Who, in the final analysis, were the women of Acadia and New France, of British North America and Canada? What were their major concerns and interests, their problems and achievements, joys or sorrows? It is our hope that some answers to these questions will emerge from our documents and that they will spur us on to look for more—to find out who we were and are, and who we might become.

Alison Prentice,
Series Editor

ACKNOWLEDGEMENTS

We have been looking for historical documents on the lives of Canadian women for six years now, always with pleasure although sometimes for longer hours and with quite different results than we had expected. The sources we have consulted rest in repositories across the country. We could not have found nearly so much, nor of such great variety and quality, without the help of friends, archivists, and colleagues who checked old file boxes and left their own work to do ours, tracing down obscure references and half remembered clues. Paula Bourne, Bettina Bradbury, le collectif Clio, Marg Conrad, A.W. Currie, Marta Danylewycz, Jean Dryden, Micheline Dumont-Johnson, Nadia Eid, Chad Gaffield, Sandra Guillaume, Linda Hale, Kent Haworth, George Henderson, Isabel Kaprilien, Marie Lavigne, Anne MacDermaid, Marvin McInnis, Diane Matters, Tom Nesmith, Janice Newton, Michael Owen, Keith Ralston, Barbara Roberts, Shirley Spragge, George Tompkins and J. Donald Wilson all helped in this way. Over the winters' writing and revising Pat Schulz, Alison Prentice, Ida Smith, Christine Johanson, Sally van Luven, Shirley Harmer, Veronica Strong-Boag, Rebecca Coulter, and Janice Dickin-McGinnis offered us advice, encouragement and thoughtful criticism as did our colleagues in the Department of History and Philosophy of Education, Ontario Institute for Studies in Education, the Department of History, University of British Columbia, and the Department of History, Queen's University. The typing and retyping continued so that it seemed without end. Karen Donnelly, Barbara Latimer and Beulah Worrell did this work speedily and in good heart and to them we are especially grateful. The book relied heavily on research funds provided by the Ontario Institute for Studies in Education.

Reasonable efforts were made to trace the owners of copyright for all documents. They are acknowledged throughout the book immediately above the relevant citation. Without their generous assistance, *Canadian Women on the Move* would not have been possible. The spelling and grammar of the original documents have been retained but punctuation has sometimes been added for clarification.

Beth Light
and Joy Parr
Toronto, 1983

INTRODUCTION

The Canadian women who lived in the last decades of Victoria's reign, through the years of Laurier and the First World War, are difficult to see through the traditional historian's lens. They have no political history in the conventional sense. There was none of their sex among those who drafted the British North America Act nor among the nation's voters in the half century thereafter. At its beginnings the new nation existed only in its political dimension. The Confederation was frail and improbable, a union urged by the weary British upon a scattered array of communities whose distinctive economic foundations and cultural priorities seemed less likely to draw them together than apart. There is a national history of men in politics from these earliest days, but a national history of women is almost fanciful. There was no common Canadian womankind in 1867.

If women were without political rights, they were not immune from political events, nor uninfluenced by the transformations normally charted in the history of men. In 1867 four colonies joined together in the new Confederation, Ontario, Quebec, New Brunswick and Nova Scotia, the latter two under protest. The new political entity was to be melded not from stable constituent parts but from disparate elements, each of which was undergoing considerable flux. The central Canadian provinces were still predominantly rural but Ontario was facing strong competition and a weakening demand in its traditional export markets for wheat. The lands of Southern Ontario had been settled. The new farms of Muskoka were not faring well and prospects further north seemed even less promising. Along the Saguenay and St Maurice of Quebec opening new lands was a hard struggle. Reluctantly the limits of agricultural settlement in the region were being defined. Although new urban frontiers were opening, the manufacturing sector remained small, and the prospects and necessary patterns of city life unfamiliar. The Maritimes were leaving a time of considerable prosperity based on international trade and looking to the region's coal to replace wood as the foundation of the local economy.

Confronted with the need to change, British North Americans of pre-Confederation times had most often moved on. In the early nineteenth century, migration to Glengarry and Cape Breton had given Scots crofter communities another generation's reprieve from the market economy. In the following decades movement away from the St Lawrence had allowed settlers of the valley, both English and French, to continue in their pioneering farming patterns. The ways in which Canadians of first generation after Confederation reacted to the growing constrictions upon their traditional ways of life were similar. They looked to the north and west, to the lands occupied by native peoples and the widely separated outposts of fur trade society. Or they looked south to familiar jobs in ship-building and domestic service or to temporary wage work in American industry for cash to shore up the family fortunes at home. But everywhere they found change. The market economy, the capitalization and mechanization of production, the partition of home from workplace, of producer from consumer were transforming life in farm and city, separating and increasingly differentiating the material and social circumstances of women and men.

The western lands already sustained complex communities. Until about 1811 the women of fur trade society were native people or the mixed blood descendants of Amerindian women and European men. The arrival of white wives in the early nineteenth century began to erode the social position of traders' country-born companions. The factors' new spouses changed the material culture of the north west, bringing with them the accoutrements of gentry family life—musical instruments, china, and furnishings. In both Red River and the northern posts white wives allied with Protestant clergymen to insist that the more flexible marriage customs of fur trade society be replaced by genteel domestic forms and values, by a circumspect sexual division of spheres, a scrupulous restriction of sociability to those of similar social station, and firm domestic segregation of servants. These changes, combined with the close Victorian associations between dark colour and low rank and missionary assertions that Christian religious practice and sacraments define moral conduct, cast unchurched mixed-blood women and their families outside the newly forming respectability. Even in the late nineteenth century vestiges of this hypergentility remained among women in the north, perhaps a reaction to its disparate cultures and the surrounding wilderness. Young white women raised along the Mackenzie and the Athabaska were sent to Montreal or abroad to learn to be exemplary ladies.[1]

However, as long as the fur trade remained the primary economic activity of the western interior, Métis or Indian women were valued for their skills in the preparation of pemmican and pelts. In 1870, a portion of the western trading lands was transferred from the Hudson's Bay Company via the British crown to the Dominion of Canada. The fur trade ended, and with it the mixed economies of hunting, gathering, grazing, and cultivation, which had sustained the mixed-blood families of the west. The land claims of the Métis, founded on the Indian blood of their mothers, were extinguished by grants of land and scrip and the special role of Indian and mixed-blood women in the fur trade economy vanished with the hunt.

The new women of the west were Ontarians, the wives and daughters of rural families looking for lands fertile enough to sustain the familiar rotations in grains and yield surpluses sufficient to provide farms for their sons and dowries for their daughters. In the Legislative Assembly, the men who represented them crafted a school system and institutions of municipal government modelled on those of the old province. In each locality women set about to reproduce the traditions they had left behind, the missionary societies, Bible classes, teas and suppers attached to religious fellowship, the temperance organizations, women's institutes, and less formal networks through which medical knowledge and the craft skills of domestic life were shared. The Mennonites and Icelanders who arrived soon after Manitoba entered Confederation remained apart in their new communities and the old francophone families of the Red River Valley were pressed outside the mainstream. For a decade and a half the lands to the west of Brandon, Manitoba, attracted few white settlers. The railway connection with the east was complete in 1885 but the CPR seemed in no great rush to secure traffic.[2]

Yet in the farms of the west, as in those of maritime and central Canada, important changes were taking place. Domestic production was no longer self-sufficient; efficient home manufactures incorporated tools and materials purchased on the market, and sent certain parts of the production process to specialists outside the home. Women still hand produced their own and their children's clothing, and the family's knitted outerwear, socks, and stockings from purchased textiles and yarn, but spinning and weaving were no longer done by the hearth. Some town merchants took the eggs and butter a farm woman produced for sale on account toward the needles, fibres, and fancy grocery goods she needed for home manufactures. But the lingering barter system provided only a small cushion against so substantial a change. In each household new sources of cash income had to be found. Men turned their rural carpentry, masonry, and cheesemaking skills to part-time village wage work; girls and women used their domestic competence to supplement the household income by cleaning schools or township halls and serving or doing laundry for hotel or restaurant keepers in neighbouring towns. In fruit-raising districts, they took jobs picking and packing for neighbours who had expanded their holdings to meet growing urban markets. Two kinds of work had developed: work away from home for wages and work in the home that contributed to the family well-being but did not have an easily reckoned worth in cash. Wage work was most often men's. The other work, invaluable but without price, became more characteristically women's.

Through the eighties the industry of central Canada grew and diversified; iron and steel stimulated by the railway builders, farm machinery by the capitalization of eastern mixed agriculture and the prospect of new lands opening in the west, cotton and woollen textiles, boots and shoes and furniture by the tariffs of the National Policy and the hope that the domestic market for these goods would soon be large and healthy. Until 1901, however, there were still more Canadians leaving the Dominion each year than newcomers arriving; on balance the United States was still more the land of opportunity than her northern neighbour. Inside Canada a large migration from country to city and from agricultural to manufacturing and service employments was underway.

Sometime between 1911 and 1921 the population balance shifted toward the city, and since then Canadians have been predominantly urban dwellers.

For skilled working men the rising preeminence of factories as work-places entailed both a loss of autonomy and a devaluation of their labour. For women as for unskilled men this transition offered certain advantages. The variety of female employments increased. In the minds of young women factory work offered, if anything, more independence than the alternative, domestic service. And even meagre industrial pay was more ample than the merely token wages of the hired girl. Against these gains, the new female wage earner had to weigh the greater insecurity of employment, the numbing intensity of the work, and the separation from family that urban jobs frequently entailed—a shifting balance that led many to return, when opportunity offered, to the more domestic and rural patterns of their mothers. Or using an alternative strategy rural women who stayed in the cities with wage-earning husbands and teenage children continued to practise their country skills, keeping a cow, some chickens and pigs, and a backyard garden to maintain for themselves the family status attached to productive labour and partially protect their households from the vagaries of the market economy. Still, handling cash had become an important part of household management. The impact of industrialization was greatest upon female employment in Ontario and Quebec; in the Maritimes the manufacturing enterprises which had flowered in the eighties soon faded. In British Columbia the base of the economy remained the resource sector and the opportunities for paid non-domestic work for women were few.[3]

Educational institutions were being pressed to accommodate more women. In Ontario at Confederation, girls might attend high school, but the Latin options required for advanced studies usually were closed to them. Across Canada, beginning in the Maritimes, the gates of the universities gradually opened in the next two decades, first in arts, then in the sciences and medicine. These opportunities, combined with a growing number of places in nursing schools and teacher training programmes, drew many more young women to prepare for their entrance and bargain with their parents to keep part of their teen years free for studies. In the 1870s there were more girls than boys in the high school, for example, of Orillia, Ontario. This central Canadian pattern would have been a heartening sign were it not for the fact that young women found themselves needing certificates and diplomas to compensate for their gender in competition with young men with fewer credentials.[4]

Many of these young women did not intend to linger long in the labour force. The pattern that union organizers noted with frustration among female industrial employees[5] was also common among the growing number of women qualifying as teachers, nurses, stenographers, and physicians. Women tended to be sojourners in paid work. The unshakeable cultural conviction that child care must be done by women and the absence of both well funded crèches and cadres of willing nannies forced a choice between parenting and pursuit of a career upon female students, skilled workers, and professionals, a choice that their male peers were never obliged to face.

This dilemma became more stark as young women contemplated lengthy and expensive preparation for the newly opening professions. Their writing about the possibility of pursuing a career, a new nineteenth-century word for a life long vocation, shows the combination of anticipation and regret evoked by a decision between irreconcilable alternatives. No longer was marriage the only life long commitment a woman might make. In Ontario in 1901 fifteen per cent of all professionals were women, in 1921 nineteen per cent, yet the work of wife remained, unlike that of husband, a full-time job, and could be combined with any other career only with great difficulty.[6]

The persistence of this enforced choice between career and marriage is not easily accounted for on material grounds alone. Crude fertility rates were declining in both rural and urban Canada. So, too, was household size; in the countryside by .81 persons (from 5.7 to 4.9), in the cities from 5.1 to 4.6 persons between 1871 and 1921.[7] A woman at home had fewer children to care for and could expect to live longer, perhaps four years longer in 1921 than in 1881. Sewing machines and factory-made textiles simplified the home production of clothing. Men's garments were available for purchase used or ready-made. Gas stoves and tinned goods eased the burden of food preparation. More accessible municipal water supplies and chemical cleaning preparations made doing laundry at least somewhat less arduous. Yet in the face of all this demographic, technological, and economic change, the image of ideal womanhood remained largely unaltered. If anything, the aspect of the image least consistent with the new realities of women's lives was reinforced. The ideological sanctification of motherhood as the fount and essence of female nature grew stronger as the need to bear many children decreased and the choice to rear large families grew less common. The cult of domesticity and the emphasis upon the homemaker as efficient consumer and modern manager filled the void left by women's lost role in economic production, as did rising standards in *child-care*. And a species of social mothering, of maternal feminism, safely filled the space left when the demands of political radicals and educational reformers for equal rights for women were turned back.

In the mid-nineties came the first signs that the ethnic balance of the Dominion might be changing. Between 1891 and 1901 the number of British-born in Canada decreased while the number of Europeans and Asians in the country almost doubled. With free land in the United States no longer available and transatlantic shipping rates falling, Canada's export economy thrived, and both Canadians and immigrants found the Dominion a more attractive stopping place. The newly arrived southern and eastern Europeans settled principally in the prairie west, the Asians on Vancouver Island and the lower mainland of British Columbia. They assumed jobs native-born Canadians were unwilling to do, took up lands native-born Canadians were unwilling to settle. Yet very quickly an uproar arose against their presence in the Dominion.

In discussions of the 'immigrant question' issues emerging from the productive and the reproductive spheres were linked. Both urban and rural Canadians of British descent had begun to have fewer children, the decline in rural household size being especially marked. These longer established households were not engaged in labour-intensive family work. Parents facing many market choices began to reckon more closely the costs of shelter and schooling for many offspring. The Ukrainians, Hungarians, Poles, and Russians, who were more typically embarking upon pioneering subsistence agriculture or locked in low-paid urban work, were untouched by this demographic transition, proud and insistent upon retaining their old world cultures. In their circumstances children were still a source of material support. In the nineteenth-century English Canadians had feared that they would be outnumbered by the Québécois, *la revanche des berceaux*. In the early twentieth century European newcomers were feared for the same reasons, and the problem was labelled 'race suicide' a term that emphasized the choice by English Canadians to have fewer children. Maternal feminists saw the solution to this problem not in raising larger 'Anglo-Saxon' families, but in social reform.[8]

The reform movement they supported was broad in compass. It included plans for change in the structure and servicing of cities, pleas for clean water, pure milk, better sanitation, campaigns for child welfare legislation, against crinolines and constricting corsets, for the establishment of better rural schools and agricultural extension programmes, for the abolition of blood sports and the tavern. Most women initially perceived their participation in reform work as an extension of their domestic role as wife and mother and entered the social purity campaigns as good moral influences, the public health movement as concerned nurses to their own families, urban reform as homemakers to the city at large. Other women were drawn to reform by the same broad range of predispositions that drew men to these activities—radical political ideology, patriotism, xenophobia, religious belief, class hatred. Among the leadership of women's reform movements, professionals figured prominently—doctors, teachers, and academics, women who were experts, who legitimated their demands for change by reference to their training, and urged that scientific standards of efficiency and philosophical criteria for equality be applied to social policy. The values of the professionals had broad credibility among middle-class women and their arguments became widely accepted justifications for reform.[9]

World War One heightened the emphasis in the reform movement upon patriotism, and upon maternity. The conflict carried so many young men away that there could be no denying the interdependence between the cradle and the sword. For some women this was a matter of pride; for others the contradictions between blood-shed and Christian values evoked shame. The war drew women to recognize and then affirm their place in public life in other ways, as workers in munitions plants, replacements for farm boys gone overseas, tendentious recruiters through white feather campaigns against luckless lads who remained behind. The Union Government gave the female relatives of soldiers the vote in order to secure conscription.

Between 1916 and 1920 Canadian women received the vote in all jurisdictions except Prince Edward Island and Quebec. Thereafter we might expect that they would have found a firm place in political history. This has, of course, not been the case, a circumstance that seems best related to vagaries in social formations not so conventionally political—the socially endorsed division of labour that made child care an exclusively female responsibility and thus made married women too busy for political work, the continuing definition of public life as unladylike, and the curious fears for social stability associated with the release of women from the private sphere.

The chapters that follow are organized by stages in the lives of women rather than decades in the life of the nation. The label for this sort of analysis, the life cycle, is borrowed from biology. The categories into which the discussion is grouped, beginning with childhood and ending with old age, remain vestigially biological. In discussions of the late nineteenth and early twentieth centuries (when disease created age- and sex-specific mortality rates that held a commanding influence over women's lives and deaths, and when female productive labour required bodily strength that varied with physiological maturity) this modicum of biological determinism is not inappropriate. So long as reproduction remained a woman's primary social function, and in both its physical and cultural aspects her special responsibility, menarche and menopause were conspicuous turning points in a woman's life. This is not to say that biology was destiny for women, but rather that the society of the time gave reproduction such precedence that this aspect of life governed all others for women, rather as colour bars once governed the mobility of American blacks or taboos about the disabled govern the independence of the physically handicapped today. Biology created reverberations in the lives of girls and women that society magnified into deafening commands.

Though female toddlers were more hardy than males, more likely by a considerable margin to survive the first five years of life, generalizations derived from adult body size were read back upon early childhood. Girls were described as more frail, and bound by more restrictions upon their physical activity than boys, barred from school in winter when older boys attended, lest their delicate constitutions be damaged by the foetid and turbulent atmosphere of the classroom. Similar biological allusions were used to restrict female access to employment. A broad range of job-related activities—standing, sitting, standing in a warm place, sitting in a cold place, focusing upon a task requiring a high degree of mental concentration, coping with the monotony of repetitive factory work—all were considered deleterious to female reproductive capacity, and therefore inappropriate as women's work. And on more than one occasion the polling booth was described as having an environment so noxious that women ought to be barred from voting on medical grounds.

The particular cultural demands made upon Canadian women on the basis of their gender were in every case mediated by separate and distinct opportunities and disabilities bequeathed by class, region, and ethnicity (what people at the time would have called race). Within each stage in the life cycle an intriguing diversity of female experience emerged. And in the end, these patterns became of more compelling interest than the biological. The malleability or rigidity of these patterns tell us much about the resources women might use to remake the world that had been made for them, to break the spurious prominence given to biology in their lives.

NOTES

1 Sylvia Van Kirk, *"Many Tender Ties": Women in Fur Trade Society, 1670-1870* (Winnipeg, 1980) and Jennifer S.H. Brown, *Strangers in Blood: Fur Trade Company Families in Indian Country* (Vancouver, 1980).
2 W.L. Morton, *Manitoba: A History* (Toronto, 1957) and Nellie L. McClung, *Clearing In the West, My Own Story* (Toronto,
3).Susan Mann Trofimenkoff, "One Hundred and Two Muffled Voices: Canada's Industrial Women in the 1880's," *Atlantis,* III (1977); Bettina Bradbury, "The Family Economy and Work in an Industrializing City: Montreal in the 1870s," *Historical Papers* (1979); le Collectif Clio, *L'Histoire des femmes au Québec* (Montreal, 1982); and Star Rosenthal, "Union Maids: Organized Women Workers in Vancouver, 1900-1915," *B.C. Studies,* XLI (1979).
4 Margaret Gillett, *We Walked Very Warily* (Montreal, 1982); Ramsay Cook and Wendy Mitchinson, eds., *The Proper Sphere: Women's Place in Canadian Society* (Toronto, 1976) Chapter 3; Chad Gaffield and David Levine, "Dependence and Adolescence on the Canadian Frontier," *History of Education Quarterly,* XIII (1978).
5 Wayne Roberts, *Honest Womanhood: Feminism, Femininity and Class Consciousness among Toronto Working Women, 1896-1914* (Toronto, 1976).
6 Janice Acton *et al,* eds., *Women at Work: Ontario, 1850-1930* (Toronto, 1974) 280.
7 A.J. Pelletier, F.D. Thompson, and A. Rochon, *The Canadian Family,* Census Monograph No. 7 (Ottawa, 1931) 30.
8 Carol Bacchi, "Race Regeneration and Social Purity: A Study of the Social Attitudes of Canada's English-Speaking Suffragists," *Histoire sociale/Social History,* XI (November, 1978) and Linda Kealey, ed., *A Not Unreasonable Claim: Women and Reform in Canada, 1880s-1920s* (Toronto, 1980).
9 Neil Sutherland, *Childhood in English-Canadian Society* (Toronto, 1976); Richard Allen, *The Social Passion: Religion and Social Reform in Canada* (Toronto, 1973); G. Stelter and A. Artibise, *The Canadian City* (Toronto, 1979); Barbara Latham and Cathy Kess, eds., *In Her Own Right: Selected Essays on Women's History in B.C.* (Victoria, 1980); L. Kealey, ed., *A Not Unreasonable Claim.*

CHAPTER ONE

CHILDHOOD

A rosy glow lingers around our image of late Victorian and Edwardian girlhood, eyelet-bordered pinafores over blue gingham dresses, full berry pails set down by a broad shady tree, kindhearted tears for the poor animals in a Beatrix Potter tale, years of innocent isolation from the adult world, a time to nurture the modest tenderness of womanhood. By the late nineteenth century the identification of childhood, especially girlhood, with purity and sentiment was almost complete in middle-class British Canada, an association imported with illustrated Sunday school primers and the *Girls' Own Annuals* from rural manses and the homes of England's gentry.[1] Nonetheless, Canadian women lived far from English country gardens and the rearing they gave their daughters diverged frequently, by preference and necessity, from the high Victorian ideal.

One feature of Canadian girlhood consistent with the British gentry ideal, and present across class and regional differences in the Dominion between Confederation and the end of World War One, was its family setting. For young girls, independent experience outside the shelter and parental discipline of their families was much more limited in this period than it had been earlier, when novice servants were sent off to apprenticeships at age seven or eight, or than it would be later when children of the same ages typically spent six or seven hours daily in school.

Although common schooling was widely available in eastern Canada by the 1870s and followed quite closely upon settlement in the west, the preeminence of family responsibilities meant that attendance requirements could not be strenuous. Nor could the penalties for truancy, which did not exist in all jurisdictions, be rigorously enforced. Country girls saw less of the classroom than their brothers because housework and child care knew no seasons. The snow-covered fields freed boys from home to attend school during the winter months. In cities, like Hamilton, whose economies were based on heavy industry, parents urged boys to take up available jobs as soon as they were able, but because employment for girls was more scarce, parents allowed them to remain longer in school. In textile towns and in the garment-making districts of cities, this pattern was reversed, girls being the first pressed into wage work in the family interest. For all children, the needs of the home had first call upon their time and these calls were gender determined. Patterns of school attendance formed as the mirror image of a sexual division of labour were in place even for youngsters of tender years.[2] Children's time remained family time; priorities at home determined when they might be released for other activities.

Reformers feared the disintegration of kin ties in the growing cities, but there too family authority dominated the lives of children. Because the move from country to city was full of risks, family help was extremely important in the search for lodgings, for work, for the way to live an urban life.[3] City households often included a number of adults. In addition to their parents, the children of working-class city families had to accommodate demands from other kin; for example, cousins passing through in search of work and the aunts with whom they stayed when their mothers were ill. Middle-class children, too, learned to defer to the succession of older relatives who boarded in their parents' homes.[4]

The first child-protection laws, allowing provincial agents to intervene in troubled families and asserting the state's rights to custody, date from this period. The model Canadian legislation, an Ontario act of 1893 called "The Children's Charter," was especially designed to limit parents' rights to introduce their children to thievery and prostitution; this statute governed girls under 16 and boys under 14. Through the nineties, in English Canada children's aid societies became a popular urban philanthropic activity, their volunteers confident that the separation of parent and child was often in the child's interest. But the practical influences of these policies remained small. Parental and broader social opposition, supported by contrary pronouncements from American authorities, soon discredited radical intervention between kin, so that the emphasis—if not always the practice—shifted from having agencies supplant family rearing to having them support it.[5]

In city and country a child's leisure companions were usually kin. Girls played with their sisters and brothers. Although they met other children at school and in Bible class, connections with peers were less important than responsibilities to, and for, siblings. Thus a child, especially a female child, was almost never beyond the watchful guidance of family, and as she grew older, almost never without a younger brother or sister, tugging at her skirt.

Separate municipal playgrounds were not generally established until the early twentieth century, probably because neither play, nor the creation of a space solely for children and separate from family were particularly acceptable by earlier standards. Rhymes, photographs, and finger games offer glimpses of children absorbed in a separate youthful world of imaginative play, yet for most girls, even in the early twentieth century, being young was not a state apart from, but a preparation for, mature and responsible womanhood. That preparation involved two kinds of learning: absorbing the demeanor, bearing, manner, and character appropriate to one of her gender and class, and acquiring the practical skills required in a girl of her cultural background and material circumstances.

Across the country, schools with separate entrances and segregated playgrounds for girls and boys testified to the unanimity with which Canadians of European descent regarded childhood as the training ground for separate spheres. Although their particular experiences differed, girls' recollections of their early lessons in womanliness share a starkness tinged with discomfort. Evelyn McLeod, an American child on the Canadian prairies, remembers limits on her play imposed by the requirement that young ladies never soil their pinafores, and her introduction to modesty's bleakness through painfully tight braids. The female children of powerful propertied city families learned through shaming that their bodies were to be primly covered, their lips sealed, their thoughts pure, and their minds always attentive to the words and needs of others. As a girl in Alberta, Anne Anderson learned from her mother the special responsibilities of Métis women for devoutness and family harmony, even though in that culture she recalled no sexual division of labour among children until they entered their teens.[6] But, in this respect, the Métis were atypical among Canadian families.

Most families in the late Victorian and Edwardian periods introduced their youngest members to the sexual specificity of work and held up, as objects of derision, newcomers such as the Doukhobors who did not follow the same conventions. In rural communities of western European derivation, girls learned domestic tasks, cooking, baking, the rudiments of housework, sewing, laundry routines, and helped with poultry and dairy work, but except in the farm-making stage or in emergencies thereafter, were ordinarily excluded from the fields, the terrain reserved for their fathers and brothers.[7] (The exception to this pattern was the tending of herds—a dreary, lonely task, which seems to have fallen to both girls and boys aged 9-13.) The schools shored up these divisions in the early twentieth century by instituting vocational training programmes, which provided domestic science for city girls and carpentry and metal-working for city boys.[8]

Technological change substantially altered the skills required of rural girls and through the period home production became increasingly integrated with factory production. In the 1870s, mothers would have taught their daughters the whole process by which floor coverings were made for the home. In 1893, Mary-Louise Pickering sewed cloth scraps together for the carpet weft but the weaving would have been done by an outside artisan. By the end of World War One the hand-made rag carpets had almost entirely faded from use. At the turn of the century, girls and women still prepared fleeces in the home, but sent the fibres on to a factory to be woven into blankets.[9] The girls who no longer learned to spin or weave acquired other skills, often involving machinery made outside the home. By the 1880s most farm households had sewing machines with which to make Mr Timothy Eaton's yardage into clothing and linens. By the early twentieth century girls used the family cream separators to prepare milk for local factories.[10]

The effects of expansion and innovation in industry were most marked in urban working-class households. The path of technical change in manufacturing was uneven. Certain processes were easily mechanized, breaking the control of skilled artisans over the production of an ever-widening range of goods. There were, however, many tasks too delicate for early steam-powered machines to perform, too complex for machines that could not do more than one task, but not too complex for a child. Particularly in urban centres specializing in textile production and garment-making in the seventies and eighties, new jobs in home manufactures were created for female children, making these city girls immediately valuable contributors to family income, just as their cousins on the farm were. Young girls learned from their mothers to finish the lapels and buttonholes on factory-made clothing, and to make boxes, flowers, and other fancy goods to serve the broadening middle-class taste for ornamentation. In textile mills girls carried supplies to operatives whose machines could not go untended, and stood by to mend throstles and threads difficult for older workers to reach.[11] As machinery was refined, these ancillary workers were displaced, as the skilled artisans had been before them. The state made city truancy enforcement more rigorous, and female children found themselves detached from the labour process and in school. They were unlikely to be able to replace their contributions to the family income by peddling small goods, selling papers, or running messages, as their brothers might, because across the country municipal regulations concerning street work were firmly discriminatory against girls.[12] Thus the city fathers tried to teach girls from urban working-class families the lessons about lady-like clean pinafores and modesty that country daughters learned from their kin.

NOTES

1   For British writing in this vein see M.W. Hughes, *A Victorian Family* (Oxford, 1977); Gillian Avery, *Nineteenth Century Children: Heroes and Heroines in English Children's Stories 1780-1900* (London, 1965); Francoise Basch, *Relative Creatures: Victorian Women in Society and the Novel* (New York, 1974); Alec Ellis, *A History of Children's Reading and Literature* (Exeter, 1968); Bob Dixon, *Catching Them Young: Sex, Race and Class in Children's Fiction* (London, 1978); Barbara Frankle, "The Genteel Family: High Victorian Conceptions of Domesticity and Good Behaviour," unpublished Ph.D. thesis, University of Wisconsin, 1969. See also Anne S. MacLeod, *A Moral Tale: Children's Fiction and American Culture 1820-1860* (Hamden Ct, 1975) and Anne Douglas, *The Feminization of American Culture* (New York, 1977) Introduction.

2   Ian E. Davey, "The Rhythm of Work and the Rhythm of School," in Neil Macdonald and Alf Chaiton, eds., *Egerton Ryerson and His Times* (Toronto, 1978); Michael B. Katz and Ian E. Davey, "Youth and Early Industrialization in a Canadian City," in John Demos and Sarane Spence Boocock, *Turning Points* (Chicago, 1978); Frank Denton and Peter George, "Socio-Economic Influences on

School Attendence: a Study of a Canadian County in 1871," *History of Education Quarterly* (Fall 1974); Susan Houston, "School Reform and Education: The Issue of Compulsory Schooling, Toronto 1851-71," in Macdonald and Chaiton, *Ryerson;* David Jones *et al, Shaping the Schools of the Canadian West* (Calgary, 1979); J. Donald Wilson and David Jones, *Schooling and Society in Twentieth Century British Columbia* (Calgary, 1980).

3 Michael Katz, *The People of Hamilton, Canada West* (Cambridge, Mass., 1975) chapter 5 and for finely crafted British research on the same theme, see Michael Anderson, *Family Structure in Nineteenth Century Lancashire* (Cambridge, 1971).

4 The role of kin not parents in the lives of children is analyzed in Bettina Bradbury, "The Fragmented Family: Family Strategies in the Face of Death, Illness and Poverty, Montreal, 1860-1885," in Joy Parr, ed., *Childhood and Family in Canadian History* (Toronto, 1982), and the importance of urban family ties is noted in Margaret Conrad, "Recording Angels: Private Chronicles of Maritime Women, 1750-1950," Canadian Research Institute for the Advancement of Women, *Papers,* IV (November 1982).

5 Neil Sutherland, *Children in English-Canadian Society* (Toronto, 1976) parts one and three; Richard Splane, *Social Welfare in Ontario* (Toronto, 1965); Leonard Rutman and Andrew Jones, *In the Children's Aid* (Toronto, 1981); Dennis Guest, *The Emergence of Social Security in Canada* (Vancouver, 1980) chapter 5; Constance B. Backhouse, "Shifting Patterns in Nineteenth Century Canadian Custody Awards," in David Flaherty, *Essays in the History of Canadian Law,* vol. I (Toronto, 1981) 240-41.

6 The best study on the Métis family in the period covered by this collection is Marcel Giraud, *Le métis canadien* (Paris, 1945); for the earlier nineteenth century, see Jennifer S.H. Brown, *Strangers in Blood: Fur Trade Company Families in Indian Country* (Vancouver, 1980).

7 Rosemary Ball, "A Perfect Farmer's Wife: Women in Nineteenth Century Rural Ontario," *Canada: An Historical Magazine,* III (1975) 2-21; Joy Parr, *Labouring Children: British Child Immigrants to Canada 1868-1924* (London and Montreal, 1980) chapter 5.

8 R.M. Stamp, "Adelaide Hoodless: Champion of Women's Rights" in Robert S. Patterson *et al, Profiles of Canadian Educators* (Toronto, 1974) 213-232; Alice Ravenhill, *Memoirs of an Educational Pioneer* (Toronto, 1951); Lucien Lemieux, "La fondation de l'Ecole Ménagère St. Pascal, 1905-1909," *Revue de l'histoire de l'amérique française,* XXV, 4, (May 1972) 552-7; Susan Mann Trofimenkoff, *The Dream of Nation* (Toronto, 1982) 123.

9 The Corrective Collective, *Never Done: Three Centuries of Women's Work in Canada* (Toronto, 1974) 80-85; Dorothy Burnham, *Keep Me Warm One Night: Early Handweaving in Eastern Canada* (Toronto, 1972).

10 Allan Bogue, "Ontario Agriculture between 1880 and 1890 with Special Reference to Southwestern Ontario," unpublished M.A. thesis, University of Western Ontario, 1946; D.A. Lawr, "The Development of Ontario Farming, 1870-1914; Patterns of Growth and Change," *Ontario History,* LXIV (December 1972); Helen C. Abell, "The Adaptation of the Way of Life of the Rural Family in Canada to Technological, Social and Economic Changes," in *The Family in the Evolution of Agriculture* (Ottawa, 1968); Grace Rogers Cooper, *The Invention of the Sewing Machine* (Washington, D.C., 1968).

11 On the unevenness of technological change and its effect upon the labour process, see Raphael Samuel, "The Workshop of the World: Steam Power and Hand

Technology in Mid-Victorian Britain," *History Workshop Journal,* III (Spring 1977) 6-72; for this pattern in late nineteenth-century Montreal, see Bettina Bradbury, "The Family Economy and Work in an Industrializing City, Montreal in the 1870s," *Historical Papers/Communications historiques* (1979) 77-86.

12 Susan Houston, "The 'Waifs and Strays' of a Late Victorian City: Juvenile Delinquents in Toronto," in Joy Parr, ed., *Childhood and Family in Canadian History* (Toronto, 1982).

1 THE FAMILY AND THE INSTITUTIONAL EXPERIENCE

CHANGING ENVIRONMENTS

In our quest for material dealing with the experience of girls in post-Confederation Canada, we were constantly aware that the clearest childhood recollections document some kind of disruption in the writers' lives. Grace Casey George's reminiscences are typical of this point, emphasizing as they do happy disruptions such as the constant activity of visiting or receiving visiting relatives, or the more momentous "breaking up" of her home in Colborne for the unknown experience of Northwest Mounted Police posts after 1887. About her new life in the north west, Grace's descriptions raise an additional theme. She vividly recounts her education in the public school and at home with her mother. As was the case in British North America, mothers often continued to be formally involved in teaching their children when weather, distance, or the lack of a school prevented formal public schooling.

Northwest Territories, 1876-1890
Reminiscences of Grace Casey George, Acc. 70,207/2, 1-4, Provincial Archives of Alberta.

I was born in Colborne, Ont. on August 29, 1876 and have early recollections of going to Rice Lake via the narrow gauge railway to Harwood from Cobourg....

My grandmother Casey had a summer home on Tick Island, just off shore from Harwood, and also lived in Port Hope, where I spent many happy times with her when a child. She died in 1885, and my next vivid memory is of a visit from Aunt Mary (Hudsbeth), a very strikingly beautiful woman with brown eyes and white hair, and a witch at telling fortunes with cards. She foretold that there was an appointment coming soon to my father which would mean a breaking up of our home in Colborne and moving far away. And to be sure a short time later, on October 2, 1886 came news of father's appointment as an Inspector in the N.W.M. Police.

This was quite an upheaval. My mother was born Caroline Strong in Colborne and all her roots were there, as well as my father's. He was a born soldier and the appointment pleased him greatly. He was terribly disappointed not to have served in the recent N.W. Rebellion....

Our first journey in a pullman car was quite an event. We were three girls, aged 10, 8 and 3, and all slept in the upper berth. I don't know if there were dining cars in those days, but we had a substantial lunch basket and fared very well. There were no quarters available for us at Regina where my father was posted, so it was arranged that mother and daughters would stay off in Winnipeg with old Colborne friends living there. The Bruces were able to put us up and we boarded with them on Colony Street until my father found a small house just outside the barracks at Regina.

I had started to school in Winnipeg and life was quite interesting. Dr Benson's sons had a dog trained to haul a toboggan and it was thrilling to ride on it across the prairie, and there was lots of that in those early days.

We parted from our good friends and arrived in Regina on New Year's Day 1887. The train arrived some time in the early hours of the morning and the porter had forgotten to awaken us. My father came on board and found us still in our berths—so the train had to wait while we were bundled up and stowed away in the box of a police sleigh, covered with Buffalo robes and driven to our new home....

Our home in Regina consisted of five rooms: sitting-dining room combined, kitchen and three bedrooms, a stove in each room except the third bedroom where we children slept on a homemade affair that took up most of the space so no room for a stove. The Winter of 1886-87 was one of the coldest on record in the West, and to make matters worse there was a coal famine as the narrow gauge railway from Lethbridge to Medicine Hat where it joined the main line was completely blocked. Coal was rationed out in sacks and our house being so small and ceilings very low we suffered less from cold than any of the people in barracks. Blizzards were frequent and many were lost and frozen to death. They had to string a rope from the barracks to the stables as otherwise the men got lost just going that far when a blizzard was blowing. We used to enjoy going to the musical rides in the drill hall on Saturday afternoons. Life was quite gay, with balls, etc. in barracks and town. They only had one road to town in those days so if you met a sleigh whoever had to turn off the road upset in the deep snow. It was soft so no bones broke, but in after years they had two roads so that discomfort was avoided. The snow drifts were so high we children found it great sport climbing onto the roofs of the houses, and they made grand slides too. Then when the thaw came in the Spring and the mud! I expect our mothers had a time with us as of course we liked to play in it. There were quite a number of children in barracks: Commissioner Herchmer's daughter Birdie and three sons; Supt Deane's two daughters and three sons; Supt Allan's two daughters and one son; and Sgt Major Belcher also quite a family. Some had a governess. Mother taught us for the short time we were in Regina as my father was transferred to command the Post at Edmonton in May 1887. We travelled to Calgary by train and from there by police team; two-seated democrat for us and a wagon for our baggage. It might be interesting now to say how little in the way of household goods we had in those days. Mother always kept her sewing machine—our only piece of furniture. Bedding, linen, dishes and cutlery and our clothing were all our worldly possessions....

To go back to our life in Fort Edmonton, there is much I could tell. My sister Clare and I first attended a public school. Mr Stiff was our first teacher, succeeded by a man named Martin who proved to be anything but the sort of man to be in charge of little girls, and was later on summarily dismissed for misconduct. My father had taken the matter up with the Board but getting no satisfaction we were sent to a Roman Catholic school which at that time was just being opened by the nuns. Many of our nice girl friends also were sent there.

Margaret and Lou Taylor became our close friends as their home was at Lac Ste Anne where their father was in charge of the Hudson Bay post and we had several very interesting trips to visit them. There were three sons—one afterwards became the well-known Eddie Taylor, Manager of the Hudson Bay store in Calgary, and later partner of Lougheed and Taylor. I might say here that I probably would have married him had not my father ruled that neither I nor my sisters could be engaged until we were twenty years old, so in the meantime I changed my mind about Eddie....

CHILDHOOD IN EDMONTON

Anna Laura Robertson, the author of the memoirs excerpted below, was only seven years old when she travelled from Seaforth, Ontario, to her new home in Edmonton, yet her reminiscences make clear the impression which the event made in her life. Her memories of play, education and leisure activities provide an indication of other highlights as she matured in the growing city of Edmonton.

Alberta, 1883-1899
Memoirs of Anna Laura Robertson Harrison, Acc. 70.207/1, 1-3, 8-9, 16-20, Provincial Archives of Alberta.

My father, Walter Scott Robertson, had gone to Winnipeg a few years earlier and from there had driven to Edmonton by team and wagon, though many at that time had made the long journey with ox and cart. He returned to Seaforth [Ontario] and immediately had a return of his old trouble, asthma. As he had been quite free from this while in the West, he decided at once to return to Edmonton, which he did, my mother and family to follow as soon as a home could be made ready.

What it must have meant to my mother, I only realized much later, leaving friends as well as all the comforts which the early pioneers had to give up, but I can't remember ever hearing her complain.

There were six children: Harry 17, Nel 15, Carrie 13, Fred 10, and I (registered Anna Laura but christened Annie Laurie) 7, and my small brother Bobby, 2.

To us, or at least to me, it was wonderful riding on the train for days, eating and even sleeping on the train. What more could a small girl want? Eventually we reached Winnipeg where we were met by a distant cousin of my father's, Alex Macdonald, who took us to his lovely home but told mother he had bad news for her. The telegraph lines were down between Edmonton and Winnipeg and it was impossible to get a message through. Of course, I didn't realize at the time what this meant to my mother. Uncle Alex, as we called him, advised her to return to Ontario as it was then late in September, I have many times since heard my mother say the happiest day of her life was when she received the telegram saying my father would meet her in Calgary on a certain date....

We reached Edmonton, population then between two and three hundred, October the third, 1883. Here there was a ferry to take us over the Saskatchewan River (though I have forded it many times since), but our camping days were not over as the house, which was to have been ready, was without doors and floors. A big tent was put up and a floor laid. In this we lived until the house was ready.

To go back to my childhood in the big house on the hill, I have many happy recollections. We all had horses to ride, Indian ponies. But we did not ride astride as the girls do now. We rode on a side-saddle and loved it! However, we walked to school along the top of the hill.... [The school] consisted of one room, heated by a Hudson's Bay stove. A pail of water stood near the door with a dipper hanging above and I can't remember any epidemic being caused by us all drinking from the same dipper. I have never forgotten one tragic day in the school room. It was Bobby Burns Day and our good Scottish teacher thought we should celebrate it, so he asked if anyone knew 'Bonnie Charlie'? Most of the pupils stuck up their hand so I did too. "All right, Annie, you sing it." I managed the first four lines, then how I wished the floor would open up and take me in. I can still see those broad boards with their wide cracks but they refused to open up. Then the teacher came to the rescue and suggested they all join in the chorus. It saved the day and also taught me a lesson.

The children came to this school from all directions, and the only contact we had with each other would be in school. Consequently, I spent most of my young days with older people and as my parents made their home open house to the many young men away from home and as we had the only piano in the town, and my brother and sister played, many evenings were spent singing songs and dancing. I can't remember when I learned to dance. There was always a shortage of girls so I would be treated quite like a grown-up and asked to dance. Of course I loved it! I still can feel the bitter disappointment I had one night. It was a special event. Others were coming and my dress and slippers were put out and I was told I could come down as soon as Bobby and Grace had gone to sleep. I laid down and went to sleep and didn't wake till the party was over, my dress and slippers there to remind me of what I had missed!

Now to go back to those early days. For those pioneers who had vision they were having their dreams materialize. Settlers arrived in numbers, many coming overland from Calgary as we had done. However, in 1891, the Calgary and Edmonton Railway, known as the C. and E., was built through to the south side of the river. As there was no bridge over the Saskatchewan at that time, the train was met by buses from the north side and the passengers brought to Edmonton in style, usually with a four-horse team. In 1902, a bridge was built at what was known as the lower ferry and the same year the Edmonton Yukon and Pacific Line joined with the C. & E. and brought the traffic to Edmonton. In the meantime, the south side became known as Strathcona. The rivalry was very keen between the two towns, especially where sports were concerned. You must remember we were just towns, no big stadium from which to watch a game, more often standing by a fence surrounding the players. On one occasion I was standing watching as our Edmonton players came on the ice. They wearing new sweaters, each displaying a big 'E'. a Strathcona girl standing near me said: "Yes, 'E' for idiot!"

The girls played hockey too. I was captain of the team when in my teens. We played against Strathcona too. Looking at the photograph now, I realize that I am the only one of the team left. We girls also curled but skating and dancing were our chief amusements in the winter.

By 1893 Edmonton had grown to the extent that a number of theatrical troupes were coming to town and in that year my father built what was known as Robertson Hall. Companies would come and play different plays each night for a week or more at a time, famous musicians and well known actors among them. The hall had a beautiful floor so was also used as a ballroom. As I was then in my teens I was generally one of the party, always went with a brother but didn't always go home with him. We always had programmes and as there were many more men than girls there, one's dances would generally be engaged ahead of time. But in any case there would be a line-up waiting as we came out of the dressing-room so one would have extras and extra extras three or four deep. I remember my first evening gown. It was a mauve silk with deep chiffon frill falling off the shoulders and outlined with violets at the top—my first long dress. Pages could be filled about the gay times we spent in Robertson Hall, such times as when the Old Timers held their ball and decorated the walls with valuable furs and had teepees on the stage; and other occasions when a freighter, who played wonderful dance music on a whistle, would come to town and an impromptu dance would be organized, my brother Harry often playing the piano. Then, of course, some of the old timers played the 'fiddle'. We never called it a violin but [it made] grand dance music. The Hall was burned down in 1906, and though I was then married and mother of your Grandad, I was at the dance the night of the fire. We were having coffee when a fireman came up to tell us that a building at the back of the hall was on fire and we had better go out for a little while. We jokingly marked our cups of coffee and went to the street to watch the fire department, but the water tank was empty and the fire swept through the building and nothing could save it, so what started as a gay party ended in a sad group saying goodnight and going home.

Now I must again turn back the clock and tell you about our camping days at Cooking Lake. It was said that it had been called that as the Indians made it their stopping place between Beaver Lake and Edmonton. Though only about twenty miles south-east of Edmonton, when we first had a camp there it would take a long day to make the trip. No regular road, just trails, and as the farmers moved into the country it would often mean finding a new way through each trip. At first we camped in tents, two or three families making up a party, all joining around a huge campfire in the evening and singing the latest popular song or reciting a funny verse. One I can remember, as one of the party couldn't see why we laughed:

Go ask Papa, the maiden said,

Now the young man knew Papa was dead,

Also the wicked life he'd led,

So he understood when the maiden said

'Go ask Papa'.

After a year or two my father had a house built of spruce logs and called it 'Spruce Lodge'. It still stands and is used by his granddaughter (his daughter Carrie's daughter). Many jolly times were spent in it....

HOMES FOR GIRLS

For children who were homeless or whose families could not or would not support them, homes like the Girls' Home in Hamilton or the Kingston Orphans' Home met a real need. These agencies were fairly typical of similar institutions in urban centres across the nation. The following report on the Hamilton Girls' Home and the selected minutes of the ladies' committee of the Orphans' Home and Widows' Friend Society in Kingston reveal the vision of appropriate practical and moral training for girls advocated by the institutions. Of particular interest in the following documents is the interplay of parental and institutional control over the lives of the girls involved. It is also worth noting the continuous demand of residents of both regions to take in boys and girls aged over ten to be employed as servants.

Hamilton, 1894
"Girls' Home, Hamilton," Proceedings of the Ontario Conference on Child-Saving. *Ontario Sessional Papers, No. 29 (1895), 58-9.*

Miss M.H. Simpson, Secretary of the Girls' Home, Hamilton said:

The Girls' Home at Hamilton is for homeless children of the city between the ages of four and fourteen. It is not for Roman Catholics because these are cared for by the sisters of that church, and neither is it for orphans because there is a Protestant Orphans' Asylum in another part of the city, but with these exceptions, the homeless children, the fatherless, the motherless, those whose parents are in hospital, or jail, or lunatic asylum, or roaming perhaps as tramps free from parental anxieties—congregate in the Girls' Home, there to be clothed and nurtured largely at the public expense. The city, besides an annual grant to the institution, pays $2 a month for those destitute ones who are sent in by order of the mayor, but these are very few, most of the children being brought in by relations. In many cases one of the parents is a respectable member of society, who having signed an agreement to pay a small monthly sum varying, according to circumstances, from $1 to $3 a month, faithfully continues to do so as long as the shelter of the Home is desired, whether it be for a few months only or for several years. There is a tendency on the other hand amongst some parents to pay considerably less than the amount thus agreed upon, and when the committee believes this is owing to inability to do better it overlooks the deficiency, reflecting that after all this is a charity, and charity must be exercised accordingly. But when payment is discontinued altogether for no excusable cause then the charity aforesaid takes on a fresh complexion, and the Home assumes the exclusive control of the child, ignoring the parent's authority, as under these circumstances, it is empowered to do by the agreement signed on entrance. The girls thus thrown on the hands of the committee are placed at a suitable age with families in the country, and indentures are signed binding them to remain till the age of eighteen with their employers, who are bound on their part to supply board and clothing and to pay $5 annually to the Home to be held in trust till the term expires. During the last five years the girls thus placed out have been about five per cent of those discharged. The indentures by no means prevent a girl from leaving her employers should the connection become undesirable for either party, for when this is found to be the case a transfer is effected as soon as possible; but if a place is left without permission the annual $5 held in trust for the girl is forfeited and her connection with the Home is at an end. When this occurs it is almost invariably owing to the influence of those parents whose claims have been ignored and from whom the whereabouts of their daughters has been concealed—a concealment often productive of hostility on the part of the parents both to the Home and the employers. This is the most painful and unsatisfactory feature of the Home work; and the knowledge that the difficulty has long been shared by similar institutions is not in itself helpful. In most other respects results are satisfactory. There are usually about fifty children in residence; and from time to time girls, having attained the age of eighteen, draw their money, varying from $20 to $35, and are reported to be doing credit to those who brought them up.

•

Kingston, 1889-1911
Orphans' Home and Widows' Friend Society, Kingston. Minutes, Queen's University Archives.

1889 Semi-monthly meeting July 23rd—9 members present.... Meeting opened by Miss Gildersleeve. Sec. read a letter from Mr & Mrs Miller expressing their appreciation of the kindness shown them [their children] by the Com. while they were in charge of the O.H. [Orphans' Home]
Woods has decided that his daughter Emily should remain in the O.H. The 3 Aylesworth children come in on the 19th. They can be given out when a suitable home offers. Sec. to write Mr Clarke that the usual charge for children in $1.50 per month. The Com. in this case are willing to take a smaller sum.
Several applications rec'd for Children between 11 & 14. None now in the Home to give out.
Mrs Ring whose boy was admitted at the last meeting now asks to have her daughter aged 9 admitted. Granted.
Minnie Bearance to be allowed to go to her Aunt's in Storrington for a week.
The meat & bread supplied to the Home are not satisfactory. Mrs Gould to interview both Butcher & Baker.
Mrs Britton to order the Coal from Mr Smith—30 tons. The usual allowance of wood to be asked for from the School Board.
Miss Grahame brought Katie Kers back to the Home on the 15th. She was very troublesome for a few days after her return but the Matron says she is improving.

Monthly meeting Jan. 14th 1896
Members present—Mrs Fraser, Mrs Britton, Mrs Gildersleeve, Mrs Waddell, Mrs Rogers, Mrs Rossie, Mrs Richmond, Mrs McC_____, Mrs Robertson, Mrs Waldroce, Mrs Richardson, Mrs S_____, Mrs Kent, Mrs Noel Kent, Mrs Machar, Mrs Mackie, Lady Cartwright, Miss Pecever, Miss Robertson, Miss Spaugenberg, Mrs Duff
Meeting opened by Miss Gildersleeve.
Minutes of last meeting read and confirmed....
Mrs Rogers read a letter from Rec. Mr Young giving some particulars of the Mcdonald children. Ellen has left the Greers & is now again with Mrs Preston. Her great fault is untruthfulness. Mrs Fortune has sent Charley back to the Home but has kept Ethel. Charley is not to be given out this winter. Hollings-

worth a farmer near Lansdowne would like to take him, if the place is still open for him he may go in Spring.

Ernest Beach a boy aged 3 whose father is dead & mother sick in the Hospital is to be admitted.

Mrs Kent suggested that the relations in England of the child Knox should be informed that he is being cared for in a Charitable Institution The Sec. authorized to communicate with them.

Application by the Anglican Clergyman Arden for the admission of several children (Walmesley) from that place who are quite destitute. They can be received.

Mrs Storcus has proved a worthy assistant to the Matron. It was decided to pay her at least $8 per month.

Treasurer reported the Expenses for the month—$400—Mills $48—Bread $27—Meat $13. Paid $56 for 3 years Insurance for $7500—Bills to be paid— For putting in the Electric Light & $100. For the Kitchen Range $190. Stove for heating the water & other items $48....

Visitors—Mrs Waldron, Miss Noel Kent, Miss Robertson, Miss Pecever....

Monthly meeting of the Orphans' Home Committee held May 9th 1911.
Mrs Skinner in the Chair and opened the meeting.
Members present 14...

Derry	Mrs Derry took her little girl out of the Home May 6th & paid $11.00 that she owed.
White	It was moved by Mrs Calvin seconded by Mrs Brownfield that Mrs Chown write Mrs White Newboro that we have no girl ten or twelve to give out....
Page	Grace Page has gone to her aunt in Gananoque. Five children have been taken to the Hospital sick. Miss Terrier & Miss Wilder want six more tables for Kindergarten. Mrs Strachan moved seconded by Mrs Gildersleeve that they be bought. Carried.
Wood	An application from a Mrs Wood wanting three children placed in the Home. Mrs Skinner made enquiries & they were not satisfactory. Mrs Chown to write her that she better take her children to the Country to live with her father & uncle.

A SIBLING RELATIONSHIP

From most of the preceding documents one can unearth evidence about the relationships between girls and their parents. Occasionally one can also discern the support and companionship that came from sibling relationships, but rarely to the extent in the following letter from a New Brunswick girl, away from home at a convent school, to her brother.

Montreal, 1910
Barry Family Papers, Letters of Molly Barry at the Villa Marie Convent in Montreal to her family, 1910-1913, Provincial Archives of New Brunswick.

Montreal, Canada
November 13th 1910

Dear Charlie: I have been intending to answer your letter ever since I got it but this is the first chance I have had. I never knew that in addition to your other innumerable talents you possessed that of letter-writing. You should not neglect this talent so please exercise it by answering this letter as soon as you can spare any of your valuable time.

Friday evening I received Paul's letter with the clipping from the *Gleaner* telling of your great stunts in athletics. I always knew you were good for something, although just what that something was I never found out until now. I wish I had been at the game; it's just my luck to miss it. But I suppose this won't be your last time.

What has happened to Rita? [her sister] I have not heard from her for quite a while....

There are so *many, many* things of interest to tell you that I hardly know where to begin. I suppose I could tell you all about the girls here but I know you would not be at all interested in that unless you have improved since I left. Is it true that Francis Hawthorne is going to give a dance? I suppose you will say "How in the dickens do I know," but I am willing to bet that if there is such a report you know as well as any of the girls. Boys always pretend they never listen to any gossip but they manage to collect a lot just the same....

2. WORK

DOMESTIC TRAINING

A.W. Currie grew up in Middlesex County, Ontario, the only son in a family of five children. His father died when he was eight years old and most of his childhood recollections are of a female-headed household, a fact that may account for his special perceptiveness about women's work. Below he recalls the British North American practices for the domestic training of girls, which continued late into the century as a vital method to prepare young women for service and marriage.

At the turn of the century, when this photograph was taken, fuel for heating and food preparation was a major item in the family budget. For poor families the cost of coal must have been prohibitive. The gathering of coal that had fallen from railway cars was work that children, such as the young girls pictured above, could easily do to help out. Rail yards were often near working class neighbourhoods. Girls foraging in this way amidst heavy moving equipment in patrolled railway company yards must have had to be quick witted and fleet of feet.

Credit: J.J. Kelso Collection, Public Archives of Canada, C-85579.

Ontario, 1885
A. W. Currie, Growing Up in Rural Ontario, *10, Queen's University Archives.*

In a house like ours without a separate kitchen or laundry room and where most tasks were done by hand rather than by machinery, an observant small boy inevitably picked up a lot of information about housework. Girls acquired even more because at an early age they could be of great help to their mother. Later on, they were told that if they wanted to make a good marriage—and what farm girl didn't; there was almost nothing else to look forward to—they would have to learn to keep house. Much scorn was cast on one girl who, after marriage, would phone her mother to learn how much sugar to put in apple sauce. Nowadays some city girls hardly know how to boil water without burning the pot or kettle.

In my mother's day there was an additional reason why a farm girl had to learn to run a house efficiently. She was expected to work as a maid for a couple of years before marriage in order to get cash for her hope chest, sometimes called heaven-knows-when-but-not-soon-enough-to-suit-me chest. Mother recalled one such girl who did most of the cooking, washing, bed-making and cleaning for a farmer, his wife, their three small children, and the hired man. For this, she was paid $4 a month, which she received in four instalments. When a month with five Saturdays rolled around, she told mother who was visiting at this home that unless she got a dollar for that week she would quit. This happened about 1885....

LEARNING WESTERN WAYS

Among the rarest documents in Canadian women's history are those that present a picture of childhood and youth written during those years rather than recalled at a later date. We are fortunate that a thoughtful grandmother in Ontario preserved the letters she received from her fourteen-year-old grand-daughter, Maryanne Caswell. First published in 1952, Maryanne Caswell's fascinating letters have been republished as *Pioneer Girl* (Toronto, 1964, rev. ed. 1979). The letter that follows is Maryanne's first description of her life and work at her new home in Clark's Crossing, Saskatchewan.

Clark's Crossing, Saskatchewan, 1887
Saskatoon Star-Phoenix, *11 September 1952. From* Pioneer Girl *by Maryanne Caswell,* ©*1964. Reprinted by permission of McGraw-Hill Ryerson Limited.*

May 8, 1887
Clark's Crossing, Saskatchewan

Dear Grandma,

First day was Sunday. We were awakened from our promised long sleep, that there was no room to move till we have folded our bedding. We dressed and were shown how to fold and put our bedding out of the way.

Uncle John made flour porridge. Aunt Patience fried eggs in lard with bread. We had breakfast. After helping to wash the dishes and learning how to feed calves from a pail in which we were to coax the calf to drink after inserting our fingers in its mouth, we were glad to sing hymns to Aunt Patience's playing on the organ she had brought from Cherokee, Iowa.

By and by, Martha and I, wearying for mother, stole quietly as we could to Uncle Rob's where the others of the family had slept and were to stay until we had our own shelter, as it might be.

The ravine was lovely in its dips and curves deepening to the river, the water pleasantly gurgling on its way in the evening shadows. Aunt Frankie, with Wallace, met us at the top. Our family had rushed down to us at the bottom. We like Aunt Frankie. She is kind and pleasant to us. We had a dainty supper, helped wash up, then played skipping stones with the children on our way to the river. Neither Wallace, nor Uncle John's Albert can talk yet, though they soon will have made friends with us quite readily....

[The] next week was a busy one for each of us. Father sowed his White Russian wheat on his last year's breaking; the peas, oats and flax on Uncle Joe's land. I was shown how to handle the oxen, to harrow a good seed bed while father sowed from a big bag tied round his waist. All went well till I came to the end of land, turning too short the harrows tipped up on the oxen's back, frightening them into a run. I hung on to the rope halter shouting "whoa" till father came to release the harrows, explaining the serious effect to us if the oxen had gotten out of control. My hands were burnt with the rope. Mother made a salve of Balm of Gilead (black poplar) to heal my blisters.

With willing help and hindrance, we assisted mother to plant the roots of rhubarb, currants, strawberry, iris, and others we had brought with us from Palmerston. The garden seeds got under the ground. Our food to prepare, the care of Andrew and Mabel, many new chores to learn, the wandering cattle to herd as they wander far, and helping father get ready for a trip to Moose Jaw (for supplies), gave us no time for repining and wishing we had stayed at Heath's out from Moose Jaw, or, as Mr Alexander tried to persuade father, remained nearer the railway.

When looking for the cattle beyond the north ravine, we saw an ox-team with wagon standing in the slough. They had run away with their owner, Mr Mears, an Englishman, on his way from Saskatoon to Prince Albert. He was soaked to the hips, trying to coax the stubborn, difficult beasts out. He told us where the cattle were, and as later we drove the cattle to Uncle John's Kraal*, we heard singing. The ox-team was tied to the fence, and bedding spread out to dry. Aunt Patience was at the organ, Mr Mears in scanty attire was singing rustily, "Bringing in the Sheaves"—with us it was bringing home the cattle. They sang "Pork and Beans and Hard Tack," the "Pembina," "Red River Girl." Aunt Patience sang, "There is nothing in this World but Trouble and Dirt."

They were having fun, though.

Love from all of us,

Maryanne

_____

SADIE HARPER'S DIARY

Sadie Harper, the fifteen-year-old daughter of a Shediac, New Brunswick, family, began a diary on New Year's Day, 1890, which she would keep for eight years. A selection of her entries for January of that year presents a picture of local activities and life experiences from the perspective of this young woman. Although her days seem preoccupied with the weather, the round of visits and other social events, and the health of relatives and neighbours, one important aspect of her life emerges. This is the necessity of her work for the household when their domestic leaves to marry. Her work in that capacity required her to absent herself from school.

Shediac, New Brunswick, 1890
Sadie Harper's Diary, January 14 to January 24, 1890. MYY 476, Provincial Archives of New Brunswick.

Jan. 14. Thurs. Fine and cold. Mamma is not very well. May went down to the Point. Aunt Deanie was a little better. Helen quite sick and George very sick and poor Winnie was just taking La Grippe. Poor Mrs McKillop who died yesterday looks very natural. She died very easily. The Influenza is spreading here. Nellie got a long letter from Annie Lo in Luton, England. Win went to her music lesson as usual and went to Mrs Lawton's to practise. Jim White came up in the evening and stayed until quite late. Election is the order of the day.

Jan. 18. Sat. May was in bed all day. She was pretty sick and Miss Morrison came up in the aft. and stayed to tea. Bloise and I went on quite a snowshoe tramp. Our servant girl left today to get married and my work now is to clear

_____

*[An enclosure for sheep or cattle, South African in derivation.]

off the breakfast, dinner and tea tables and any extra work I am asked to. In the evening Miss Morrison, Winnie, Ted, Gertie and myself went to the Taits to attend a political meeting. The speakers were Mr Stephens and Mr Powel and heard a fine speech from the latter and I think if the ladies were to vote he would be sure to get his election. Dr Belliveau and his bride returned tonight....

Jan. 22. Wed. Fine but cold. I did not go to sch. today as there was plenty of work to do at home. Nellie and May do very well at cooking. Though May says she hates it. This aft. Mr Baird called and Mrs Webster and Aunt Kate and Aunt Maggie were up and Mr Ayer was in for a little while. Mamma seems quite better today. I forgot to say that I was to the supper last night and had a very nice time. Quite a number were there and all seemed to enjoy themselves. We did not have tea until late. Uncle Frank came up in the evening for awhile. I am reading a book from the sch. library called Square and [?] or building the House. It is quite nice.

Jan. 23. Thurs. It is a lovely bright fine day out and not very cold and there is lovely sleighing. Winnie is a good deal better and went down to the factory with *papa* to help him write in the office as Albert Webster is not up yet. He has La Grippe pretty bad. I did not go to sch. today but stayed home to work and work I did. I don't know how many times I wished to be back in sch. only that I had not my lesson prepared as it was Latin and Roman history. Poor little Edna Pavel died yesterday and Mrs Pavel is very sick. We heard today that old Mrs Welling up at the cape was very sick also and she had a paralytic stroke. Mamma is feeling very well. She is setting up in her bedroom having her tea and the tea table is waiting for me to clear it off and again sit down. I read until bedtime.

Jan. 24. Fri. It is fine and a little cold. I did not go to sch. today as we have no girl yet and no hopes of one. I think it is dreadful. It is run here and there keeping pots from going dry and letting things burn and so on. I think I am getting to be quite a cook and I like it quite well. Today I cooked the meat for dinner. It was pork and had to go on about half past nine and then you had to watch that it didn't burn and keep turning it over which was pretty hot work. But that is not all—but I won't bother telling about them. This aft. I washed out the cup towels—my work. Poor Duff is in for La Grippe, I guess. He has such a bad headache and shivers and Bloise also is sick and this evening just after tea which I was clearing, they both had their feet bathed in hot water, then came the howling about it being too hot. The sch. had just one session as there were so few there nearly every one with La Grippe or waiting on them. Winnie is reading aloud to Mamma in her room. Mrs Edmond's letter which came today. Albert Webster is a little better and Winnie will be down in the office until he is back. Poor Mr Dickie died yesterday aft. and Mrs Pavel is reported to be dying. It is so sad, and Mr Sweenie is very sick also with the famous disease. Nellie went for a drive with Teddie this afternoon down to the Point so good night for now.

SEWING

The needle skills that nineteenth-century girls learned at school and in the home had obvious uses in domestic production. These skills could also be applied to earn some extra money for small luxuries or for emergency situations. For the thirteen-year-old Mary Louise Pickering, whose first diary entry is printed below, work at rag sewing for five cents a ball would provide money to purchase a present for her mother's birthday.

Portage la Prairie, Manitoba, 1893
Norman Williamson, ed. The Diary of Mary Louise Pickering-Thomson (Altona, Man., n.d.), 1.

It is the twenty third of January 1893 and a Monday. I have decided to keep a diary. However I do not suppose that it will be at all like any one else's diary. I am not starting it in the conventional way either, for all the others I ever heard of were either commenced at the beginning of a New Year, on their birthday, or after some great event. Mine is simply started on a Monday, without any of those requisites. I am Mamie Pickering, a girl thirteen years of age. I live with my Papa and Mamma, a dog and a cat, in a house just within the town of Portage. Mamma is down town and Papa is at work lathing the new part which was added this fall. I am supposed to be sewing rags for a carpet. I don't like that work at all and the only reason I do it with anything like pleasure is that I have been promised five cents a ball for all I sew. I have $1.35 owing me now and I want to make up $5.00 before the 22nd of May, which is Mamma's birthday and I want to get her a ring. I have just called Papa to feed the chickens for I have a sore throat and can't go out. I suppose I had better go back to those rags. When Mamma came home she brought three papers, so I had some reading to do, however there was nothing interesting. I have made another ball of carpet rags so with the one I made before that means ten cents. It also means that I have only to make 71 more balls.

"LEARNERS"

Technological change and mechanization combined with a consumer demand for ready-made clothes greatly expanded the textile industry of late nineteenth-century Canada. In textile and garment-producing centres, manufacturers found a youthful female labour force in the daughters of the urban working class. As the Federal Commission on the Sweating System discovered, these girls were often exploited in factories or in the home manufacturing system.

Report Upon the Sweating System in Canada, *Canada Sessional Papers, No. 11, 1896, 10, 12-13, 16.*

There cannot be said to be an apprenticeship system in the ready-made clothing trade. "Learners" are employed—usually young boys and girls—but the employer is under no obligation to teach them a trade or any part of one.

...I learned of one contractor, engaged in making pants and vests, who makes a practice of employing "learners" who engage to work for him without wages while they are learning the trade. Those learners, usually girls, are kept at some trivial and easily mastered work, such as pulling out basting threads, sewing on buttons, or running up seams on a sewing machine, and then, when the term for which they agreed to work without wages expires, they are discharged, without having had an opportunity to learn any trade by which they can earn a livelihood, their places being filled by other "learners" who are in turn defrauded out of several months of work and time. It is not easy to determine just what effect the existence of such an "apprenticeship system" may have upon wages, but it is abundantly evident that when fair employers are forced to compete with those who take advantage of the opportunities which such a system offers to the unscrupulous, the effect must be detrimental....

The piecework system is probably more usual where women and children are employed than it is among male employees, but the division cannot be said to be on sex lines. Having regard, however, to the fact that all work done in private houses is done on the piecework system and is mainly done by women, it is evident that much the greater part of the clothing made under the piecework system is made by women...

The number of females in the ready-made clothing trade is relatively greater than the number of males, and, as a consequence, as the production of ready-made clothing increases in comparison with the making of ordered or custom clothing, the number of female employees becomes proportionately greater than the number of males. For the same reason, and in about the same proportion, child labour increases as compared with adult labour....

The development of the "sweating system"—including in the term the contractors' shops and the home-work system—has been coincident with the business revolution which has, within a quarter of a century, changed that industry from one in which the proportion of custom-made goods to ready-made was about as nine to one, to one in which the proportion of ordered clothing is probably not more, [than] if as much as, forty percent. The development of the ready-made industry by the subdivision of labour has rendered unnecessary the employment of so great a proportion of specially skilled handicraftsmen and made it possible to give employment to less skilled and cheaper labour....

———————

SUMMER WORK

As was the case in rural and resource society in British North America, after Confederation a girl's labour was highly valued and contributed to the family economy. Ada Williams worked on the fish flakes, made winter feed, picked wool, pulled vegetable garden weeds, and culled berries during her school vacations at West Jeddore, Nova Scotia around the turn of the twentieth century. Although some of this work, such as wool production, was divided on the basis of sex, the work of both girls and boys was valuable and essential for the survival of the family. While these reminiscences may seem to recall the practices of 1800 rather than 1900, one significant difference emerges. Technological advances in the wool industry had meant that the picked wool, which formerly had been carded and prepared for spinning by the household women and children, was by 1900 sent to the mill for processing. Over time, girls and women would lose the skills and knowledge required in this process (and later in others) and become increasingly dependent on consumer goods.

West Jeddore, Nova Scotia, c. 1900.
Grace Forsythe, ed. Tales of the Yesteryears: The Writing of Mrs. E.S. Williams, West Jeddore, 1888-1977, Book I, *44-45, 70-71.*

In childhood years, when the little one-roomed schoolhouse was closed for the summer holidays, all boys and girls had special work planned. Everyone worked for a living, children included. There was no money coming to the homes as a help. No family allowance.

The fisherman had to salt their fish, then dry them for market late in the fall. Everything seemed to be the hard way, but taken for granted as part of their living. So there was fish to be washed, pressed, dried and tended on the flakes or rocks. Hay had to be made for winter feed for the cattle. I worked with Owen, [her brother] who said we made a 'good team'.

Sheep shearing was always a gala day for the boys who went around the heads of the Cove, rounding up the sheep for the pens prepared by the men. After the shearing, came wool washing. It fell to the girls to pick wool and help the mothers get it ready for the carding mill at Smith Settlement. Many hours in the lovely month of June were spent in picking that wool! The mail driver took the bags of wool to the mill where it was made into rolls ready for spinning.

Then, out came the spinning wheels, and the whirr and buzz of the busy wheels were heard over the Cove. Some of the women gathered at a vacant house where their spinning wheels could be set up and left for a stormy day or any spare hours.

A fine sunny day meant working in the hayfield or weeding the garden. I remember weeding the vegetable garden until dusk, after which my bedtime lunch was a thick slice of bread and molasses with a glass of fresh buttermilk while I rested weary bones on the big rock that still 'grows' by our back door....

WONDERFUL CHILDHOOD DAYS

Anne Anderson was born in 1906 in St Albert, the daughter of a Scottish father and a Cree mother. She grew up speaking Cree and English and learning of both cultures. Her engaging account of her youth underlines the important emotional and work role of the eldest daughter in a growing family and also suggests the nature of the mother-daughter relationship that developed.

St Albert, Alberta, 1906-1920s
Anne Anderson Papers, Acc. 77.236, Provincial Archives of Alberta.

I must think back 60 years or so, oh, really is it that long ago. I picture a large weather beaten log house that belonged to my parents....

Yes, I see hand made tables, chairs, wooden beds, benches and wide shelves. Good, strong substantial furniture they had to be. The memories of 5 younger sisters and 2 rather spoiled, younger brothers. Tiny tots playing and so happy....

After romping about all day the children were ready for bed in early evening, so Mother took over the washing of each child and oh how beautiful were those clean little faces and those cheeks that reminded me of red apples. It was my turn to put them to bed, generally 3 in a bed, according to age and size. "Do not forget their prayers," were Mother's words....

We appreciated quietness after all our little darlings were in bed. It was peaceful and quiet. Mother and I would do mending, darning, patching or do beadwork. Then Father would come in from his barn after tending to chores. Then I was told to go to bed and believe me I was dead to the world in a few seconds. I would hear Mother and Dad speaking softly in Cree and French until Father decided to hit the sack. Mother often times sat until midnight to finish her sewing.

Mom and Dad always planted a large garden, they labored from early morning till late at night, appearing ever so happy at all times. Never did I see or hear my parents quarrel or disagree. We truly had a happy home environment. Were lucky children indeed. Mother was the spanker and we were really scared of her. Dad never laid a hand on us but he lectured us and made us understand....

I had two older brothers 13 and 15 years. Mother trained them to do cooking and caring of kids also. They were good bannock makers....

When the boys were old enough to work Father was very concerned with them. Mother likewise with her daughters....

I often think of all the responsibility left on my shoulders at such an early age. Luckily I never contracted any illnesses. I was hardy and strong. Hard work never kills anyone is the saying. I really believe this. As I mentioned before that there were six girls in our family. Mother had a daily program mapped out for us from Monday to Saturday. We were taught sewing, washing, baking, beadwork, moccasin making and tanning hides. Our daily routines of work came to us automatically without being told, but sewing was supervised by Mother. We made shirts for men and boys and suits for small boys, made from old suits. Then came dresses, aprons, petticoats, undershirts and pantys in all sizes and descriptions. I still see the neatly pressed suits for my little brothers and they looked so nice and fit so well.

Saturday afternoons were generally quilt making times. We girls who could make neat stitches made the blocks. We were also taught to make tidy knots. When blocks were made they were sewn together into a quilt top. Then Mother put the interlining and lining, by tacking them neatly with colored wool. The edges were bound with colored material. They looked very nice and as each one grew to adulthood, we were given a nice quilt. We were proud to have one of our own. Only after we proved to sew a neat stitch were we allowed to sew on the machine. We older girls felt it was like a graduation.

This went on year in and year out and our family steadily increased. I dearly loved to hold a new baby brother or sister. After all had seen the baby and kissed it, it was placed in the swing where he spent his first six months. When I attended grammar school, there was not much time for play. I thought of Mother and what she was doing. Did she need help! Being the eldest girl, I fully understood, with our family that care and supervision was needed at all times. I felt I should be there to help her. My dolls were my little brothers and sisters and real live dolls they were! I never had a doll of my own, and often I longed for a real pretty doll of my very own....

Our Father was taken by the Great Spirit very suddenly one day when a ruptured appendix was not diagnosed properly. This left Mother to raise 10 children, a baby of 5 weeks old. I believe we were all doomed without our dear father but somehow we survived.

After experiencing several months in a fatherless home I decided to go out working to help Mother with a bit of cash. This all happened in September. In the following spring I got a job in a home with 12 children. I fitted into a large family as it was home life for me. But poor Mom I would say, out there with such grief to bare by herself. Often I was in tears thinking of her. I had visions of saving a few dollars of the meagre earnings, I would give Mother and be able to get dolls and toys for Christmas, as I knew exactly what a sad Christmas we were faced with. I found the lady of the house a very kindly woman. She cared for the 4 youngest children. I had full charge of the milking, cooking of meals, baking, butter making and sandwich making. We went several miles to feed hungry, working men at the adjacent farmland.

I was always provided with 2 helpers and a horse and buggy. Each month I was taken home to see my Mom. Here I was so proud to hand over my $35.00 I had earned. She sure appreciated this and I continued to work until fall harvesting was over. I found it heavy work but enjoyed it. From 4 a.m. we were up and fed men and away they went to work. Then we prepared vegetables for dinner. Washed breakfast dishes and then milked nine cows with the help of 2 teenagers. Then we separated the milk and put what we needed for the day away, also the cream. It was a wild merry go round, but as a teenager it was equally fun and hard work.

My Mother was my idol. I wanted to be like her as an Indian. To be proud of her race and language and so capable in no matter what she did. I believed to be a treaty Indian was great. I married a treaty Indian therefore and became full status with treaty rights....

----

3. SCHOOLING

MRS LAY PRESIDED

In the following document, a woman recalls her education between the ages of 12 and 14 at Mrs Lay's school in Montreal. Private schools of this type, accepting day and boarding scholars, proliferated in the third quarter of the nineteenth century in Canada's commercial towns and cities and are evidence of the desire of the burgeoning middle class to educate their daughters in the accomplishments and values suited to their lives as adult members of that class. The influence of such education and of female directors, like Mrs Lay, made an obvious imprint on the girls who attended these schools.

Montreal, 1870
Dougall Family Papers, MG 29 C34, Public Archives of Canada.

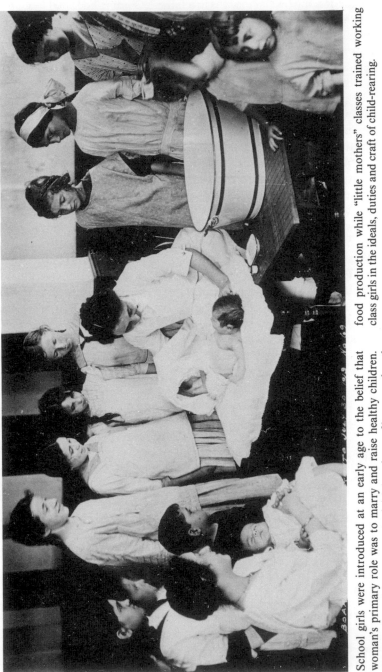

School girls were introduced at an early age to the belief that woman's primary role was to marry and raise healthy children. Home economics classes emphasized the science of housework and food production while "little mothers" classes trained working class girls in the ideals, duties and craft of child-rearing.

Credit: Little Mothers' Class, Board of Education No. 69, City of Toronto Archives.

The school, of about 100 day girls and 20 boarders, was known as Saybrooke Hall, and was kept by Mrs Lay, a Southern lady of refinement and intelligence and imbued with a strong religious spirit. She had been a school-mate of Frances Willard, and a literary society in our school was called the Willard Society. At its meetings the elder girls took part in monthly discussions and had regular business meetings. Many of the girls later, with this training, became secretaries of church and other societies.

Every morning began with prayers, when Mrs Lay presided on the platform surrounded by her dozen or more teachers. On Monday mornings the girls were grouped according to the churches they attended. The group—say from St Andrew's Presbyterian Church—would be told to stand up, and girls would be singled out and asked to repeat the text and all they could remember of the previous day's sermon. Then the group from the English Cathedral, and so on. Fear of not being able to respond made us form the habit of close listening that I, for one, have never lost. On Friday mornings our favourite Scripture texts were asked, and each one had to be ready as we never knew who would be called upon. I think careful Bible reading came on another day. Mrs Lay's influence over her girls was of the highest order. We were early sent away to Edinburgh, but Mrs Lay's influence with me is outstanding, and so many of her pupils to this day show the effects of her early training.

"THE BOREDOM OF EVERYTHING"

Many Quebec girls received their primary and secondary education under the tutelage of nuns at convent schools. The strict education at these schools was highly credited by contemporary parents and observers. However, for some young women, like Henriette Dessaulles, the structure of this religious education must have been narrow and confining. The following extracts from Henriette Dessaulles' journal are testimony to the critical mind and spirit that she brought to her religious education. This questioning attitude and liberal thought continued in her later life as she pursued a career in journalism, writing for *Le Devoir* under the name of "Fadette."

Quebec, 1874-1875
Louise Dechêne, ed., Journal d'Henriette Dessaulles, *Montreal, 1971, 25, 36, 67.*

24 September 1874

Oh! The boredom of everything the last few days, it would be a sin to try to keep the memory of it. Sister du P.S., who I so little like, was sick, in the infirmary, it was a little turkey of a postulant who replaced her and she performed the miracle that I spent the time regretting the absence of our teacher. At that time, I studied a little, I did my work to rid myself of it, I questioned the turkey enough to make her sick with fear, because she did not always know what to make of my questions or of my arguments, to her credit....

24 February 1875

A singular little incident this afternoon. I was a bit tired and absent-minded during class.

Questioned three times on the history of England, I answered indifferently and without enthusiasm: with regard to the quarrels between Henry II and Thomas Beckett, I finished by saying that the latter must have been punctilious and quarrelsome and that I would have been curious to see another version of the history than the one we were learning. I could have pulled off the Sister's headdress and I would not have achieved a better effect and naturally I replied that way to tease her. She ordered me to be quiet, which I quietly did, and I pretended to sleep the rest of class. After the meal, she brought me alone with her and wanted to know where those "dangerous ideas" came from. I looked at her and told her that it was a whim, that I did not believe a word I said....

30 September 1875

Soon it will be retreat...but I hate it!...to convert me?...Oh, no, that's a phrase that one! To be alone and tranquil! I am tired of my classes, of my music, of the others, of myself, of everything. Of God? But yes, it is stupid to say maybe, but that's the truth, however stupid it may be! to be incapable of saying a good prayer, to dislike His work, it is perhaps this horrible thing that I call "tired of God."

I am forcing myself however to continue, whatever the cost. I study, I pray, I talk, and when the night comes, I sleep and I am rid of it all!....

WINTER SCHOOL DAYS

Most Nova Scotia girls would have received their book learning in schools like that described by E.S. Williams below. However, not all learning at school was confined to books. From the laughs of other students at her clothing, this young girl learned the distinctions of class, while from her escapades in winter play she learned the lessons of friendship with other girls. E.S. William's schooling did not last very long. The family's need of her help in caring for younger siblings took precedence over attendance at school.

Nova Scotia, 1895
Grace Forsythe, ed. Tales of the Yesteryears: The Writing of Mrs. E.S. Williams, West Jeddore, 1888-1977, *Book I, 34-36.*

My school days began when I was about seven years old, in 1895. Being the third child, I was launched forth under the protection of Annie and Owen. Memories of that long tramp over snow and ice make the walk seem endless. Being bundled up heavily with clothes made it all the more difficult. Drawers had to be tucked down around the ankles, and over them were heavy knitted stockings of homespun wool from Papa's sheep. Petticoats of flannelette were an added protection. My dress was a brick-colored homespun, woven by Aunt Annie Stephen and made by Mama. The top was plain to the waist, long sleeves, a few gathers around the waist, and a trimming of velvet around the neck to stop the itching. Over all that I wore a hand-me-down coat. My woollen stocking cap was tied down with a "cloud", a long scarf crossed in front and tied in the back, leaving eyes, nose, and mouth clear. My mitts were hand-knit wool, and on my feet I wore hand-sewn moccasins made by Papa, who was a good hand at making them. They were moose or cow hide, treated with cod liver oil to make them more durable and waterproof. A coating of mutton fat also helped, and completed the job.

Not all children wore such an outfit, but we from the Cove were fishermen's children. We suffered many disdainful glances and remarks, especially when the heat of the stove brought out the aroma of cod oil. Annie and I had this outfit for the first years of school, but styles had changed by the time the younger girls went. In summer we went barefoot.

There was no physical drill in the schools then, as a walk of more than a mile over all kinds of roads in all kinds of weather, snow banks to plough through, was all the exercise needed for one day....

...during the winter months it became extremely cold following a heavy rain. On the hillside among the trees ice was bulging out in all directions. A brook remained clear enough where we could fill our water bottles for cleaning slates and for drinking. One noon hour Rhoda Doyle, Florrie Baker, Millie Richardson, and I decided to coast among those trees. We would crouch, or hunch, sliding from one tree to another. We were having a wonderful time until I missed grabbing a tree. I flew over the downhill ice and struck a rock or jagged piece of ice, with the result that the knee of my wool stocking and long drawers were badly torn and my knee skinned. I decided not to mention the accident to anyone, and the girls promised not to.

By the time school was out, and I started the long walk home, my knee was in a sorry state. When dusk came, the little oil lamp was lit in the living-room with Mama attending to the latest baby. I got out in the kitchen by the old

Waterloo stove, uncovered my knee and applied a liberal dose of turpentine. It was agony for a while, as the turpentine was like fire on the raw flesh. By the time Mama smelled the turpentine and came out to the kitchen, I was weeping bitterly. She washed the wound to try to relieve the burning, but the water only made it worse. I was laid up for days, as my flesh was cooked and covered with blisters. That taught me to leave ice and trees alone....

Teachers of those years were real heroines. In a one-roomed school, with a stove in the middle, children three in a seat at times, and often 100 enrolled. She stood on the platform with her pretty crisp white apron trimmed with embroidery over the shoulder covering her clothes as a protection from chalk dust. Her dark skirt was ankle or floor length, and was worn with a pretty white or colored blouse. Teachers of years gone by were held in high esteem by parents, thus instilling the same respect in their children.

I didn't get very far in school, as I was more or less Mama's helper at home. Annie and Amanda were studying to be teachers and by 1900 there were four younger children. My pet subjects were geography and book-keeping, and I was keen on spelling matches which the teachers often had. I used to watch the teacher trying to explain geometry to the older students, inwardly vowing I would never try to learn or understand that. After I left school I used to read and practice writing on my own at night by the light of the oil lamp in my room....

SCHOOL DISCIPLINE

Although educational writers frequently questioned the ability of female teachers to exercise appropriate classroom discipline, Marjorie King was obviously impressed by the authority of the teachers she remembered from her primary schooling days at Whitby.

Whitby, Ontario, 1908
Marjorie James King, "Schooling in Whitby Ontario, 1908-1918."

My family moved from Toronto to Whitby in 1908, when I was six. I had already attended Kindergarten and the primary class in Toronto, and could read quite well, having been taught largely by the phonetic method. I suppose I must also have had some experience with numbers. At any rate I was quickly moved from the "baby class" in Whitby to Junior First, or Senior First, I'm not sure which. These would be equivalent to Grades I and II of the present method of naming classes.

The teacher was Miss Woodhouse, known as "Peggy Woodhouse". She was short, and as broad as she was tall, and could move remarkably nimbly on her small feet concealed beneath her floor-length skirts, almost as if she had been on casters rather than feet, when she had occasion to belabour a wrongdoer with her stick.

All the teachers used sticks for punishment except the principal, who used a rubber strap. Miss Woodhouse's stick was a longish, widish black ruler. Miss Borrowman's was a sort of cane or switch that might have been cut from a tree. Corporal punishment was used fairly infrequently and fairly formally in front of the class, and consisted of strokes on the palms of the hands. Miss Woodhouse was the only teacher I remember who used the stick to rap knuckles or shoulders in the ordinary course of the days work. Incidentally, corporal punishment was confined to pupils in the primary or "public" school, and girls very rarely received it....

4. EDUCATED BY HOME AND SOCIETY

BATHING CONTEST

Eunice M.L. Harrison was born in 1861 in British Columbia. She received her education at a number of Victoria private schools, at St Ann's Academy and at a finishing school. During those years she was trained to be a refined lady by women she recalled as "English gentlewomen of the old school." Eunice Harrison also recalls participating in a bathing contest described below in opposition to the lessons of her schooling and her parents' authority.

British Columbia, c. 1870
E.M.L. Harrison, "Pioneer Judge's Wife," 18-19, Eunice Harrison Papers, MG 29, C54, Public Archives of Canada.

Then was held the first bathing contest on the coast, if not in the whole of Canada. Of course it wasn't called that and it wasn't open to the public.

Mrs Dietz from San Francisco, who was living in Moodyville, and was known for her pleasant foibles and wealth, engineered a contest and got a young doctor from Moodyville to examine and measure the girls who numbered about fifty. They had assembled there from the various districts on a holiday.

I surmised that my parents in Victoria would rather object to my taking part in such a novel diversion, but I could see no harm in it. A friend finally persuaded me to enter.

The physician lined us up and measured us from head to toe, amidst much merriment, in which the inevitable chaperone heartily joined.

I was very surprised when I was declared the winner, and more so when awarded a handsome gold prize about Fifty Dollars, for no one knew that a prize was to be awarded.

When I told my parents they were extremely annoyed and made me promise to never engage in such things again.

———————

ETIQUETTE AND ADORNMENT

The teenage years were a mixture of childhood dependence and adult responsibility for Mary Louise Pickering, a Portage la Prairie girl. By the age of thirteen, Mary Louise was expressing hopes for a future teaching career, an interest in the young men in her neighbourhood, and an increasing independence of thought in her diary. There is also an increasing interest and acceptance of the lessons of etiquette and adornment that she had learned.

Portage la Prairie, Manitoba, 1893
Norman William, ed., The Diary of Mary Louise Pickering-Thomson *(Altona, Man., n.d., 18-19).*

1893
May 31—Wednesday: I ironed this morning and hunted up all my fancy articles for my room and threaded my beads and made them into a string for my purse and put a new piece on my handkerchief box. I put the handkerchiefs in their box and my jewelry into its case and arranged my work basket and ripped off the blue ribbons on my garnet velvet bag and put old rose ribbons on it. I tied my little glass bottles together and made them look pretty and I put my ribbons in a drawer of my little bureau; my laces in another and gloves, girdles, purse and hair pins in another. Put the silk, satin, plush and velvet pieces into my boxes and packed them all into my big wooden box. It took nearly all day.

[When she was finished, Pickering made a list of her possessions. In doing so, she left us a clear description of the wardrobe of a girl her age living in western Canada.]

Dresses: Navy Blue Cheviot, Ribbon Trimmed, Red Blouse Waist, Grey Gored Skirt, Pink Shambra Dress, Cream Blouse, Honey Suckle Print, Lace, White Muslin, Embroidery, Fawn Cashmere, Silk, Nunsveiling, Poplin, Pink Flannelette, Blouse, Cream and Red Sailor Blouse.

Coats: Grey Corduroy Ulster, Grey Corduroy Cape, Fawn Coat, Brown Cloth Jacket, Grey Persian Lamb Muff, Grey Persian Collar, Red Tee Wool Tie, Cream Wool Tie, Cream Scarf.
Jewellery: 4 Rings, 1 silver Bar Brooch, 1 Gold Small Brooch, 3 Common Brooches, Locket and Chain.
One Dozen Common Handkerchiefs, Six Fancy Handkerchiefs, Handkerchief Box.
Hats: Grey Persian Lamb Cap, Grey Cloth Cap, Fawn Felt Hat, White Leghorn, Trimmed Rose Wreath, Sailor Black Straw, Black Straw Velvet, Trimmed Wind.
3 White Undershirts, 1 Winter Undershirt, 1 Medium Undershirt, 2 pair Canton Flannel Drawers, 3 Pairs Conor Drawers, 2 Red Flannel Shirts, 3 Ribbon Sashes.
Hair Ribbons, Bows and Laces without number.
Writing case, pincushion, leather purse, plush purse, Ladies Companion, needles, thread, buttons, black velvet girdle, brown kid gloves, untanned kid gloves, silk gauntletts, corded silk gauntletts, black cashmere gloves, blue cashmere cuffs, kid mitts, cashmere stockings, winter stockings, two trimmed night gowns, 1 common pair boots, 1 pair best kid boots, 1 pair cardigans, 1 pair spring rubbers, 1 button hook, books, 1 glove buttoner, knife, etc. Contents of writing case—toothbrush glass, 1 bottle Hayt's German Cologne, scissors, work basket, scraps of work at odd times.

[To this list Mamie adds the following rules of etiquette for young ladies.]

Table Manners
Take your seat quietly at the table.
Sit firmly in your chair without loling, leaning back, drumming or any other uncouth action.
Unfold your napkin and lay it in your lap.
Eat soup directly with a spoon.
Be careful to make no noise in chewing or swallowing your food.
Cut your food with your knife.
But the fork is to be used to convey it to your mouth.
Break your bread, not cut or bite it.
Your cup was made to drink from, and your saucer for to hold your cup.
When you have finished the course lay your knife and fork upon your plate with the handle toward your right hand.
Wipe you nose if necessary but never blow it at the table.
It is almost unnecessary to mention that the table cloth is not the place for your salt.

Better to be too late for the steamer or the railway train than for dinner. Snobs sometimes wore gloves at the table; it is not necessary that you should copy them.

TO BE A LADY

Evelyn McLeod's memoirs are important for two reasons. First, they detail the frequent family arrangements made for children who lost their mothers or both of their parents. Second, the reminiscences briefly outline the philosophy which dominated the training of so many Canadian girls—their education to be ladies.

Consort, Alberta, 1909
Evelyn Slater McLeod, "Restless Pioneers", Acc. 77.39, 1-2, Provincial Archives of Alberta.

WHEN I FIRST SET FOOT on the grasslands of Alberta I was nearly six years old. We were one of 19 families and some single men, who had filed claims for homestead land the previous fall and who, in the spring of 1909, had come to take possession. Most of us were from Benson County in the State of North Dakota.

I was the daughter of Ray Slater and had joined the family of my great-uncle Wesley Williams and his wife Ellen (who were childless) when my mother died the previous year. There were five of us children and we were fortunate, for each was taken into the home of a relative.

My Uncle Wesley, 60 years of age at that time, was a kindly man of medium build with bright blue eyes and ample moustache. His wife Ellen, 12 years younger, was of English ancestry and had taught school prior to their marriage. She was quite good-looking in a stern way—her gray-green eyes complementing her severe mouth. Her everyday gingham and Sunday challis were in the style of the period, which was to the ankle, covering well the upper part of her high-topped shoes. Aunt Ellen took good care of me. My hair was braided so tightly I had perpetually raised eyebrows and I was not permitted to make mud-pies because I would soil my pinafore. Her tongue was caustic. She was a stickler for good manners and was determined that I should grow up to be a lady, an eventuality to which she referred often....

Although she could not be even ten years old, this young Quebec girl is portrayed by her photographer as a pensive adult woman in the idealized setting of the parlour.

Credit: Collection Musée des Grondines, N 175-125 Décor 863, Archives nationales du Québec.

"WHEN I GROW UP, I SHALL BE A NUN"

Jeanne Brassard's childhood, described below by an English observer, was probably fairly typical of that experienced by other rural French Canadian girls. She was already aware of the different roles of men and women through observing her parents and brothers but she drew on the models of the nuns who taught her at the convent school to define herself.

St Aniel, Quebec, c. 1915
Jessie Sime, In a Canadian Shack *(Toronto, 1937, 109-112).*

Jeanne wanted a sister. Indeed it was her confiding to me that she had had enough of boys that first drew us together. (Not that I had had enough of boys: I have never yet had a sufficiency of them.) She hoped that "it" would be a girl. "Such a companion for me!" she said sighing. "Boys are so noisy. *Ils font tant de train.* When I grow up, I shall be a nun. But I would like a little sister now. She would be company." I must offer Jeanne the tribute of a little section to herself, for though she was not subtle, I have never again met anyone like her. She stands out in my recollection as always neat, amazingly neat, as if she had dropped from Heaven like that and stayed just so ever since. Her abundant dark hair, which her mother always found time to arrange in ringlets, fell down her back, midway to her waist, in a thick clustering—mane is the only word I can think of; each ringlet was, as it were, to itself and remained miraculously in place, the whole lying heavily on her shoulders. In front it was parted and brushed to each side evenly at the temples, so that you can see the brow, broad and placid already, the well-shaped ears, the dark, calm eyes, the lovely rounded cheeks of childhood, and the mouth which, if God, as the saying goes, gives us all the rest of our face, we form for ourselves. Jeanne was right, I believe, in thinking herself already a little nun. She did what she had to do methodically, with no fuss. She liked set hours for set duties. She was useful, industrious and in her own way cheerful. She was never put out, that I saw, except occasionally with the boys. I don't know that I have ever before or since my acquaintance with little Jeanne Brassard seen anyone who had a vocation for a sisterhood as she had. She seemed in a way pre-ordained to be a nun: you felt that if she married she would be led astray and be unhappy. The days should tick themselves away for her by the Convent clock. She would not be a mystical nun but she would be a useful one. I see her now, approaching me with our milk-jug in her hand; it was usually she who measured out the fresh-drawn milk for me. I see her sedate smile "Bonjour, Madame." She spoke well: the nuns at the Convent School were "real French"—*vraies Françaises de France,* as the habitants said—and she copied them in every-thing. Did she look an anachronism in that warm, bare, French-Canadian kitchen? Not exactly. She just looked a nun in miniature, and she would have looked that anywhere.

———————

CHAPTER TWO

NEITHER CHILD NOR WIFE

Living alone was the most rare of conditions in the late nineteenth and early twentieth centuries. Even though central Canada was being fundamentally transformed by the growth of industry and migration to the cities, changes often associated with rising individualism, there were really no housing forms to accommodate a single person of either sex living alone. The more economic life changed, the more social conventions demanded established family patterns, stability, and continuity in life at home. Single men had long lived away from kin in Canadian bunkhouse communities. Domestic forms did not so firmly govern males. But by the early twentieth century, more young women were challenging convention by taking up rooms in boarding houses in town and going away from home to work or to school. With the home no longer the centre of production, families were smaller. There were fewer children to demand care from teen-aged daughters. Among poorer families, the household's greater need for purchased goods pressed older offspring into the paid labour force. In more prosperous homes the shift from home production offered daughters time to cultivate religious and cultural interests or to seek further formal education. The sight of young women outside the home, the streets, the factories, and the lecture halls was profoundly unsettling for many Victorians—and the more the range of young women's activities broadened, the more censure was levelled at a life outside the discipline of family or some surrogate for kin.

There were a variety of ways in which young women might respectably pass the time between childhood and marriage. In late nineteenth-century agricultural Ontario some girls stayed at home, or worked in households nearby, marrying later than their mothers had because in difficult economic times the founding of a new family required many years of thrifty preparation. Maritime and Quebec women frequently lived with kin in New England, sending money from their factory wages home, often going home themselves when the time for marriage came. For some, this period involved training and the practice of a craft or profession outside their parents' household but under home governance. Student and qualified teachers lived with kin or boarded with other families. The same was the case for seamstresses and, of course, for domestics. Thousands of *Québécoises* spent this time as novices with religious orders, protected from both secular temptation and material insecurity.[1] The handful of privileged women enrolled at Canadian universities lived either in strictly regulated residences, such as Sir Donald Smith's Royal Victoria College at McGill, or in specially designated boarding arrangements like those developed at Queen's. In nursing, the female profession with the fewest economic and social barriers to entry, young women were housed within hospital complexes under stern patriarchial regimes.[2]

There were pleasant aspects to this carefully protected sojourn. Le collectif Clio tells us that for many young Québécoises time as a novice was a serene period of communal labour before marriage.[3] The account in chapter three of the rollicking tucking frolic in Cape Breton suggests that the family watch on unmarried sociability offered a comforting sense of order and support in the succession of generations.[4] But parental restrictions could be vexing. In her diary Jessie Low records the frustration of a young woman bound to the tea service in the drawing room while the wide world waited at the door.[5] There is a hearty shout of rebelliousness in the writings of many young Victorians. "In a sense, girls were the first adolescents." Because women were, by the ideals of Victorian culture, always to remain partly children, dependent, vulnerable, and emotional, growing girls more quickly pressed against their limits of acceptable teenage behaviour than did growing boys. Females were more frequently labelled precocious. Their pubescent sexuality evoked fear and demanded restriction from public view. Their every activity outside the home seemed to imperil their qualifications as future guardians of the hearth. Thus, the penalties for adolescent acting out were severe. If she wished to make a respectable marriage, a young woman whatever her class had little choice but to accept the conventional terms of trade, offering her labour cheaply, or at no price, and living in modest confining decorum under familial discipline.[6]

Because Christian values were most closely identified with the domestic sphere, the late Victorians demanded strict piety from young women. Church functions offered girls an irreproachable reason to be away from home, within evangelical religious practice an emotional release, and among all denominations a chance for sociability outside the family circle. But devoutness also schooled women to an accepting and obedient demeanor, the appropriate nature for the guardian angel wife Ruskin described tending the walled garden of family life.[7]

Christian obedience implied obedience to older kin. That part of a young woman's life which existed apart from family—her studies, her work, her friends—was residual, contingent. Domestic claims took precedence, drawing the young printer away from the press to the kitchen, the medical student from the laboratories to the drawing room of a lonely mother, the writer to the untended hearth of a young colonial relative. For unmarried as for married women no calling was higher than the care of family.[8]

Standing in for mothers and aunts to care for children, the elderly, and the ill, however, required traits inimical to the image of fair and marriageable maiden, so that in her late teens a Victorian girl began to live out the perplexing tension deeply embedded in nineteenth century womanhood, between dependence and self-reliance, emotionality and calm competence, frailty and strength. Some found the burden of these diverging expectations so great that they escaped into hysteria, a passive and therefore possible, if only marginally acceptable, way for a young woman to call attention to her predicament and claim relief from her pain.[9]

Medical perceptions of women's physical limitations emerged in large measure from these social conventions of female passivity, vulnerability, and limp-wittedness—and served in turn to reinforce them. Indeed as declining family size, increased life expectancy, heightened convictions about Christian stewardship, and liberal individualist predilections toward equality seemed to release women, young and old, for more activities outside the home, physicians provided influential justifications for female confinement to the domestic sphere. They argued that women's brains weighed less, a product of their evolutionary specialization in reproduction and that this difference was physical proof of lower female intelligence, a pragmatic ground to limit female education. They posited a fixed amount of energy within growing girls' bodies so that young women who chose to concentrate upon their studies or take up wearying employments weakened their developing wombs and imperilled their futures as mothers. Such activities seemed ill-considered in any case as after puberty the fickle humours of the menstrual cycle were thought to make girls unsteady students and unreliable workers outside the home. Thus the bonds of domesticity and devout motherhood drew closely around girls even in the decade before marriage when they were more likely than at any other time in the life cycle to be spending work and leisure time outside the home.[10]

Stark contradictions troubled girls, especially working-class girls, in this time of life between families. Although propertied observers, among them Lady Aberdeen, believed that women needing to earn a living were best protected by employment as domestics, young servants were vulnerable. They lived inside households but outside the incest taboo. Even the best-intentioned of mistresses were poor defenders of their maids' interests, their loyalties torn by their own need for labour, the misunderstandings emerging from cultural differences across class, and the fact that employers' obligations to family always took precedence over those to household members. Service was never a haven of sexual safety.[11]

Neither, as the century wore on, did a position in service seem very much like home. In rural areas or commercial towns when hired girls worked for neighbours, when their own families were connected to those of their employers by trade, religious fellowship, or long association, community standards had demanded that the distance between a young maid and her mistress be minimized, consistently in public presentation if less commonly in practice. But, by the 1890s, urban servants were more often immigrants or migrants from distant locations employed to clean, cook, and care for children, to be sure, but employed also to signify, by the differences between their own demeanor, clothing, and class background and those of their masters, the social station of the household. This change turned earlier companionable ties between mistress and maid into a narrow formality. The city servant was further isolated in the early twentieth century as the development of suburbs set her workplace further from the shops and entertainments where she had formerly met her peers, in a smaller more efficient house where she worked alone.[12] The bourgeoise claims for domestic service were increasingly implausible, the non-domestic alternatives for young women seeking work increasingly attractive.

Technological change and pay differentials between the sexes increased the industrial demand for female labour in the late nineteenth century. The feminine domestic virtues of politeness, patience, obedience, and physical grace also made girls attractive as retail workers, office clerks, and employees in service industries. By 1900, for example, most telephone operators in Canada were female. All of these jobs paid more than domestic service so that girls with meagre family resources wishing to pursue respectable aims, to assist their kin financially, or to save a small stake for marriage, turned more often to 'not very respectable' jobs in commerce or industry as the period wore on.[13]

Middle-class women's groups, particularly the YWCA and the WCTU, responded by establishing urban hostels for single working girls. Some factory owners provided residential accommodation for their female hands. Department stores often required as a condition of employment that their clerks demonstrate that they had safe lodgings. At the end of the period, in war-time, the state pressed this transition further, attempting to change public attitudes toward female work outside the home by describing as loyal actions that had recently been labelled unladylike, and asking the public censor to cover-up reports of female vulnerability on the streets and in the workplace, aspects of a labouring girl's life that physicians and bourgeois feminists had lately accentuated.[14]

NOTES

1   David Gagan, *Hopeful Travellers* (Toronto, 1981); Margaret Conrad, "Recording Angels: Private Chronicles of Maritime Women, 1800-1950," Canadian Research Institute for the Advancement of Women, *Papers,* IV (1982); Marta Danylewycz, "Taking the Veil in Montreal, 1850-1920: an Alternative to Migration, Motherhood and Spinsterhood," paper presented to the Canadian Historical Association, June 1978, London; Micheline Dumont-Johnson, "Les communautés religieuses et la condition féminine," *Recherches Sociographiques* (janvier-avril 1978) 79-102; Susan Mann Trofimenkoff, *The Dream of Nation* (Toronto, 1982) 123.

2   Margaret Gillett, *We Walked Very Warily, a History of Women at McGill* (Montreal, 1981) chapter 5; Margaret Street, *Watch Fires on the Mountains* (Toronto, 1973); The Corrective Collective, *Never Done, Three Centuries of Women's Work in Canada* (Toronto, 1974) 88-89; Stanley Frost, *McGill University 1801-1895* (Montreal, 1980) 251-59; Hilda Neatby, *Queen's University* (Montreal, 1978)

132-33, 206-10; Elizabeth Smith, *A Woman with a Purpose,* edition prepared by Veronica Strong-Boag, (Toronto, 1980).

3   Le Collectif Clio, *L'Histoire des femmes au Québec* (Montreal, 1982).

4   See "Community Matchmaking," in this chapter.

5   See "Planning and Account-keeping," in this chapter.

6   Joseph F. Kett, *Rites of Passage* (New York, 1977) 133-43; Walter E. Houghton, *The Victorian Frame of Mind* (New Haven, 1957) 348-52; similarly for the United States, Bernard Wishy, *The Child and Republic* (Philadelphia, 1968) chapters 3 and 14 and provocatively for an earlier period, Philip Greven, *The Protestant Temperament: Patterns of Childrearing, Religious Experience and the Self in Early America* (New York, 1977).

7   W.E. Houghton, *The Victorian Frame of Mind,* 348-52.

8   See for example the case of "A Pinafored Printer" in chapter 5 of this book; Alice Ravenhill, *The Memoirs of an Educational Pioneer* (Toronto, 1951); the autobiographical sketch of Maude Abbott included in chapter 5 of this book under the title "Struggles for Higher Education." Mary Electa Adams also followed this pattern, see Elsie Pomeroy, "Mary Electa Adams: A Pioneer Educator," *Ontario History,* XLI (1949) 106-17.

9   For general discussions of this pattern, see Carroll Smith-Rosenberg, "The Hysterical Women: Sex Roles and Role Conflict in Nineteenth-Century America," *Social Research,* XXXIX (1972) and Alan Krohn, *Hysteria: the Elusive Neurosis,* published as monograph 45/46 of *Psychological Issues* XII, Numbers 1/2 (1978) chapter 4. See also "Problems of Adolescence from a Medical Perspective" in this chapter.

10 Wendy Mitchinson, "R.M. Bucke: A Victorian Asylum Superintendent," *Ontario History,* LXXIII (1981); Carroll Smith-Rosenberg and Charles Rosenberg, "The Female Animal: Medical and Biological Views of Women and Her Role in Nineteenth-Century America," *Journal of American History* (Sept. 1973); Wendy Mitchinson, "Historical Attitudes toward Women and Childbirth," *Atlantis,* IV, (1979); Wendy Mitchinson, "Medical Attitudes toward Female Sexuality in Late Nineteenth Century English Canada," unpublished paper presented to the Canadian Historical Association Annual Meetings, Saskatoon, 1979; Wendy Mitchinson, "Gynecological Operations on Insane Women: London, Ontario, 1895-1901," *Journal of Social History,* XV (Spring 1982) 467-84; Carl Degler, "What Ought to be and What Was: Women's Sexuality in the Nineteenth Century," *American Historical Review,* LXXIX (December 1974) 1467-90; Linda Kealey, ed., *A Not Unreasonable Claim* (Toronto, 1979) 8; Daniel Scott Smith, "Family Limitation, Sexual Control and Domestic Feminism in Victorian America," in Mary Hartman and Lois Banner, eds., *Clio's Consciousness Raised* (New York, 1974) 119-37; Carl Degler, *At Odds: Women and the Family in America from the Revolution to the Present* (New York, 1980) chapters 2, 3, 4, 9, 10, 11, 12.

11 Genevieve Leslie, "Domestic Service in Canada, 1880-1920," in Janice Acton *et al,* eds., *Women at Work* (Toronto, 1974) 94; Leonore Davidoff, "Mastered for Life: Servant and Wife in Victorian and Edwardian England," *Journal of Society History,* VII (1974) 406-22. On the vulnerability of young British immigrant servants in Canada, see Joy Parr, *Labouring Children,* 114-18; on the relationship between illegitimacy rates and women's occupational distribution, see Louise Tilly, Joan Scott, and Miriam Cohen, "Women's Work and European Fertility Patterns," *Journal of Interdisciplinary History,* VI (1976) 447-76.

12 We are grateful to le collectif Clio for suggesting this point. Their work on Quebec

women includes an extremely valuable discussion of the varieties and changing conditions of work in domestic service. See *L'Histoire des femmes au Québec,* op. cit. Also on domestic servants in nineteenth-century Toronto, Montreal, Quebec City, and Halifax, see Claudette Lacelle, "Les domestiques dans les villes Canadiennes au XIXe siècle: effectifs et conditions de vie," *Histoire sociale/Social History* (May 1982) 181-207.

13   Janice Acton *et al,* eds., *Women at Work, Ontario,* 72, 267, 280, 281; Joan Sangster, "The 1907 Bell Telephone Strike: Organizing Women Workers," *Labour/ Le Travailleur,* III (1978) 110; Corrective Collective, *Never Done,* 96-101; Parr, *Labouring Children,* 126-28.

14   Wendy Mitchinson, "The YWCA and Reform in the Nineteenth Century," *Histoire sociale/Social History* (Nov. 1979); Suzann Buckley, "British Female Immigration and Imperial Development: Experiments in Canada, 1885-1931," *Hecate: Women's Interdisciplinary Journal* (Jan. 1977); Barbara Roberts, "A Work of Empire: Canadian Reformers and British Female Immigration" in Linda Kealey, ed., *A Not Unreasonable Claim* (Toronto, 1980); Barbara Roberts, "Sex, Politics and Religion: Controversies in Female Immigration Reform Work in Montreal, 1881-1919," *Atlantis* (Autumn, 1980); Barbara Wilson, *Ontario and the First World War, 1914-18* (Toronto, 1977) XXXIX, 103.

1. GROWING UP

ENTERING WOMANHOOD

The emotional and physical changes that attended the teenage years are frequently hidden between the lines in diaries of young women. But, in the case of Susan Crease, a Victoria, B.C. girl, one encounters specific references to a general dissatisfaction with her life, her family, and herself. Her Sunday, April 11, 1871 reference to her "first attack" may be a rare entry noting the beginning of her period.

Victoria, British Columbia, 1871 and 1873.
Susan Crease's Diaries, Entries of April 5, 9 and 11, 1871 and September 25-27, 1873. Crease Family Papers A/E/C86/C864. Provincial Archives of British Columbia.

5.19.71
I am 15 years old a great dunce & very ugly and cross. I have lost my dear pet baby Harry. I am not happy O God make me more so. I am no longer bright and lively but dull and stupid O that they loved me more but I cannot repine. I have more than I deserve I must be grateful and thankful & love them more. Dear Jesus teach me to do so.
Fine weather
however

9 Friday I am going to stay at Yale with Mrs Bushby for some weeks
11 Sunday My first attack....

September 1873
25th B & I went to school and I have been grumbling at having to do so because it will prevent my going with the Duponts on their camping expedition as well as because it prevents our seeing Miss C Dupont whom I love very much. Dear Mama is not very well and looks tired. I wish I could help her but her heart is barred against me so that she hates to see me.
26 Went to Teachers' meeting Aunt E walked round Beacon Hill & home with me.

27 *A dreadful* day. We have all been busy house cleaning. Dear Mama is quite worn out & I have been tiresome and impatient. Mrs Y came. Also Mr & Miss Dupont.

While the argument that young women needed protection of their health as the future mothers of the race was frequently put forward to restrict female entry into higher education or public work, the same argument expanded female opportunities to participate in physical education and leisure sports. Bicycling, basketball, skating and hockey gained popularity in the late nineteenth and early twentieth centuries as acceptable appropriate exercise for young women and many towns, such as La Tuque, Quebec, boasted women's leagues.

Credit: Club de hockey féminin, La Tuque, Collection Clermont, Jeanne d'Arc, N673-123, Archives nationales du Québec.

PROBLEMS OF ADOLESCENCE FROM A MEDICAL PERSPECTIVE

As a student at Trinity College Medical School in 1873, Archy McCurdy kept extensive notes of the lectures presented. From the excerpts below a picture of medical teaching on the subject of adolescent women emerges. It is worth noting the connection made at the time between menstruation and weakness in young women as well as the differing effect of this weakness for factory girls as opposed to "indolent and luxurious" young women.

Toronto, Ontario, 1873
Notes from Trinity College Medical School, Archy McCurdy, 1873 Mott/ Norwich Collection, MS 280, Public Archives of Ontario.

Anaemia is want of blood and other fluids, the pallid look of the countenance, colourless look of the lips, developing into dropsy and diseases of the heart. Factory girls are very much subjected to this disease, and girls at the time of the menstrual period, brought on by wearing thin shoes, and from wet feet.
Menstruation, Signs of
....It [menstruation] usually occurs every 4 weeks or every lunar month. It is said to be unlike other blood of the body. There is a change in their [women's, presumably] whole system, the breasts are developed, the voice musical, and her manners more womanly. In some places a prejudice exists that meat handled or salted by them will become tainted....
—When menstruation ceases or is suppressed in females, they will have discharges from the nose, finger ends, the appetite is for unusual things such as pickles, slate pencils..administer a purgative of aloes.
...By many people, the *moon* has been supposed to have an influence over the menses, but such is not the case, as females are known to menstruate at all periods....
After the menstrual period ceases, the genitals loose their size and become atrophied, hairs make their appearance on the face, the voice changes, the breasts dry up and the whole body assumes the masculine form....
Hysteria This disease manifests itself in a variety of forms, either emotional or assumed. The disease is confined almost to females from the ages of 15-20 years, yet persons of 50 are occasionally subjects—old maids—childless women, widows. At the menstrual period the disease is very marked, and its attacks occur generally at that time—also at the first period of gestation. Young, vigorous girls—actively employed seldom or never have this disease; but the indolent and luxurious are prone to it. It occurs occasionally among males if addicted to masturbation or venereal excesses or depression of any kind. Startling news may occasion it.
Symptoms It may assume the form of any disease—a want of control of the faculties, hyperasthesia, disasthesia, irregular muscular action—also it never affects the subject if alone. The patient laughs, then cries, chokes, does not

froth at the mouth—the patient falls but takes care not to hurt herself. Breathing irregular, palpitation of the heart. The patient is conscious, but fails to answer the questions that are put to them. The disposition of the patient is variable, either depressed or exceedingly hilarious.
Treatment—Dash cold water in the face....

———————

A DUTIFUL DAUGHTER WRITES HER MOTHER

When Mrs Dougall went with her eldest daughter to New York, she left partial responsibility for the household in Montreal to her daughter, Lily. While Lily had charge of shopping, meals, and supervising servants, she was not made party to the financial aspects of household management. This same in-between status was evident in Lily's own mind, as her letters show, when she considered her role and status in the world.

Montreal, Quebec, 1878 and 1880.
Dougall Papers, Public Archives of Canada.

May 20th, 1878
I do not see how the expenses here are to be arranged, but, as you say, that is none of my business. At any rate I am of age, and I am not going to leave you alone any part of the winter. Not that it makes much difference being of age in a world where one must just do what seems right and nothing else.

Christmas, 1880
Dearest Mother,
I have always had the notion all my life whenever any great pleasure happened to me that my mother was praying for me. This much at least is true, that I know you always do pray for me.
I have been very happy lately in having found a firmer footing in the Christian life than I ever had before. I have been very blind all my life to truths that, as your daughter, I should have known when I was a child. I thank God every day for giving me such a Father and Mother. No wealth or position that you could possibly have given us could have been as much to us as the lessons your life and patience have taught us.
Goodbye, dearest mother
Your loving daughter,
Lily.

———————

PLANNING AND ACCOUNT KEEPING

As the daughter of a Lanark County Anglican clergyman, Jessie Low was trained to the manners and responsibilities of young womanhood. Her diary for 1892, written while she was still at home, reveals something of the frustrations these might entail for a teenager who was more interested in politics and drawing than in tea serving. By 1894, however, Low had moved to Ottawa where she began a life-long career as a civil servant. Her personal accounts for that year show how well she had learned her lessons of family and social responsibility as she contributes some of her wage to her mother and attempts to acquire the elements befitting a young woman's wardrobe.

Ontario, 1892-94
Jessie Low Diaries, Low Papers, MG 30 D35, Public Archives of Canada.

1892
Jan. 1 Friday

   The first day of the new year is nearly over. It has been quiet enough. David (uncle) who has been here since the day after Christmas, went off on the ten o'clock train and we went to service at eleven and had lunch about one. I was working at my drawing this afternoon when Mr Reeves called. Mamma and Annie received him and I had to give him some tea to my disgust. I hate serving anything....

   We had great excitement here last night on account of the election to Parliament. Mr Jamieson, the member of Lanark has been appointed to a judgeship in the west and so a new election had to be gone through. Mr Rosamond, our man, got in with over 400 majority. (It shows, however, that the Conservatives are just as strong if not more so, than ever.) It is considered a tremendous victory and is a very important one as it is the first since those scandals at Ottawa which the Grits make so much out of. Of course we all know who are to blame. Sir John Thompson and the Hon. C.H. Tupper spoke here in the Hall last Tuesday night. Annie was up at Pakenham and Papa Mamma David and I went. I don't know when I enjoyed anything so much in fact we all did. Those speeches were splendid....

July 24th. 1894

On hand	$3.00
Rec'd ———————	$25.00
Total	$28.00
Paid Mrs Galloway	$17.00
Gave Mother	5.00
Paid for ticket home	1.30

Paid for corsets	1.00
Paid for gloves	.75
Paid for shoes (mending)	.60
Paid for stamps	.25
Gave Jessie Austin	.25
Paid for nets	.20
Paid for ribbon and thread	.13
Paid for polish	.15
Paid for hat (trimming)	1.15
(Balance for collection and stamps)	.22
Total	$28.00

Sept. 25th	tooth powder	.10
Sept. 23th	collection	.10
Sept. 29th	Liquorice powder	.05

"WE WERE GETTING VERY RESTLESS"

The events and emotions in the transition from girlhood to womanhood are rarely explicit in the historical documents we have been able to unearth. In most cases, one senses restlessness with dependence and the desire for social contact outside the family combined with a certain amount of fear and retrospective thought. The following excerpts from Helen Carmichael's New Brunswick memoirs are unique in presenting a picture of these emotions and of a mother's understanding and sympathy with her daughters. They are also unique in providing evidence of the extent to which the consumer economy had penetrated the resource economy of New Brunswick.

Five Fingers, New Brunswick, c. 1918.
Helen Carmichael Dodge, My Childhood in the Canadian Wilderness, *(New York, 1961) 44-49.*

I think that winter my sister and I started showing resentment at having to share a room with all our sisters and brothers. We were getting older now. We looked the mail-order catalogues over a dozen times a day, wishing for something new. Everything we had was homemade.

By now we were more company for Mother. We talked about spring and when we would get out of the woods again.* Mother felt confident that it would be our last winter in camp. She could see we were getting very restless. It

*[The Carmichaels lived in a New Brunswick lumbering camp.]

was no life for young girls. She told us that if we would only bear with her for the rest of the winter, she would talk over leaving with our father. We contented ourselves as best we could....

Time was slipping by. Christmas was fast approaching. My sister and I had mentioned on several occasions to Mother how we would like very much to spend Christmas in the settlement. We had scanned the Eaton's & Simpson's mail-order catalogues for new clothes. After some very long debates with my father, it was finally decided that we could go to the settlement for a few days at Christmas.

First, we sent off a hurried order for new clothes. This time it would be real shoes, instead of moccasins, and a dress and coat that Mother didn't have to spend hours making. I never will forget the day the tote team came with the package. We were so excited, we could hardly wait to undo it. Then we nearly wore our dresses out trying them on. The shoes were high black laced ones, and we also had black stockings. It was so wonderful to imagine everything coming from a store!

We were to go by tote team a few days before Christmas and return the day after the holiday. This would be our first Christmas away from our sisters and brothers. Of course, they still believed in Santa Claus, but by now we three older children did not. I wanted so much to take my brother Steward. As he was only thirteen months younger than I, we had been together constantly. I would have felt much safer if he were with me, but no argument on my part would change my mother's mind. She thought he was too young; and besides, she needed him at home to help with the work while we were away.

Early next morning we were up, put hay in the bottom of the sled, put blankets over that and covered ourselves with fur robes. Tucked in my sister's pocket was the money for our expenses, along with a message for Mrs Furlotte, who ran the hotel, asking her to keep an eye on us. If there were to be a dance, the message said we could go.

It was an all-day ride. We were both cold and hungry when we arrived long after dark, but to our amazement everything in the hotel was decorated. There was a huge Christmas tree in the lobby, with hundreds of candles burning on it. I am sure we must have stared, for we had never seen anything so beautiful before. After we had feasted our eyes on the tree and the surroundings, we were shown to our room by a very young boy who could not speak English; but he managed to make us understand what was needed.

For the first time in our lives, we stood in the centre of a room that was to be our very own for two whole days. There was a bureau, a bed, and chair. We didn't dally long in our room, though we put our few belongings on the dresser and hung up our new coats. Although there was no heat in our room, we didn't mind.

We went down to the lobby, where a large pot-bellied stove stood in the center of the room. Everyone was standing around it getting warm, so we joined them. It was very delightful just standing there and listening to people talk. Those who could speak English tried very hard to make us feel at home. During the evening we learned that Mrs Furlotte's two nieces had arrived that afternoon; in addition, some of the younger men had come down out of the woods to celebrate the holiday. We were sure to have a good time.

When supper was ready, everyone marched into the dining room. We all sat together at one big table. The main topic was the dance, which was to be held the following night at the house next door. We were entertained that evening in the hotel. Music was furnished by a phonograph. We made a couple of trips to the only store in town, where I spend most of my allowance on real gum. It seemed so good after having chewed nothing but spruce gum all my life.

Then, of course, everyone was going to midnight mass, so we had to go along. We had never been in a church so late at night before. It, too, was beautifully lighted by candles. When we got back to the hotel, we were all taken to the kitchen, where we feasted on pork pie. This, too, was a treat for us, but with French people it is a must at Christmas. By now we had had a full day of new experiences....

2. THE DOMESTIC EMPLOYMENT OF YOUNG WOMEN

ON THE MOVE AS A SERVANT

By the 1880s, a number of charitable organizations were involved in assisting young British girls to emigrate to Canada for placement as domestic servants. Between 1885 and 1893, Charlotte Alexander was a leading figure in this work. The following excerpts from the records on Jane Collis are drawn from Alexander's papers, which also included revealing letters from the young woman.

Ontario, 1887-91
Charlotte Alexander Papers, MG 29 C58, Vol. 1 & 3, Public Archives of Canada.

JANE COLLIS: Age about 17. Came to Sutton early in April 1887 from Miss Mittendorff's Home.

1887: Clayton House, Epsom.
Been with Miss M. 9 years. Miss M. wrote she is "of the real East End type. Has a bad father & one sister in a bad house, but she herself is perfectly steady & innocent. It would be such a blessing for the poor child to be taken away from her relatives." Went to Canada with the party in May. Placed in a situation in Toronto, Mrs Bleasdell, 550 Church St, May 27. $6 to begin $8 when suitable. Came back to me June 27 with letter saying she was "good &

obedient but had no idea of work or responsibility." Went with me to Brampton, July 9, Saturday. Had tea at old Mrs Carter's. Mrs Hunter daughter of old Mrs C. took her home with her saying she wd (would) on Monday place her with a neighbour who wanted a servant. Good Christian home. J.C. did not like the place. Went July 16 to Mrs D.E. Starr, Brampton. July 20 called to see me on her way to Muskoka with Mrs Starr. July 28, Mrs. Starr wrote "doing very well with the children—think with training will make good servant—Does not appear to understand much about housework." Aug. 22. Mrs Starr wrote "Jane has greatly disappointed me.... Most of the time she is utterly useless, wild as a hare". &c. "She may possibly do better". &c. September left Mrs Starr & went to Mr & Mrs John Lawse, farmers, Eversley, P.O. near King (RyStation). Began well, Mrs S. was sorry afterward she had parted with her....

March 1890

c/o Mrs Eden Smith
34 Salisbury Avenue
Toronto

Dear Madam,

I thank you for inviting me to the party and staying at your house for the night and paying my fare. I am getting on better now than I was at first, as I am getting to know my work. Mrs Smith has such a pretty baby and it is growing so fast. I was so pleased when I found I was near Sarah I see her every Sunday after Sunday School and sometimes in the evening & Nellie Gates. Mrs Smith lets me go every Monday evening to Confirmation class at St Simons Church & Nellie Gates and I got confirmed February 15, Saturday evening and went to communion the next morning at 8 O'Clock. Annie Hughes came out of the Hospital in January I do not know where she is now. I daresay you are busy now in getting more girls ready to bring out with you in May I will conclude now hoping you will have a safe journey.

I am
Yours truly,
Jane E. Collis

c/o Mr C.W. Magee
Bradford PO
Ont
1891

Dear Madam

I do not know how to thank you enough in words for all the kindness you have done me, when you said goodbye to me, then I wanted to thank and shew that I was grateful to you, but I could not find words enough to express my gratitude for all you have done for me. I have improved better in health though the work is hard, in drawing up water from the cistern and carrying water to

and fro and milk from the barn, when I have been bending my back along time when scrubbing or doing any other thing, I have a pain in the centre back of my shoulder. We have some visitors here from the States just at present. They were to come two weeks ago they stayed longer in Toronto than what they expected to. Harvest has just begun and each day seems to find more to do. We have not begun our new potatoes or green peas yet. Ours is to come. Toronto nearly had her share. I have been to church once since I have been here and I went in buggy to know my way. Its too far around to walk there and to go through the fields to make it shorter would soon wear out my clothes. That is the nearest church to us. Did Alice Robinson leave her place in Bradford. I should like to leave here at the end of my month in September as have not been feeling at all well. I have had headaches and faint feelings and then had a slight continual tooth and gum ache from Thurday evening to Saturday evening and Friday night I was awake all night when I lie down in my bed I felt ill, with the heat of the sun when picking berries all the afternoon and the tooth and headaching all the time. Next morning I did not feel bright for working in the afternoon when the most of the work was done I laid down for an half an hour. I and everybody else has as much butter as they want, five eggs and one cup of warm milk I have had as yet, in the place of tea. I had cold milk not now though. I will draw this letter to a close now.
I am
Yours respectfully
Jane Collis

c/o Mr C.W. Magee
Bradford PO
1891

Dear Madam,
I am very sorry in not staying here a year but I am not satisfied with having least wages during winter, I'll stay till the end of fall if you wish it or till September 15th. Will you please tell Matron I received her letter that I began to answer it. But I think it will not be written in time for her as she is going to England so soon. I hope you will all have a safe and happy journey to England I am in haste—please excuse bad writing.
Jane Collis

THE ISOLATION OF SERVICE

Cannington Manor, the large estate located in the Northwest Territories, has recently been declared a national historic site. The manor was built by the Humphry family in an attempt to recreate English country life in remote

Assiniboia and may appropriately be called a gentry folly. If her letters are any indication, it was certainly seen as a folly by Martha Morgan who worked there as a domestic servant. Morgan, whose earlier service experience included large households in Tunbridge Wells, left Cannington quite quickly to join friends in upstate New York finding the work and the isolation of Cannington Manor too much to take.

Northwest Territories, 1892
Martha Morgan Papers, MG 29 C85, Public Archives of Canada.

annington Manor
Assinibioa
NWT Canada
Sunday 17th, July

My Dear Namesake
I cannot tell you how pleased I was to get your letter I saw Mortlake Postmark I could not think where that was I had quite forgot your writing I had your letter July 15th I have only had one letter from home since I have been here well I must tell you I don't like this country much for it is so dreadful quiet there is nothing going on it is a nice country as far as that goes but there is not many people about no Chapel no Sunday School I have to Church we go every Sunday about 6 or a dozen of us in the waggon it is too hot to walk the Church is 2½ mile First time I was driving I thought I was going to Break my neck there is no roads here like England only like roadways across a field they are called trails every driving affair is different here all the seats seem to work on springs till the Jogging is less felt I quite enjoy it now every Sunday. We have been very busy Spring cleaning as they call but I told them it was past Spring cleaning it was Summer cleaning I never saw a house in such a filthy state, never. One thing they are not very particular; the knives had not been cleaned for 6 weeks. This Family are from London they have only been out here 4 years this October. The Boss was a Shipbuilder in England. He was going back in the world that's why he came out here because he has so large a family an they can stand a better chance to provide for themselves the girls don't like this so well as the old Country...

Cannington Manor
Assinibioa
N.W.T. Canada
Sunday 21st 92

My Dear Martha
I was very pleased to receive your letter Friday August 19th. Also I got a letter from Miss Thomas & one From Mother & one from Mrs Jones...we get

letters twice a week now. I am sorry you are miserable. for I know the feeling. it is a *peculiar* feeling O really it is something past describingly dull here for sometimes I feel as if could not stop here not a single person I know but worse than all there is so few people round here. Sunday is a perfect miserably day. I could go where I like but there is nowhere to go or anything to be seen so I dont see it any use to go out all the Boys go up to a lake to Bathe every sunday the Eldest son makes the only amusement he is playing the piano or Banjo every night and singing very funny songs. there is only dancing thats about the most that goes on here the Eldest daughter & Son goes lots of nights till about 3 o'clock in the morning there's nothing for servants. Mrs Humphrey leaves England for here August 26th. so I shall soon see what she is like But I have made up my mind not stay here longer than my year which is not 9 months now. Thank goodness but I can tell you I have a good place a splendid place for grub we get plenty of sweets and pastry every day never go without pudding for dinner we have only 3 real meals a day. no supper Breakfast 7 Dinner 12:30 and the evening meal at 6 or half past. every person cut their own luncheon sometimes we have afternoon at 4 it does seem such a relief to have no supper to get because I can do what I like after tea. o if I was near a Town I might see something....

Cannington Manor
Sunday 23rd
Assinibioa N.W.T.
Canada

My Dear Namesake
I received your kind letter a fortnight tomorrow also I had your Photo the following week after the other letter... I have sent you just a skip* of the wedding that was here. It is taken by the Eldest Son he cannot take Photographs well if you will send back he is going to mount it for me. Standing in the back doorway is the Bride and Bridegroom so called Slopers next our Boss and the best man... Mrs Humphreys is very quiet sort of person you can never tell what those sort of people mean but she is realy very kind to me. She makes a lot more cooking and washing. We wash once a fortnight. The daughter always helps and she does the ironing but I have to iron all the starch things I have had a lot of collars and white shirts all the summer. The boys call them Boiled rags. But is for my good I have learned more here than I have ever learned before. girls can get in laundry In Montreal from £3 to £4 per month.

---

*[photograph]

BLUEBERRY PICKING SEASON

The daughter of a Scottish father and a Cree mother, Anne Anderson tells the story of her adolescent years and provides a picture of the responsibility and reward of a young woman during the annual blueberry season. Her earlier memories of childhood work appear in Chapter One as "Wonderful Childhood Days" (pp. 00).

St Albert, Alberta, early 20th Century
Anne Anderson Papers, "Blueberry Picking Season," Acc. 77.236, Provincial Archives of Alberta.

When the berries were ripe everybody went picking, sometimes family groups would go together. However I always dreaded this season. I knew I would soon be left on the farm to care for my little brothers and sisters while my folks were gone. However I had older brothers but they also had chores to do such as milking, feeding the hogs and gathering eggs.

There was a lot of preparation to go on a berry picking trip. Father would get a team and wagon with a good wagon box. It was half filled with hay and in this every available box or trunk was taken. The hay would help from mashing the berries on rough roads.

Finally they were gone and this meant a week or 10 days I would a mother, nurse, housekeeper and chore girl. There was always a baby left to tend to and I often felt the responsibility that was on my shoulders was more than I could cope with. However nothing ever happened while my parents were gone. We survived but were we glad when we saw the pickers coming home. I can still see the many boxes of delicious blueberries that we were so fond of. Some were sold and others we canned for our own use. We were all paid by getting new clothes. I generally got a new dress and the boys got overalls and we sure appreciated this. This went on for many years as money was made in every available way possible. This was a yearly job for me.

But as the new homesteaders came into the country the blueberry patches quickly disappeared. Today they are quite scarce but to me those days were truly happy memories of a family where there was not much time for play and the love and respect we had for our parents.

LAUNDRY WORK

By 1902, when Ada Williams sought work in Halifax as a domestic servant, the conditions of such domestic employment had undergone a considerable change across the country generally. Most servant girls were no longer the daughters of neighbours residing in the same community. By the last decade of the nineteenth century, domestics were immigrants from Britain or Europe or migrants from more distant rural areas. With this change came an alteration in the relationship between mistress and servant typified by a distancing between the two in working conditions, class, and, perhaps, age. The household worker found herself not only physically isolated but also emotionally isolated from the companionable household work that had frequently characterized British North American households.

Halifax, Nova Scotia, 1902
Grace Forsythe, ed. Tales of the Yesteryears: The Writings of Mrs. E.S. Williams, West Jeddore, 1888-1977. *Book I, 96.*

The summer I was 15, I went up to Halifax to look for work and earn a few dollars. I found a job doing housework, where I had to wash a huge pile of clothes every day while the mistress sat and watched me. I stood it for one week, and left. She refused to pay me anything, and was very angry. I went down to the waterfront and got on Capt Weston's vessel and started for home.... I walked down home in the thick fog, and went in the house just as Papa was having his breakfast. "I had to come home, Papa," I said. "The work was so hard, and I was homesick." "Come in child. Come in," he said. "We might as well all starve together."

IN AND OUT OF SERVICE

The following brief biography provides an unusual glimpse of two early twentieth-century Alberta women and their two very different approaches to life. The author, Mabel Whitney Morrison, was the wife and manager of a relatively well off household where Mamie was her first house-maid in Vegreville, Alberta, in 1910. Despite differences of class and outlook, Mamie and Mable developed a firm and enduring friendship.

Vegreville, Alberta, 1910
Judge F.A. Morrison and Family Papers, Mabel Whitney Morrison, "A Child of Nature," 1930, Acc. 78.220, Provincial Archives of Alberta.

When Mamie first came to work for me I was very dubious concerning her. She did not impress me very favorably. She had a sloppy, untidy appearance and a face that showed nothing in the way of character. But I was desperately in need of help and I was glad to have found a girl who was not a foreigner. I decided to give her a trial and told her if she were not satisfactory I would not keep her. She appeared to be satisfied with this arrangement so she was duly installed as maid of all work in my busy home. I had two small children and lived in a brand new western town. We had no modern conveniences. Our drinking water was procured from the pump in the back yard. The water was excellent but the supply was limited, about six pails, a day, so all water for household purposes had to be hauled from the river....

Contrary to my expectations she turned out to be a very capable girl and an excellent cook. Since that time I have had many and various housemaids but not one could cook like Mamie. Her meals were most delectable. She knew how to make the homely potato into a variety of delicious dishes. Her meats were done to a turn, she had the knack of concocting the most toothsome desserts, in fact, she put artistry into her cooking. There was no monotony in Mamie's meals.

She was strong and good natured with a fine sense of loyalty. The children adored her and she adored the children. I knew when Mamie was left in charge of them that they would not be neglected or abused. She was with me three years and during that time I was never angry with her. True, she was careless about certain things, she might break a choice bit of glass or china or tear my precious linen but somehow it was never her fault. There was always a sense of harmony in her way of working. She never complained, she had a pleasant voice, an infectious laugh and was never noisy. She took life as she found it and life was good.

One day, however, the unthinkable thing happened; Mamie failed me. During the dinner I rang for service. No Mamie answered. I rang a second time. Still no Mamie. Exasperated I went into the kitchen, half expecting to find her fainting or dead. But instead I heard her gay laughter outside the back door. My mingled feelings of anger and curiosity led me to peek through the window. There I saw our mounted policeman in all his colorful uniform, mounted on his handsome horse, very obviously showing off for Mamie's benefit. Her eyes were so filled with delight and laughter that I hadn't the heart to disturb the romantic scene. I served the dessert! Later when Mamie said she was sorry but she had not realized the flight of time I offered no reproof.

This, apparently, was the beginning of her first romance. The policeman was very attentive and Mamie's laughter was lovely to hear. Not very long after this incident another catastrophe occurred. I awakened one morning and wondered at the silence in my household. I looked at my watch. It was only 7.30 and the children were still sleeping. But, where was Mamie? There were no familiar noises coming from the kitchen! I sensed danger! In fact I so far forgot myself as to suggest to the man of my heart that he go and look in Mamie's room. I had to go myself. I found the room empty and the bed had not been slept in. Just as I was contemplating calling up the fire department I happened to look out of the window. There was Mamie hurrying home, presumably to get breakfast. I stood still and waited. She came in looking a bit worried and tired. Before I could speak she said, "I'm sorry but Jack (the policeman) is sick and there was no one to do anything for him so I stayed and took care of him. The doctor told me what to do." I asked what was wrong and she told me that it looked like pneumonia. I suggested the hospital. Mamie said, "No, he cannot afford to go to the hospital. Anyway I'm taking care of him nights." I started to remonstrate and reason with her but she quietly told me that if I did not let her nurse him "nights" she would leave me. "I'll do your work", she said and she did. Jack lived. Not long after this our policeman was transferred to another town and life went on uneventfully.

One day, out of the blue, Mamie announced that she had decided to go back to her native state. She was tired of the quiet life in our town. She had formed a friendship with another girl who hankered for the bright lights so she persuaded Mamie to go travelling. It was spring. She went and we missed her.

I have often been told that I always get everything I wish for, so one very hot day in the following summer I wished hard for Mamie to come back. No sooner said than done! I looked out of my window and saw Mamie coming towards my home! Yes, she actually came back. The next day we had forgotten that we have ever been without her. She simply told me that she had discovered that other women were not like me. So, you see, we formed a mutual admiration society.

It wasn't long before Mamie had another beau, Jim, the barber. During the following winter Jim spent many an evening in my kitchen so I was not surprised when Mamie proudly displayed an engagement ring. Truly the way to a man's heart is through his stomach. They decided to be married in the spring. I helped make the trousseau and when the big day arrived I sent them away with a smile on my lips and a tear in my eye. When would I ever find another Mamie?

About seven years later she came to me again. We now had moved to the city, Edmonton, and my family were growing up. The early days of my married life in the little town seemed far away. One morning I was called to the telephone and a voice said "Do you know who's speaking?" I had to admit I didn't know, so the voice said, "This is Mamie." Well there is only one Mamie so I said for her to come and see me. She came and told me all about herself. Jim and she had gone to live in Minnesota and were very happy and moderately prosperous. She had a little Jim with her but his Daddy had died of diphtheria and so they had come home. She had been fortunate enough to find a good place to work. She was housekeeper for an old bachelor who owned a big farm in the neighbouring country. It was a very fine farm and a fine house with the modern conveniences. She ran the place as she pleased and was allowed to have her small son with her. She had come to town to do some shopping and wanted to see me. I could not see that she had changed much. When she left I told her to come and see me any time she was in town.

Two years later she did come again. Still I could not see much change in her but she had a real story to tell me this time.

She was now the mother of another son; the bachelor was his father. About two months back she had been very ill with flu and the doctor had said that she could not live. So, in order to legitimatize his son the bachelor had married her on her death bed, as he thought, but Mamie thought differently and lived. The Bachelor took the flu and died So Mamie was a widow with a fine home and two sons. "I'm tired," she said, "I'm through with men, they're no good. No I'm well fixed and I intend to stay that way". That sounded reasonable to me so she went home promising to call on me again.

She came again, a year later, looking a bit bedraggled but with same cheerful smile on her face. We talked for a while but I could see that she had some news so I helped her out by asking a leading question. Yes, Mamie had weakened and had married the hired man who had worked on the farm. I had seen him years ago when he was a "no good" in our old town. I was genuinely sorry to learn this but Mamie was as cheerful as ever saying that Scotty wasn't half bad. She finally told me that she had mortgaged her property and they had moved back to our old town where her old friends lived.

I later heard that she and her husband were very hard-up but they never missed a country dance. Her two children were healthy little ragmuffins and Mamie goes out working by the day. I would be willing to wager any amount of money that she still cooks wonderful meals.

SCHOOL CARETAKER

Among the variety of legal documents that have survived to the present, the employment contracts signed by Canadian women are a useful source for the comparison of local conditions of work. The following Quebec example outlines the duties and wage of Miss Clodia Roch who was hired in 1910 to clean and maintain the local school. Although the work required would have been strenuous, paid service of this type had advantages over domestic service; namely, the independence of residence and a greater degree of independence of work.

Longue Point, Quebec, 1910
Engagement du personnel en généralités 1906 à 1910, 2-3-2-2, Longue Point. Archives of the Montreal Catholic Schools Commission. Translated from French.

The year one thousand nine hundred and ten, the nineth day of May.

Before Mtre JOSEPH ALFRED BEAUCHAMP, notary for the Province of Quebec, undersigned, residing in the village of Beaurivage de la Longue Point and practising in the city of Montreal.

APPEARED:

The Commissioners of schools for the municipality of the parish of Longue Point, in the County of Hochelaga, acting for and representing at present by Joseph Pierre Deschatelets, Esq., doctor of the village of Beaurivage de la Longue Point, duly authorized to this end by a resolution adopted by the said commissioners of schools the eighth of May current 1909,

Of the first part;

And Miss Clodia Roch, of legal age and aware of her rights, residing actually at Berthier,

Of the other part;

These parties have agreed to that which follows, to be understood:

The said party of the second part promises to the said parties to do or have done the work outlined below during the course of the next school year beginning the first of June next (1910), to be understood:

1. To clean the classes of the girls' school of the said village of Beaurivage de la Longue Point as often as the school law requires, except the washing of the floors.

2. To remove the snow from the sidewalk situated opposite the school and in the yard of the said school in such a manner that the sidewalks are never obstructed;

3. To remove the snow and ice which might accumulate on the roof and galleries of the said school.

4. To light and heat the stoves or furnaces of the classrooms in such manner that the temperature of the classrooms will always be healthy, and to take into the said school all the necessary fuel to this end and which will be supplied by the said commissioners.

5. The said commissioners will pay to the said Miss Clodia Roch for the execution of the above tasks the sum of twenty-five dollars payable in ten equal payments, monthly and consecutive in the sum of two dollars and fifty cents each, of which the first payment will be made the first of October next (1910) and be continue from month to month until the total payment....

WHO WILL KEEP HOUSE?

During the pre-Confederation era, most young women learned housewifely skills such as cooking and sewing by watching and helping their mothers in the home. It may have been the case after 1870 with the increased attendance of girls in schools and their increased paid employment outside the home that training and practice in domestic skills lessened. Certainly an erosion of ability was observed by and concerned middle-class reformers who sought domestic servants.

1913
Royal Commission on Industrial Training and Technical Education, Report,
Canada, Sessional Paper No. 191, 1913, 366, 376.

The Local Council of Women would like to see service in the home lifted to the
same plane as the profession of nursing. The Council does not believe the
home should continue to be the only place for which special training is not
regarded as necessary.

As matters are at present the better class of intelligent girls prefer to go to
work in stores or to become stenographers. The reasons they give for reluctance
to work for wages in homes are varied, such as: "If I go to domestic service my
friends will cut me;" "If in service you are looked down upon;" "I have a sister
who is a trained nurse; she seems not only to keep her old friends but gains new
ones, while I am regarded as an outsider."

If girls could pass the necessary examinations, and receive certificates
showing their qualifications for service, as a nurse does, the Council thinks
that in time it would revolutionize the household service question. At present
high wages must be paid for inefficient work. The training in Domestic Science
at little expense in their own town or city would produce a body of skilled
workers who could command the highest wages....

The Commission is of opinion that short courses of instruction and training
in housework and housekeeping should be provided. These might be of from
one to six months' duration. The pupil taking a course satisfactorily would
upon examination be entitled to receive a certificate of competence as a
"Home-helper" or "House-worker" of the first, second, and third class.

Provision should be made in Continuation Housekeeping Classes to enable
the "Home-helper" or "House-worker" who could not devote time continuously to such training, to cover the ground and obtain the certificate by
devoting one or two half-days per week to the classes.

To meet the case of housekeepers who desire to obtain competent house-help
for a portion of a day or week, or house-help which would not reside in the
home of the employer, it would seem desirable to have a trial made as to
whether that could be furnished in connection with a Middle Housekeeping
School. If a residence were part of the institution, living accommodation
might be provided at rates to cover the cost.

If a "Home-helper" or "House-worker" held a first-class certificate she
should be entitled to remuneration adequate to her training and ability. Such
workers would serve the community, in respect to housekeeping under normal
conditions of health, in a manner somewhat similar to that of trained nurses in
time of sickness. Whatever promises a remedy for present conditions in the
supply of labor available as "Home-helpers" and "House-workers" is worthy
of careful consideration and fair trial.

It is a trite saying that people are more moved by instincts, prejudice, and fashion than by judgement. The harmful notion has spread and is spreading throughout Canada that the doing of housework, and serving as a home-helper for pay, is less appropriate for and worthy of young women than serving as office, shop or factory workers. To eradicate that should engage the efforts of women and men, who all are directly concerned with home-making and house-keeping.

FARM TO CITY AND BACK AGAIN

On the relatively undeveloped prairie, children and adolescents learned in schools, if these were available, and through experiencing life. For the Norwegian-born Ellenor Merriken education took place in the formal setting of the school and through training by her mother and her daily life. The following excerpts from her recollections of her youth suggest the contours of her development until her marriage in 1920.

Alberta, 1910-20
Ellenor R. Merriken, The Nose Hills Country, *(Canada, 1960) 6-7, 27, 85.*

The next morning, we met our new cousins. They were a fine-looking bunch. They could all understand Norwegian, but did not like to speak it. Finally they got tired of translating what they said all the time, and talked Norwegian every time they were sure no one was listening. We started to school in a couple of days and were again the object of curiosity, for we couldn't speak a word of English. This was a small, one room country school by the name of Likness. There were several vacant seats and after all the other children were seated, we took those that were left. There happened to be a third grade reader in my desk, so I entertained myself by looking at the pictures, as the teacher, having eleven grades in one room, did not have much time for foolishness. She finally got around to hear my reading lesson. She asked me something, and when I did not answer, she up and hit me on the head. Kids can be very cruel, too, and we were made fun of and blamed for things we did not do, since we could not talk back to defend ourselves. This made us three stick close together, and stand apart from the rest. We learned very fast, though, and before long we were able to understand a lot of what was said; it took longer to learn to express ourselves....

Mama must have had a hard time getting used to the way of life on the prairie. She had known better times than we could possible hope for on the homestead. She cautioned us repeatedly to hold on to what culture we had inherited, and no matter how far we were from people or civilization, never to let ourselves down. Some of the things she impressed on me will always be remembered, and has been a guiding force in the right direction all my life. One of these had to do with temptation. She said, "If you are tempted to do a thing, stop a minute and ask yourself, 'Is this good for me?' You can tell. Then judge accordingly. Do what you know to be right, and you will end up being proud of yourself." She was a truly religious person, and always made the best of whatever happened. She insisted on a white tablecloth for every day, even if it was made of flour sacks, with a little embroidery in the corners. It gave a touch of festivity to a meal. On Sunday she brought out the good linen one, we always said grace before and after meals. She repeatedly stressed the importance of good manners, no matter where we happened to be....

I was nineteen, when I decided to get a business education, and set out for Calgary to enroll for a term at the Garbutt Business College. I soon realized what money I had would not cover room and board, plus tuition, for very long. The college had a list of applications from good homes all over the city, asking for girls to help with housework in exchange for their keep. This I took advantage of and was assigned to a nice family by the name of Sparling in Elbow Park. I walked the fourteen blocks to school every night and morning, and carried my lunch. Mrs Sparling set a formal table, so I always knew there would be the same huge pile of dishes waiting for me. My main duty, otherwise, was to care for two small boys every night except Sunday, when I insisted on going to church. This gave me a lot of time for study, and my progress was quite satisfactory.

I loved the city of Calgary and intended to stay on after graduation. It was the custom of the college to help secure a job for the graduate, and this they did. I wanted to go home to see the folks before I took a job, and I was granted the two weeks that I asked for. When I got home, Roy was a regular visitor; strange how fate has a way of altering one's plans. Ever since that first time I met him, I kept hoping that someday he might wake up to the fact that I was pretty nice, and take a real liking to me. Strange as it may seem, he had been thinking the same about me. It didn't take him long to convince me that I would make a better farmer's wife than secretary, so I gave up the idea of going back, and started in cooking for threshers....

———————

3. BEYOND THE DOMESTIC SPHERE: WOMANLY WORK, EDUCATION AND RESPECTABLE LIVING

A YOUNG WOMAN'S HOPES

Sophia Alice Puckette was born in Independence, Kansas, in 1885. In December 1904, Sophia left Kansas with her mother, sisters, and brothers to follow her father to Innisfree, Alberta, where he had established himself nearly a year before. Her diary for 1905, her first year at her new home, is a fascinating document. The excerpts below are a rare glimpse of a twenty-year-old young woman's attachment to her old home, involvement and work in her new community, and hopes and fears for her future life.

Innisfree, Alberta, 1905
James and Sophia Miles Papers, Sophia Alice Puckette Diaries, M843, f.f. 2, Glenbow—Alberta Institute Archives.

May 19, 1905
We planted flowers yesterday—four beds. Yesterday was Lota's birthday! She would have been twenty if she had lived. I sent a letter to Mary Roberton by Frank Bowtell to find out Mrs Bennett's address. My plan is to write to her and see if she will give me music lessons and let me pay for them in work.

Is my "career" about to begin? or am I doomed to have another disappointment?... I'm afraid I don't know exactly what I *do* want or what is good for me—...

June 15, 1905
I have been with Mrs Miller now for nearly 2 weeks. She gives me $2.50 a week. She wasn't able to do the work alone. A week ago I got a reply from Mrs Bennett. She thinks that a very unsatisfactory way to take music lessons and advises me to earn money and pay for them....

June 20, 1905 Today we made cheese and washed. I also wrote to Mrs Miller. How I should like to see her. What queer things do happen in this world. One of the queerest was today between the hours of 1 & 2 pm. My first proposal. What a hot day it has been. What an odd time of day!

I really must go to bed—Good night. I began work here June 5—1905....

Sun. Aug. 20—1905...
Our aim now is to go up [to town] either when she [Mama] gets back, or else the first of the new year of 1906. I thot last year I'd take the teachers' course but have decided this year to go to the [Alberta] College and take Book-keeping and Stenography—as it will enable me to get a position more quickly, and thus be able to earn enough to take me thru the High School.

O how I wish we had enough to take us girls thru school....

Oct. 31 ...If I had been writing this this morning I should have said "Maude & I still hope to go to school this winter"—but—another plan has been suggested. Mama thinks it might be better to let Maude stay home and take a correspondence course in drawing, thereby, leaving more funds for me—she thinks it very doubtful that there will be enough money to send us both, and wants me to go—...

Nov. 28 Well the plan is off—as usual—There is no money and I'll have to stay at home too. I'm frowning like a good fellow as I write this, I'm afraid I don't take disappointments very well. I've written to a correspondence school, but haven't any idea it will do any good....

Dec. 23 Papa is going to let me have $100 and I'm going to school, after all!

A HOME AWAY FROM HOME

The presence of young working women in the urban environment caused concern among social reformers who believed these women required protection from temptation and predatory males. Organizations such as the YWCA and WCTU or people like the concerned religious women of Halifax who opened the Temporary Home for Young Women Seeking Employment often established hostels for single working women where they could be supervised and regulated.

Halifax, Nova Scotia, 1870
The First Annual Report of the Temporary Home for Young Women Seeking Employment. *No. 171 Lockman Street, Halifax, 1870. Reprinted in* Atlantis, *V (1980), 196-200.*
It is just one year since this Home for the comfort and protection of young women seeking employment in this city was opened. It is to be traced to the sympathy and love of Christian Women for a class of their own sex, numerous and respectable, but who often, on their first arrival in the city, or when destitute of a situation, are likely to be exposed without such a place, especially if of an unsuspecting disposition, to many perils and temptations.

RULES OF THE INSTITUTION

1. Candidates for admission must be able to give reference as to good moral character by written documents from their clergymen, or some well-known respectable lady or gentleman with whom they have lived. The Matron is authorized to receive applicants without certificate for a single day, then refer such cases to the President or the Lady Visitors for the month.

2. Before admission, the Rules of the Institution will be read to each candidate, who must promise to obey them on being received.
3. All the inmates must attend family worship morning and evening, except in cases of illness or absolute necessity. Absence must be sanctioned by the Matron.
4. Cleanliness and neatness of appearance, propriety in conversation, and a hearty co-operation in promoting the order and arrangements of the house are expected from all inmates. They are expected to do their own washing and keep their own rooms in order.
5. The inmates must inform the Matron before going out, and must always be home at half-past nine, or at the latest, ten o'clock at night.
6. The Sabbath must be strictly observed in accordance with the Devien [sic] command "Remember the Sabbath day to keep it holy". It is expected that the inmates will either attend religious services in the Home, or at their own place of worship.
7. Any inmate wilfully violating these rules will expose herself to dismissal.
8. Bibles will be provided for the bed-rooms and it is hoped and expected that each inmate will read a portion from the Sacred Book, and in prayer daily ask the blessing of God, without which they cannot expect prosperity.
9. The internal management of the Home shall be in the hands of a committee of ladies from the different churches, who shall meet once a month at the Home to advice with and instruct the Matron.
10. Two of the committee shall once a week meet the inmates of the Home, and as many of the girls living at service in the city as can be spared and are disposed to attend, and give them such instruction, advice and admonition as shall be deemed suitable and necessary,—the meeting always to be opened with prayer. Once a month a clergyman of one of the evangelical denominations shall be invited to attend these meetings to give a short address and tender such advice as he may think proper.
11. The Matron is authorized to collect the Board, $1.50 per week, or 25 cents daily, for any shorter time than a week, so as to admit of no arrears accumulating.

―――――――

NORMAL SCHOOL TRAINING

The teaching profession was judged to be acceptable temporary employment for single educated women. A minister's daughter from Minnedosa, Manitoba, Annie Laycock kept a diary during her Normal School training in Winnipeg. Her diary entries record the usual arrangement for supervised boarding as well as the system of Normal School education.

Winnipeg, Manitoba, 1901
Annie Laycock Papers, Diary 1901, University of British Columbia Archives.

January 2nd.
...We got a room at Mrs Crawford's, 298 Balmoral St. at $7 per mo. And we take our meals at Mrs McCrindle at 2.50 per week.... Our room was about 12' by 15' by 10'. The stove pipe goes through the room and there is also a small registrar [sic] in the wall near the floor. We have a very good bedroom suite, and two chairs, one rocking chair the other a straight back common chair. A fairly good carpet on the floor and a very small closet. White washed walls with four small pictures as ornamentation and a door which will not shut tightly. There are four girls and one boy in the family. The oldest, a girl about 12 years of age. The baby is seventeen months old and is not very well. It is cross. We have the use of the bathroom and hot and cold water. They have a piano in the house. And I have permission to use it whenever I want to.

The first weeks.
The first week we got settled nicely in our room. The chairs were both broken but they fixed them. We only had an hour at Normal the first day and found out what books to get. We began our lessons on Friday. We were somewhat slow in getting acquainted.

The baby in this house died.... Miss Hammond, Mr Wilkie and I were sent to Miss Harns' room on Friday morning. We teach them on Monday. I teach a reading lesson. At our Normal Mr W.A. McIntyre takes up Rozenkranz, History of Education, Quick's Educational Reformers, Composition Literature, Primary Arith. Phonics, Reading.

Mr A. McIntyre takes up school management and organization. Mr H.S. McLean takes up Sally's Psychology, Nature Study and Stars, Advanced Arith., Practical Geometry, Bookkeeping and Writing. Mr Minchin takes Music every Tuesday night and Wednesday after four. Major Billmore takes drill on Tuesday night before music and Thursday after four.

Miss McDougall takes drawing Monday after four. We go to the Stoval Block for manual Training every Saturday morning from half past nine until twelve o'clock.

––––––––

FEMALE SCHOOL TEACHERS

During the decades that followed Confederation, women gradually became the majority in the teaching profession across Canada. Although teaching was generally regarded as a profession superior to other female work, like domestic service, it was not without its difficulties. In isolated rural areas, some teachers operated more than one school, as did the young ladies observed by Joshua Fraser in the Ottawa Valley. Urban educational records, like those of the Montreal Catholic School Commissioners, contain a number of letters from teachers complaining about working conditions, school heating, and especially, as Caroline Gibeau's letters show, the uncertainty of financial arrangements. While these difficulties relate to individual cases, a more subtle problem for female teachers emerged as larger school systems developed. Where several teachers were employed together, as in the graded city schools of Halifax, low salaries and status for women played an important role in the establishment of professional hierarchies that allocated to male teachers professional and financial advancement.

Ottawa Valley, Ontario, 1883
Joshua Fraser, Shanty, Forest and River Life *(Montreal, 1883) 283-85.*

The standard of education that is insisted upon now, both for teacher and pupil, is, I think, far too high for many of our school sections in the purely rural districts, and decidedly so for our isolated backwoods....
Let me instance a case in point: In the immediate vicinity of this district, in which I have pitched my tent for several months, there are two schoolhouses, four miles apart (though I think it is nearer five), between which one teacher divides her time. She teaches in the morning at one place, then takes her dinner and walks the four miles to the other school for her afternoon's work. She stays there all night, teaches in the morning and then walks back to the former place to teach and stay for the next twenty-four hours. I have often pitied these young ladies, and many a time I met them on their long weary walk between the two schools; in every phase of the execrable weather of our fall, winter and spring, in hail, in sleet, in rain, in snow, up and down the highest hills, —it had to be done, else complaint and reduction of pay followed; and a great part of the time the schools are vacant, just from the absolute impossibility of getting a teacher who has come up to the required standard.

•

Montreal, 1869-74
Caroline Gibeau to School Commissioners of Montreal, July 17, 1869 and August 12, 1874. Montreal Catholic School Board Archives.

Montral 17 July '69

The School Commissioners of the City of Montreal
Sirs;
Allow me to present a new request to you. I acknowledge with gratitude the things you have already done for me, but I know also that you are devoted

friends of education [and] by consequence the protectors of those upon whom the heavy task of teaching is incumbent and that certainly you would not want to see someone who you could assist sink under this weight. Sirs, you may judge whether I am exhausted after twenty years of teaching, without mentioning other difficulties.... My strength is so exhausted that it is impossible for me to continue this heavy task with a sole assistant. Would you please, I pray, sirs, look at my revenues and my expenses. At my good old parents' age, a thousand new necessities present themselves, the maintenance of a house, however modest it is, involves continuous expenditures, eight cords of wood without counting the three you had the goodness to furnish, two stoves to rent, a very long flu which has to be replaced frequently, a mortgage and two assistants... be the judge yourselves, sirs. I do not want to dwell on these sad thoughts dominated by my finances and the dilapidated state of my health, that would be against the precepts of our Ste. religion, nevertheless, however fleeting are these thoughts, they penetrate my soul like a sharp sword. If I could die that would not be the greatest misfortune because the live of a teacher is so unhappy... but, my old parents are alive and that stops my wish. Thus, sirs, you whom God has established to relieve some of his suffering members, allow me to pay for a good assistant so that I can withstand [life] until God gives me rest and you, sirs, will receive a new right to the blessings of heaven and to the profound gratitude.

Of your very humble servant
Caroline Gibeau, Teacher

Montreal
12 August '74

Mr. Desnoyers
(Secretary-Treasurer of the School Commissioners)
Sir,
I learned with anxiety of your new and very serious illness. I feel that anxiety for you and your wife and also for myself: because you do not know, sir, how much the uncertainty under which I have lived for some time tires me. For mercy, sir, ask the Commissioners to have the goodness to give me a positive reply and that their generous charity should inspire them to rule in my favour. Besides accommodation and food—these rooms need to be sufficiently heated, in the poor, aged there is little blood. Beside they must add in clothing and laundry, I have never done this work and cannot start at present without a miracle, for my poor old mother—judge for yourself it is over twenty years since we washed our own linen. I have been waiting but we have only three weeks left and if,... there is no arrangement, I will be forced to recommence my class and in consequence prepare myself.... I have not yet informed my music mistress who has been hired since the distribution of rates and I have two assistants in view, it is time for me to decide....

British North American women had been responsible for food preparation and preservation in the home and, with the advent of the canning industry, took up work in canning factories. In the lobster canneries of Prince Edward Island, pictured in an 1880 drawing by Richard Harris, local female hands washed and cleaned the crustaceans and filled the cans. They were paid on a piecework basis.

Credit: Drawing by Robert Harris, 1880, Public Archives of Prince Edward Island, No. 2755

In central Canada, at the George Matthews & Co. factory in Ottawa, women prepared the cans with lacquer and labels under the eyes of male supervisors. All these women, and their counterparts in British Columbia, spent long hours working in poor conditions, often without protective covering. Their situations, and those of female cotton and clothing workers, prompted the calls for protective legislation.

Credit: George Matthews & Co., Ottawa, 1907, Public Archives of Canada, PA-42289.

Halifax, 1873
Report of the Board of School Commissioners for the City of Halifax, for the Year 1879, 55.

OFFICE OF SCHOOL COMMISSIONERS, CITY OF HALIFAX

November 1st, 1873

The Commissioners of Schools for the city of Halifax, having agreed upon the subjoined scale of Salaries for the Teachers at present in the employment of the Board, as also the annexed Regulations for the payment of all Teachers who may be engaged after this date, direct that fifty copies of these regulations with the names of the Teachers, the dates of appointments, and their class of licence, be printed for the information of all whom it may concern.

1. All the Teachers who may be employed henceforward will be paid according to the scale of salaries, with the understanding that the proposed increase shall extend over a term of five years.

2. Male Teachers (Grade B) will be paid $500 a year, with an increase of $40 a year for five years.

3. Male Teachers (Grade C) will receive $400 for the first year, with increase of $20 a year until the amount reaches $500.

4. Female Teachers of Grade B will be paid $300 for the first year, with an increase of $30 a year for five years.

5. Female Teachers (Grade C) will be paid $250 a year, with an increase in the rate of $30 a year for five years.

6. Female Teachers (Grade D) will be allowed $200 for the first year, to be increased $20 a year for five years.

7. No Teacher shall be entitled to receive during any school year the annual increase provided for by the foregoing regulations, unless he or she shall, during the preceding year have maintained a satisfactory standard of efficiency—such standard to be fixed and determined by the Board.

8. No teacher shall be entitled to receive any such increase during any school year who shall not have been permanently employed by the Board previous to the summer vacation next preceding the beginning of such school year.

The Board shall have power to dismiss any teacher in their employ at any time, upon giving such teacher three months' notice of their intention so to do.

A STUDENT NURSE

The nurse-in-training faced strict regulation in her lessons, on the ward and in her daily dress and living situation as all these were dominated by hospital rules and overseen by the ever-present goverance of the superintendent. Ethel

Johns in her autobiography details the training she received at the Winnipeg General Hospital School of Nursing. Johns' later career as a nurse and her influential leadership in the profession are discussed by Margaret M. Street, *Watch-fires on the Mountains.* (Toronto, 1973).

Winnipeg, Manitoba, 1900-1902
Autobiography, 7-9, 11-13. *Ethel Johns Papers, File II-1, University of British Columbia Archives.*

At the turn of the century, the Winnipeg General Hospital, like the city itself, was undergoing rapid expansion. A new surgical wing had just been completed and duly equipped with up-to-date operating rooms. There were nineteen pupils in our class—by far the largest ever admitted to the school. We entered in a somewhat haphazard fashion, usually two or three at a time, but the day I arrived there was no companion in misery to comfort me. I was taken to a bleak little bedroom in the nurses' home with two beds in it, one occupied by a tired night nurse who groaned audibly when her privacy was thus intruded upon.

I unpacked my probationer's uniform and put it on as quietly as I could. The blue gingham dress had been made at home and, in accordance with instructions, the bodice was tight-fitting and the skirt swept the floor. I pinned on the little muslin cap, with its pleated border. My reflection in the cracked mirror that hung above the bureau was dazzling. At supper-time I was taken to the dining room and assigned to a seat at a table occupied by others of equally low estate.

At seven the next morning I was sent on full duty to Ward Three, a medical service for women. It was a relief to find that the head nurse seemed glad to see me and that she found no difficulty in giving me something useful to do. Evidently, my chief task was to respond with alacrity whenever any one of the thirty patients rapped loudly on her bedside table and demanded a variety of services that completely bewildered me. Ward Three was part of the old hospital and had not been constructed with a view to facilitating nursing service. Half-way down the corridor leading to the utility rooms were six steep steps up and down which all utensils had to be carried. By ten o'clock I began to wonder whether nursing really was my true vocation. The regular staff had vanished into the ward kitchen and were enjoying tea and toast. When they emerged, the kindly wardmaid beckoned to me and gave me a thick slice of bread and butter, plentifully sprinkled with brown sugar. "Get behind the door", she whispered, "and eat it as quick as you can. Never mind the raps. It won't do them any harm to wait a minute." I gratefully gulped down the scalding hot tea and returned to the scene of my labours.

At the end of a rather grisly week, I managed to find my way around. The head nurse taught me to make a bed and how to bathe a patient. I learned to read a clinical thermometer and to feel for an elusive pulse that slipped away from my fingers and seemed very hard to count. I could set a tray and feed a helpless patient. It was still my principal duty to answer those raps, to disinfect the bedpans in the bath tub and then to scour them in the unspeakable little sink in the utility room. I even got used to taking those six steps on the run. The hours of duty were from seven in the morning until seven at night with one hour off and twenty minutes for meals. If we could be spared, we were given one afternoon a week beginning at two o'clock. On Sundays we were supposed to have four hours free so that we could go to church. Most of the probationers didn't avail themselves of the opportunity. Our feet were too sore and our backs too tired.

When I entered the school, the newly-appointed lady superintendent had not yet arrived and, when my probation was over, there was no one to decide whether I deserved to be accepted. At last, the harassed medical superintendent looked me over and said that since they were pretty busy on Ward Three he would take a chance on giving me my school uniform and cap. A word must be said about that uniform. The dress was made of stout cotton material, blue and white checked. The bodice was lined, fitted closely and buttoned down the front. In the hideous fashion of the time, the sleeves were puffed at the shoulders and tight at the wrist. A pair of long cuffs, made of white cotton, were secured above the elbow with safety pins. The voluminous skirt of the apron was gathered into a wide waistband, and attached to it were long ties that had to be carefully arranged at the back in such a manner as to resemble a bustle. The pleated bib was stiffly starched and looked like the bosom of a shirt. It was fastened to a high surplice collar that fastened at the back of my neck and nearly choked me every time I bent over a patient....

Senior [student] nurses who displayed executive ability were put in charge of a ward and left there for months at a time, thereby avoiding the necessity of paying salaries to graduate nurses. However, it would be quite unjust to suppose that the authorities found much satisfaction in what amounted to an exploitation of the school of nursing. Adequate financial support was not forthcoming from governmental sources and the directors were obliged not only to find enough money for maintenance but also to raise funds for capital expenditure. Under such circumstances, they can hardly be blamed for regarding the school as a heaven-sent and perfectly justifiable source of cheap labour. Patients had to be nursed and nurses had to be trained—it was just as simple as that....

For a time, there were far too many changes among the graduate staff and the atmosphere of the school remained somewhat turbulent. An increasing number of students were put in charge of wards and, since their rank was arbitrarily based on seniority, they found it difficult to maintain discipline. The system was, in fact, absurd. If you had entered the school one day later than a classmate and happened to be assigned to a ward of which she was in charge, she automatically ranked as your superior officer and you were bound to obey her. You rose when she spoke to you and respectfully stood aside and allowed her to enter the elevator ahead of you. Strange as it may seem, this fuss and feathers had a certain value. Not only did it signify authority—it also fixed responsibility....

When [Isabel Stewart and I]...were in our senior year, we became involved in a critical situation. Four members of the graduate staff were summarily discharged on what seemed to the students to be insufficient grounds. A written protest was prepared by the student body and submitted to the board of directors. Forthwith, Isabel Stewart and I were summoned to appear for interrogation. We were sternly asked why we had chosen to break the contract that we had signed when were were accepted as pupil nurses and in which we had solemnly promised to obey the authorities under all circumstances. Did we realize that insubordination could lead to instant dismissal? My heart sank for I did not know what would happen if I had to forfeit my three years of training. Rather to our surprise, the ordeal ended at this point and we were permitted to withdraw [from the room]. The directors took no action and the unhappy incident was passed over in silence. Later on, we discovered that the harsh terms of the contract had been considerably modified.

A MISSIONARY

Religious revival meetings were common events in the Maritimes in the mid-nineteenth century. Meetings like the ones which converted Mrs Churchill were organized mainly by the Methodists and Baptists of the region and were designed to lead to baptism and religious renewal. The effects of such meetings and a developing religious conviction were profound on the writer of the following letters. She devoted her life and even married so that she could pursue her chosen field of mission work.

Nova Scotia, 1871-1873
Mrs George Churchill, Letters from My Home in India *(New York, 1916) 11-18, 20-25.*

Retreat Cottage, Truro, Nova Scotia,
December, 1871
...I must tell you of the great and abounding joy that has come to me this day. Mr Churchill, who is under appointment to go to the foreign field, has written and asked me to accompany him as his companion and co-labourer. At last I

am to be a missionary! For many longing years my heart has yearned to go to the heathen to tell them the wonders of God's love and grace. I think that the impulse first was born at the time of my conversion, a little girl of fourteen. How well I remember that happy time. Our home was then in Stewiacke, and through the consecrated zeal of a Mr Banks and his wife, newcomers to the community, a series of wonderful meetings was carried on, many being converted, seven of us cousins among the number. We cousins were all baptised on the one occasion, and ever since then I have wished to be a missionary....

When we moved here to Truro and I was thus enabled to attend the fine Model and Normal Schools, I prosecuted my studies for the different ranks, always with this aim in view, to fit myself for proper service. But there seemed no open door to my great Desire. We had no independent Mission Board, and few were the women who from this land had pointed their footsteps to the foreign field. When possible opportunity offered, my parents kindly but firmly opposed it, not willing that I should venture alone to such strange and distant climes. Wise and loving guides they have been to me in all else, and I was not led to override their decision in this. At such times I would say to myself—Is it the Lord calling me, or only a wish for something new and unusual—am I fitted or worthy to carry on His great work abroad—should I not instead be throwing my full strength into activities at home?... Sitting in the church choir, one Sunday, I saw two coloured men come up into the gallery, and something seemed to say to me almost as distinctly as if I heard a voice—"Who cares for their souls? You are longing to go to the heathen but why not try to save and teach these people?"

"I will care for them, Lord Jesus," I answered; and straightway that week I secured consent from the trustees to have the church open on Sunday afternoons, also visiting the "Island" where the coloured folks live, from house to house inviting them to come to a service on the following Sunday.

Large numbers attended, and the Mission became well established, many students from the Normal School assisting, and some members of the Church also giving us great aid. On week evenings I have had a night-school for any of them who wish to be taught reading, writing and arithmetic; gathering in our home kitchen at first, and as they increased in numbers overflowing into the big dining-room. It is a glorious work and I love it—something really definitely mine to do. Yet my heart has not been at rest, the old fire still burns for foreign service. So when the letter came to-day telling me of Mr Churchill's decision and asking me to share his life and labour, I felt that at last the way was opened up. And I took the letter to my family, leaving them to read it together, confidently believing that if it was God's will that I work for Him on heathen soil, He would so rule their minds to give me consent; that if He needed me there, He could raise up someone here, to care for the loved and loving sister whose long illness had hitherto made me appear necessary in the Home.... When I came down for my answer, they gave their consent, not gladly perhaps, but willingly, and devotedly....

Philadelphia, November, 1872

...You will want to hear how I am getting on in Philadelphia. It seems wonderful that Miss Eaton and I could get here at study so soon after our momentous decision. Miss Eaton is to be one of the outgoing missionaries. She is a great worker, and grand comrade. As our Board earnestly recommended that the missionaries equip themselves with the best culture possible, general and theological, Florrie and I determined we should be no whit behind our men in this preparation. Both Miss Norris who is already on the field, and Miss De Wolf who has returned on furlough, impressed upon us the great value of medical knowledge, as an aid in reaching the heathen women in their homes, so we felt we must come here to Philadelphia, in attendance upon the Woman's Medical College. It was hard to leave the home nest. A tinge of the long parting so soon awaiting us all, coloured our leavetaking at this time. My beloved sister from whom I have not been separated since the beginning of her illness, seven years ago, was loath at first to let me come, but yielded with patient and beautiful grace when fully understanding my great need of the equipment. It was sad, too, giving up my school—all those young, eager lives committed for a time to my hands to teach and fit for their place in life....

Truro, September 25, 1873.

...My last morning at home—since our marriage we have been in Yarmouth, visiting my husband's family. They received me most lovingly and I have formed with them new attachments and linked my interest in their lives. But O, how close and tender are the ties with my very own family, how hard the parting. Our breakfast together was a silent one this morning, and my Father's prayer a broken petition.

Sister Lizzie and I had our farewell last night. Hours we spent together, far into the night, talking over the old childhood days at Stewiacke, the girlhood years here in Truro, her sickness and the long weary period of pain and retirement—my teaching and mission work, my wedding-day, and the new life now stretching out for me ahead. She was very brave. We did not weep. It was rather a retrospect to record our joys and our mercies, and the seal of our mutual love. Of her own renunciation of desires and ambitions, she did not speak....

———

A DRESSMAKER

The absence of a high school and her age when her family finally moved to a farm near one prevented Ettie Miller (Cumming) from pursuing the higher education she longed for. Denied this opportunity, she turned instead to the needle skills she possessed serving first as an apprentice and later working independently in local homes.

Wellington County, Ontario, 1900-1920
M. Alberta Auger, "Dressmakers 1900-20 Era". Wellington County Archives.
Wellington County Museum, Fergus, Ontario.

My parents, Marshall and Mary Miller, lived in East Luther in Dufferin County and were clearing their farm out of the bush. I was the oldest in a family of seven. Staying in Grand Valley for three days to write my Entrance examinations was a highlight of my teens. Passing this test, I was promoted to the position of mother's helper as my parents felt there was no high school near enough for me to attend. How I longed for more learning!

When I was sixteen, my father sold his Luther farm and bought one midway between Alma and Salem. Now my younger sisters would have the opportunity to further their educations but I was too old to start into Grade 9. I enjoyed sewing and needlework, so I decided to become a good dressmaker.

I can't remember when I first sewed. As a little girl I stitched at dresses and blankets for my dolls. Often I helped Mother mend, or sewed on a button for Father...

The winter I was eighteen, Mother decided she could manage without my help so I started my apprenticeship. A Miss Davidson had a sewing business at her home in Salem. She had three apprentices that winter—Miss Jennie Bell, Miss Broham, and myself. She agreed to teach me for three months, in return for my time sewing for her. I walked two miles to and from home every day. We worked six days each week from nine till six with time off for lunch at noon. We started with easier tasks such as basting, overcasting, hemming, pressing etc. But she was very particular; there was a correct way to do each step...

Miss Davidson had 3 treadle sewing machines which we were taught to use. They were very simple compared to to-day's models. They stitched only forward but tension and length of stitch could be adjusted...

Poor lights were a real hardship for us to work by. No one had hydro; only a few Aladdin lamps. Oil was costly so lamps were never used in daytime even on a dull day. If the material was dark in color, we sat near the windows and strained our eyes.

After three months at Miss Davidson's I secured a job in the dressmaking department of Ryans in Guelph. Here for weeks, I sewed, hems only. My wages were now $4.50 weekly, out of which I paid $4.00 for board. Next, I assisted Miss Margaret Miller, a cousin of father's, who had a dressmaking business in Alma. After working for six months with experienced dressmakers, an apprentice was considered capable of completing any garment unassisted and establishing her own business.

So now I bought a used Singer machine from Miss Miller for $25 (which I used for 40 years) and started out on my own. Some customers brought their material to my home and came for fittings. More often I went to their homes and stayed for a few days or a couple weeks till I had the work completed. Wages were 75 cents a day with board included....

Patterns as we know them to-day were unheard of. Each dressmaker had basic patterns of such parts as short sleeve, long sleeve, back, front, yoke, collar etc. By taking a customer's measurements, hip, waist and length, a skirt pattern could be easily cut. Basic rules for cutting bindings, belts, flounces and frills were learned early in apprenticeship. Learning how to adjust a basic pattern to the required size was also emphasized. Most ladies kept their own basic patterns, once adjusted, for future use with minor changes....

Skirts of those days never revealed the wearer's figure. Women wore one or more petticoats (to-day's half slips). These often had rows and rows of narrow tucks and often flounces or frills 8-12" deep at the bottom. These were starched stiffly, and held the skirt in proper shape at all times. If the dress were of sheer material, a camisole often of eyelet or crocheted lace was worn to conceal such undergarments as a shirt, waist (bra) or corset. All dresses had sleeves, collars, and belts, the latter two usually being sewed by hand. Hems were also always finished by hand.

Materials we used mostly for dresses were wool crepes, linens, silks, velvets, cottons, brocades, and satins. For skirts and suits, wool serge and flannels were popular. Material when purchased was never pre-shrunk. This was always done before cutting out a garment. Shrinkage was often three inches to the yard, and material was shrunk by pressing with a warm iron and a damp pressing cloth. Dresses often had yards of braid, or lace for trimming. This was usually sewn on by hand also.

---

4. WORK UNFIT FOR THE MOTHERS OF THE RACE: MOVING INTO NON-TRADITIONAL WORK ROLES

MONTREAL'S FEMALE NON-DOMESTIC WORKERS

Industrial and commercial expansion in Montreal after 1850 created an almost insatiable demand for workers. For women, it created jobs and the opportunity for employment in fields outside domestic service. Suzanne Cross has documented women's important but docile role in the city's labour force by 1900. In the following results of a survey conducted in 1913 by the Montreal Local Council of Women, a general view of the role of women and their employment situation is presented. It is worth noting that the Child Welfare Exhibition Committee in 1912 estimated that a Montreal family of five required $952 annually to live above the poverty line.

Montreal, 1913
Miss C. Derick, "General Report on Women's Work," Royal Commission on Industrial Training and Technical Education, Report *(Ottawa, 1913) Part IV, 1975-79.*

GROUP 1: Women in Clerical and Commercial Positions
This class of occupation offers suitable employment for properly qualified women. There is a constant demand for women stenographers and clerks in business and professional firms, and within the last few years this has extended to the banks. Clerical work is congenial, the surroundings are generally comparatively good, the hours of employment reasonable, and the chance of a living wage and of steady employment is afforded. Women who have received a good secondary education and are well grounded in English, and who have had a thorough business training have no difficulty whatever in obtaining good positions, with the prospect of rapid advancement.

Women employed in banks begin at $400 or $500 a year.

Stenographers earn from $600 to $1,200 a year, in exceptional cases even as high as $1,500, although young girls may begin at $25.00 a month. The majority are handicapped by a deficient education; the lack of knowledge of their own language, of spelling, punctuation, and of elementary composition and letter writing is a matter of general comment. After short courses at one of the private business schools, these young women seek employment for which they are only partially trained. Small wonder if their work is more or less unsatisfactory to their employers; nor can they themselves ever hope to attain to the more responsible and remunerative positions. These are reserved for the exceptional or thoroughly trained woman.

In this group of wage-earners have been included the telephone operators. In Montreal there are at least 800 women employed who earn from $20.00 to $80.00 per month, according to their efficiency. These employees are trained by the Company, and the work is arranged in three shifts. Work at night and Sundays is more highly paid. Apart from the nervous strain, which appears unavoidable, telephone operating seems a desirable employment for women.

Business and commercial training—apart from the four years' course offered by the Commercial and Technical High school—is at present chiefly to be obtained in private business schools. Short courses undoubtedly appeal very strongly to the immature and inexperienced and to those who are anxious to earn a living as soon as possible. The business school not only gives the desired instruction, but quite frequently acts as an employment bureau.

The advisability of instituting short commercial courses in Technical Schools, open to those already well grounded in English, and affording a thoroughly practical business training, is, we believe, worthy of consideration. There is an ever increasing demand for such courses.

GROUP 2: Saleswomen in Shops

There are many women wage-earners in shops who come under Group 1, and some, those engaged in millinery and dressmaking, are included in Group 3. In Group 2 are included only those engaged in selling.

In the higher grade department stores there are very few girls of 14 years of age, and these few generally act as errand girls. In less highgrade establishments and smaller shops, young girls may more frequently be seen, but at present not to such an extent as some years ago, before the introduction of the various cash-carrying systems.

Comparing the position of the shop-girl with that of the girl in domestic service: —

The shop-girl has clearly defined duties, and her hours of work have a definite limit, generally from 8 o'clock in the morning to 5:30 or 6 at night (with some exceptions), all her evenings and Sundays are free, and during these leisure hours she is her own mistress. At her work she is under the same supervision and discipline as her associates; from the moment she leaves her work till she returns to it, she is practically free to choose her own society and take what recreation she prefers without let* or hindrance. She considers that her social position is superior to that of a domestic servant, and as evidence of this she is addressed as Miss (Mrs), while the domestic is called by the Christian name. Again, she is not at the constant beck and call of one individual, confined to one house and the monotony of the daily round, but goes to and from her work, and is brought in contact with an ever varying stream of life which lends an interest and even a charm to her environment.

The disadvantages, not always realized, are sufficiently grave, but might be easily obviated. She often has but scant home comforts, perhaps has to prepare her own hurried breakfast; she must face the weather at all times; in many establishments she is required to stand the whole day long, not being permitted to sit down for an instant, a requirement most assuredly injurious to her physical well being. Frequently the ventilation is extremely bad, and the employee constantly breathes a vitiated atmosphere, with sometimes extremes of temperature and exposure to draughts. Her wage is very often barely

*[obstruction]

sufficient for her maintenance, and she may have difficulty in making both ends meet. In her leisure hour she naturally seeks amusement and relaxation, only to find that, as a general rule, recreation of a desirable character is offered to her only at prohibitive prices. If she is boarding, she seldom has any place in which to receive her friends, and very often there is no one to whom she can look for authoritative guidance. And thus it is that in an innocent search for pleasure natural to all, she is frequently exposed to temptations of a particularly insidious nature, the true character of which she sometimes does not recognize till too late.

There is a distinct need for comfortable and respectable boarding accommodation at reasonable rates, for working girls of all classes. It is to be hoped that there may soon be a business women's hotel. There should also be social clubs for working girls, affording parlours and halls, where innocent and desirable recreations might be provided and where both men and women might pleasantly mingle together in a thoroughly wholesome environment.

The work being done by the YWCA is more excellent, but does not more than begin to meet the need.

GROUP 3: Women in Industrial Establishments
In this group the inquiry was addressed to seventy-one (71) establishments. In about 22 instances no report could be obtained. There was either an absolute refusal to answer, a polite but repeated evasion, or a failure to send the promised answer.

Out of 71 establishments, 49 employers responded to the enquiry; 25 different kinds of industry were included, and reports were given of 22. A table is appended giving the number of varieties of industries, with approximate number of women employees, wages, hours of employment, standard of education, etc., etc., from which particular conclusions may be drawn if desired. The more general conclusions of the committee may be summarized as follows:

In most of the industries there is very little demand on the part of the employers for girls under the legal limit. Often the work is too heavy for young girls. In some instances no effort is made to ascertain the ages of the younger employees, more particularly where there is a scarcity of hands; this is more especially the case in large mills, and it is in such cases that the labor laws need stricter enforcement.

The minimum wage in most factories is about $2.00 per week (occasionally as low as $1.75) for untrained hands. In factories new and inexperienced hands are at first put on a weekly wage while being taught the work, but are in a short time advanced to piece-work. For piece-workers there is very seldom any promotion other than increased earning power up to a certain maximum limit. Only in very exceptional cases has the worker an opportunity of being transferred to a different department or a higher grade of work. She is doomed to go on working at one little process—and her wages depend entirely on the degree of manual dexterity and unremitting industry of the individual. If she is deft and industrious and works full time, she can earn a comparatively good wage—from $10.00 to $15.00 per week. A few exceptional women in exceptional industries earn as much as $20.00 or $25.00 per week. In laundries the workers have more chance of learning the whole process and those who are skilful ironers may earn on piece-work $12 to $15 (max.) per week.

The conditions in dressmaking and millinery establishments are somewhat different. Young girls absolutely unskilled are taken in as apprentices, and not paid at all or begin with an allowance for carfare or 50 cents a week. They have a chance of learning most parts of the business, with the exception of cutting and fitting, and are paid according to their ability from $1.00 to $10.50 per week. Really skilled workers get from $11 to $25 or even $30 per week.

In the custom tailoring establishments the work is nearly all skilled and wages range from $5.00 up—the maximum for women being about $20 or $25 per week. There is a demand for skilled workers for which there is no corresponding supply here. The tailors state that they find it necessary to import labor, under great difficulties. There is no opportunity for acquiring such training at present in Montreal.

There is a demand on the part of the employers and employees alike for training in needlework and machine operating—also for skilled workers in leather and for skilled laundresses.

Employees desire opportunities for the acquirement of French or English, a better primary education, facilities for training not only in hand sewing, machine operating, cooking, millinery and dressmaking but an opportunity for obtaining such a training as would give them at least a chance of entering the various industries as skilled workers, at a fair wage. When they enter as unskilled hands, there is no prospect of promotion before them. The vast majority of women workers fall into the unskilled class—those ranked as skilled are frequently merely deft at one small process.

Factory employees place the minimum living wage at $7.00 per week, but others place it as $8 or $9 or even $10 per week, and as an ordinary worker earns from $4.50 to $5.50 per week, the average worker is not paid a living wage and is therefore not economically independent. A great many girls live at home or with friends and relatives, and in this way are boarded at low rates or contribute to the support of the family. Board outside the family cannot be obtained under $3.50 or $4 per week. The balance of the wages has to go for clothing, car-fare, recreation and incidental expenses.

Employers, as a rule, approve of evening classes, in theory at least. It is felt that the opportunity should be afforded workers of improving their education, academic, commercial or industrial. In practice, however, many disapprove strongly. They state that after working ten hours a day, the body and mind are fatigued and the evening should be spend in recreation. The strain of attending classes in the evening is too great and unfits them for the daily work.

As a matter of fact, there is small evidence of women in factories taking advantage of the evening classes already opened. It is the wage-earners of the 1st and 2nd groups and domestic servants who attend evening classes at present.

Women wage-earners are absolutely ignorant of labor laws, only being familiar with the particular conditions which affect them individually. Some of them suggest shorter hours or better pay.

Finally, in regard to the educational standards, the average shop woman has had a primary education of some sort, but seldom up to the highest grade—she can read and write and do simple arithmetic. In many factories the majority of the employees are utterly illiterate, others can barely read, or read and write with difficulty. In no single instance has the standard been considered sufficiently high. There has been an almost unanimous expression of opinion in favor of compulsory education. At present whether the child attends school or not rests with the parents; it is impossible to obtain statistics in regard to the number who never attend school. The question arises: What are the girls doing who leave school at from 9 to 10 to 14, who are not permitted by law to work in shops and factories?

SHORTHAND IS FASCINATING AS RIDING A BICYCLE

The expansion of business in the second half of the nineteenth century called for an expanded labour force with new skills. To meet this need, private business schools like the Snell's Business College in Truro, Nova Scotia, were started. Snell's ad, "Shorthand is Fascinating as Riding a Bicycle," [sic] is reprinted below. It is noteworthy that in 1895, this advertisement is addressed to both sexes equally. In later years, as business expanded and hierarchies developed, secretarial positions, requiring shorthand skills, would become the preserve of female workers.

Truro, Nova Scotia, 1895
"Shorthand is Fascinating as Riding a Bicycle," Nova Scotia Educational Association, Report, 1895.

We can teach you shorthand by mail, just as well as though you came here to the college. It isn't a bit of trouble; while you can study a few minutes or more, when convenient to yourself. This improved shorthand is as simple as A.B.C.

It is the quickest shorthand we know anything about—quickest to learn and fastest to write. Writing the vowels, as in this system, makes it easy to learn and easy to read at any time. In fact, you can learn the Permin-Snell shorthand in one half the time required...[for] some of the difficult systems—while it is better in every way.

This is justly considered a high price school. But good things cost more than cheap—and are worth more. We have improved methods for teaching—take capable young men and women right into a large business office, where they learn practically, by doing "actual business," just as it is done by other men in business. This gives real business experience and explains why graduates are in demand by the more forward business and professional men. This is supposed to be the only school of the sort in Canada.

We offer Advanced Instruction in Practical Business Affairs, in the briefest time possible and at the least possible cost. We start with the rudiments in each course: Shorthand, for office work and professional reporting; English; Typewriting; Penmanship; Book-keeping and Actual Business. Don't you know that this knowledge is the stepping stone to high positions of honor and trust? The better you are qualified, the larger salary you command and the easier to get employment....

THE DISPLACEMENT OF YOUNG MEN

It was not uncommon for men in the late nineteenth century to raise objections as women entered occupations that had previously been their preserve. For J.L. Payne who penned "The Displacement of Men" excerpted below, men would be "pre-empted" from their rightful careers if the trend to feminization continued in businesses, government, and shops.

1893
J.L. Payne, "The Displacement of Young Men", The Canadian Magazine, *I (1893) 467-70.*

The man who has his eyes open to what is going on about him cannot fail to see that the extent to which young women have entered the arena of daily work has materially contracted the range of congenial and promising employment for young men. It is observed, for example, that many of the places which young men had very properly regarded as hopeful starting-points in life, are now pre-empted by young women; and the question arises as to how far this displacement can go without creating very serious and far-reaching trouble. To my mind, the situation already wears a grave aspect, and yet it would seem to be only in the initial stage...

Nearly all classes of clerical work are passing rapidly into the hands of young women. These young women enter the office with skilful fingers, winning manners, industrious ways, and general aptness to write letters, keep books, count cash, and discharge the multitudinous duties attaching to business life. The time has gone by when it can be said they are unfitted to do as well as young men. They do their work satisfactorily and well. Taken altogether, they are neater, better behaved, and quicker than young men....

Let me present a few facts.... I know something of the Canadian Civil Service, and also the American, and from observation I should say that two young women now enter the departments at Ottawa and Washington to one young man. What is true of the Civil Service is unquestionably true of all branches of business where clerks are employed. Shops and offices are all but closed to young men, and each year the situation assumes a more fixed form. Into all the lighter branches of labor women are entering in steadily increasing numbers, to the exclusion of men. It is this exclusion or displacement to which I wish in this imperfect way to call attention, since it cannot be long until a remedy will be asked for to relieve the pressure. It is within my knowledge that competent and well-educated young men are fighting for places in the offices of the great railway companies, where, as yet, women have not entered as in other departments of work. Twenty clamor for every vacancy that occurs. The result is, that these bright young fellows, capable of doing excellent work, are forced to toil for long hours, often at night, for the munificent salary of $15 a month.... Why do young men willingly work for less than board and clothing in many instances? The answer is obvious. So many of the starting points, formerly open to them only, are now barred by young women, that those who have clerical work to sell as the means of opening hopeful avenues, are obliged to take whatever they can get and be thankful....

It may be an extreme view—I hope it is—but, if the next twenty years witness the same relative increase in the number of working girls and women as has taken place since 1870 in this country and the United States, we shall see young men doing the house work, and their sisters and mothers carrying on half the business of the land. As an instance of how the pinch is commencing already to be felt, I might cite the case of a family, consisting of two girls and a boy, all old enough to earn their living. The young man is a wide-awake, industrious and clever fellow; but, while his sisters are in good situations, he finds it impossible to secure an opening in which he could hope to make even the price of his board. This is by no means an exceptional case. Twenty years ago there would have been ten openings before him to one that exists to-day....

———————

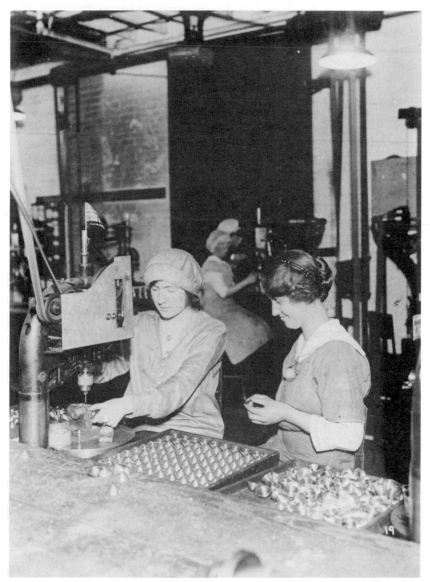

In October 1916 women were employed in manufacturing munitions for the first time in Canada. By the end of the First World War, over 30,000 female munitions workers had been employed while an even greater number of women found paid public occupations replacing men in service and manufacturing industries. The women pictured above are threading set screw holes at the Russell Motor Car Co. in Toronto around 1917.

Credit: Public Archives of Canada, PA-24639.

A MARITIME GIRL IN BOX MAKING AND SALES

While Montreal and Toronto drew young Quebec and Ontario girls to urban work, for young women in the Maritimes the industrial centres of the United States and especially Boston proved the Mecca. A.A. Brookes in his University of New Brunswick doctoral thesis, "The Exodus: Migration from the Maritime Provinces to Boston During the Second Half of the Nineteenth Century" (1978), found that by 1880 over four thousand Maritime women were employed in Boston mainly as domestics, dressmakers, tailors and nurses (p. 127). The following recollection written in 1961 by Ada Williams recreates this typical experience of many young women.

Nova Scotia and Boston, 1907-1908
Grace Forsythe, ed., Tales of the Yesteryears: The Writings of Mrs. E.S. Williams West Jeddore, 1888-1977, *Book I, 100-103.*

MY FIRST TRIP TO BOSTON, 1907
Having lived in a small fishing village until late in March of 1907, I made my debut into the outside world by a trip to the 'Land of Hope and Glory.' My eldest brother Owen was in the States and sent me $5.00 to help pay my way. I was to go to our Aunt Clara's near Boston.

After a lengthy discussion, Papa and Mama finally consented to let me take the step from the 'Home Nest.' I will admit it was with a heavy feeling around my heart and a lump in my throat that I packed my belongings for the great adventure. Packed my trunk with what? Very little. But one could not go there without a trunk! I wore the same coat, skirt and tam that had been my outfit for months....

Arriving at the dock [in Boston] I saw Owen waiting outside the gates, which made me happy. But, alas! I was not thinking of my personal appearance. When I had left Nova Scotia on April 6th, snow still covered the fields, and lakes and ponds were still frozen. I was dressed for Nova Scotia weather, but definitely not for Boston.

When disembarking, our first greeting was from some Smart Aleck shouting, "Here comes a boatload of herrin' chokers!" Owen informed me that was only one of the greetings received by Down Easters.

I was taken to Owen's boarding house for dinner, where several others from home also boarded. After a rest, we started for Aunt Clara's in South Framingham. Getting on the long street cars with seats running lengthwise, one had to be more or less conspicuous.

It was a beautiful warm day. The car was crowded with ladies all decked out in their spring finery, dresses of muslin, voile, and flower-bedecked hats; and there I sat quite conscious of my appearance. I wondered if the passengers thought I came from the North Pole.

I wore a three-quarter length tweed coat, a homemade tam, and a pair of leather and astrachan gauntlets that came up over my coat sleeves to my elbows. My black cloth skirt, well filled out with petticoats, swept the floor, three yards or more in width. It was called mohair cloth, and had almost an inch width of 'brush braid' around the bottom. My shoes were leather oxfords for which I had paid $1.50, and last, but not least, I wore a pair of handknit black woollen stockings, the wool being shorn from our sheep by Papa, then carded, spun, and knit by Mama. Beneath those stockings the lingerie worn with them was tucked in at the ankles, the latter being concealed modestly from the public eye.

The daintily dressed girls in summer finery and accessories surveyed me from head to toe. Some tittered and giggled; others, more polite, cast their eyes downward, while some raised theirs heavenward. Finally, Owen whispered, "Gosh, Ada, could you hid those mitts?" I realized I had a 'hero' of a brother. The mitts being the only thing I could hide, I took them off and sat on them! I was truly thankful for the long skirt that hid my shoes. I know my 'hero' was thankful when we finally arrived at Aunt Clara's!...

My first job over there in 1907 was at the Dennison Company, making all kinds of boxes which I enjoyed very much. After a while work got slack, so I was asked to work at a Greek ice cream parlor where I stayed until I came home in the fall of 1908.

Those months were very pleasant, as the Sculas family were fine people. I had charge of the candy counter and the ice cream 'parlour' to serve customers....

If any Smart Alecks came into the 'parlour', Mr. Sculas or his young son Johnny would slip behind my counter with me, so I was well protected. As I look back on those months, I don't think there could be a finer group to work with.

After nineteen months away from home the first time, I decided to return for the winter. In late October, 1908, I came across from Boston to Yarmouth by boat and up to Halifax by train. Leaving Dartmouth early in the morning, I travelled by stagecoach once more—a pair of horses and a double-seated wagon. Not long after we set out, a blinding snowstorm came up, a real gale from the northeast....

It so happened that the style in Boston that year was large veils tied down over our hats which were by no means dainty in size. My veil was brown, and it had never faced a Nova Scotia nor'-east snow storm....

By late afternoon we arrived at Musquodoboit Harbour at the Clairmont Hotel where the Misses Chisholm were hostesses. One of them asked me if I would like to go to a room for a little rest, so I accepted gratefully. I had to wait for the mail driver to get me safely home to West Jeddore. After changing horses, and I believe the driver, they started farther East.

I went to the room and looked in the mirror, and horrors! The snow had soaked the dye out of my Boston-brown veil, and I did resemble some one from a far Eastern country instead of Boston. I can assure you getting that dye off spoiled my complexion for a while.

INQUIRIES ON WOMEN'S WORK

Both the Royal Commission to Inquire into the Dispute between Bell Telephone Company and Its Employees at Toronto and the Royal Commission to Inquire into Industrial Disputes in the Cotton Factories of the Province of Quebec reported in 1909. Both were primarily concerned with examining strikes by telephone operators and cotton textile workers respectively but both devoted a great deal of space in their reports to the general question of women's work outside the home, arguing that such work would seriously erode women's health and adversely affect their future child-bearing and child-caring roles.

Ontario, 1909
Royal Commission Appointed to Inquire into the Dispute Between Bell Telephone Company and Its Employees at Toronto. Report. *Canada. Department of Labour. Sessional Paper No. 36, 1909: 129-131.*

The Strain on Operators

It is to be remembered in the first place that the class of persons employed as operators is composed mostly of girls and young women between the ages of 17 and 23, that persons of these years are preferred to others because of the greater facility with which they learn the work and acquire dexterity, that these are years during which the nervous and physical system of a woman is peculiarly sensitive to strain and susceptible to injury, and that harm done to, or impairment of the system sustained at that time of life is apt to be more far reaching in its consequences than would be the effects received from similar causes in maturer years. The effects moreover upon posterity occasioned by the undermining or weakening of the female constitution cannot receive too serious consideration.

The work of telephone operating does not appear to be of a kind to fit a woman for any other occupation or calling; additional significance is therefore to be given to the fact that the average time spent by operators in the service is from two to three years....

Secondly, the work of telephone operating under any conditions involves a considerable strain upon the nervous system. Some of the doctors maintained that it was not a fit work for any woman even where carried on at a moderate

rate. The faculties are kept constantly on the alert, there is a high tension on the special senses, and a certain amount of mental worry....

The special senses of sight, hearing and speech are called into operation not only continuously but constantly in a concerted manner; when not actually employed they are not resting because necessarily on the alert. The physical strain save for the obligation of sitting continuously in one position over a considerable period of time, and the reaching and stretching entailed where switchboards are large in size, or operators expected to assist with the work on boards adjoining their own is not considerable, and, to a degree, helps, to offset the effect of the nervous strain; on the other hand where there is not a proper regard for these matters the strain may be increased rather than diminished. The liability to injury from shocks, the harsh words and abuse of subscribers, the irritation caused by the intermittent glowing of lights reflecting the impatience of subscribers, the occasional buzzing and snapping of instruments in the ear, the sense of crowding where work accumulates and the inevitable anxiety occasioned by seeking to make the necessary connections whether a rush takes place, all combine to accentuate the strain upon an operator, and they are all factors more or less absent from other callings in which women are engaged....

•

Quebec, 1909
"The Employment of Women and Children". Royal Commission to Inquire into Industrial Disputes in the Cotton Factories of the Province of Quebec. Report. Canada. Sessional Paper No. 39, 1909: 16-18.

During the inquiry a considerable amount of evidence was given with reference to the employment of women and children in the cotton mills of Quebec. While it does not appear that the employment of women and children has been made the subject, save indirectly, of industrial disputes of any importance, a consideration of this class of employment would seem to come within the scope of an inquiry which has to do with the conditions of employment of operatives and the important questions of wages and hours, with which most of the disputes have been concerned. The existing scale of wages is the result of competition amongst the operatives, and the most important elements in this competition are female and child labour. It has been shown that of the operatives employed in the Quebec cotton mills 42.3 per cent are females and 26.6 per cent are persons under 18 years of age. As to the hours of labour of all these two classes it was asserted that in normal times under normal conditions, work should begin on week days at 6:15 o'clock in the morning and continue to 12 noon, resume at a quarter to 1, and continue till 6, with the exception of Saturday, when there was work only in the morning.

In determining what the maximum number of working hours should be, economic considerations alone demand that a full regard should be had for the effects of long and continuous employment, whatever its nature upon the constitution of women, and their place in the social economy of a nation. Excessive work bequeaths a legacy of weakness or disability to those who directly or indirectly are affected by it. In the upbuilding of a nation this is a factor which cannot be too constantly kept in mind.

If Canada is to have a hardy and intelligent body of producers, on which primarily her industrial position among the nations of the world will depend, she cannot view with too much caution all those factors which go to the making of a nation's manhood, and of these none are of like importance to the health and well-being of the mother and the child....

JOBS FOR GIRLS LEAVING HIGH SCHOOL

A 1913 survey of public schools in Halifax, conducted by Mrs F.W. Sexton for the National Council of Women of Canada, found that girls began to leave the school system in grade five at a rate of 20% per year. Why these girls left school, what happened to them, and what training and skills they received were also the subjects of the study as reported below. Mrs Sexton's statement documents a number of important themes. First, it points out the continuing responsibility placed on girls aged 14 to 17 for the care of their siblings and their households. Second, it illuminates the types of work available for young working-class girls in urban areas. Finally, it presents the common assumptions held by middle-class observers about the life experience of working-class girls.

Halifax, 1913
"Statement by Mrs. F.W. Sexton", Royal Commission on Industrial Training and Technical Education, Report *(Ottawa, 1913) Part IV, 1747-49.*

In Halifax there are 500 girls at home between the ages of 14 and 17. Of these, 350 have never been beyond grade 8 and very many not beyond grade 5.

Perhaps one half of such girls in Halifax and throughout Canada stay at home to take care of the other children; but from 50% to 75% of girls out of school are obliged to earn their living in some way or help at home. What are they being trained to do? They have domestic science and sewing in the public school, but no boy or girl has been able to earn his or her living on the strength of training received in mechanic or domestic science....

Leading to Unskilled Industries

Training in Halifax schools in sewing, which is necessary for any girl if she is to enter any of the trades, is not systematic or graded, but is more or less perfunctory and dilatory. The girls not at school drift about and go into unskilled trades, such as candy dipping, packing, paper and cardboard industries—all sorts of occupations that bring on tuberculosis and curvature of the spine, doing the same thing over and over again under conditions absolutely stunting and deadening. After three or four years these girls marry; and what kind of homes can we expect them to make when they have not been taught to do one single thing properly with their hands, and have been driven about amongst harmful moral and physical influences? Perhaps some of them pick up a trade, but this is increasingly difficult. Dressmakers do not want to be bothered teaching girls; they would rather import those already trained. Just when girls are at the most critical age and susceptible to influences of all kinds they are dropped into the midst of these low industrial conditions....

Tests as to Suitability of Industries for Women

The tests for industries in which a woman can engage are that they must be clean and sanitary; must have no injurious physical or moral influences or lead her away from her ultimate work of home-making; and they must offer living wages and afford hope for her advancement and development.

Investigations show that the needle industries, millinery, dressmaking, men's tailoring, etc., are the only ones for which there is definite training in Halifax, where over 1000 women are engaged in industries that are practically wholly unskilled. It would not pay to train girls to enter boot and shoe work, in fact they usually enter as stitchers, which is untrained work.

The objection to women engaging in unskilled work, such as candy-making, is that these unskilled trades are run under unsanitary conditions; that in mechanical operations the women have to use no thought, hence mental growth is absolutely stunted and ambition stifled, and the women will never reach a higher plane. As there will always be enough riff-raff to carry on unskilled occupations, why should we want to train men and women to go into these, asks Mrs Sexton. When employers cannot get women to carry on such occupations, she argued, necessity will probably cause the invention of suitable machinery. In any case, you will never be able to train all the women out of unskilled industries. She was speaking on behalf of ambitious women who must get a living wage, and who are now forced into either skilled or unskilled industries, for whom work in the former would be possible if they had the necessary training. Unskilled industries do not promise the money which is essential to an unmarried woman—firms in Halifax offering only from $2 to $4 per week, with an average of between $3 and $4 per week.

THE SWEATED TRADES

The 1896 Commission on the Sweating System in Canada spent a considerable amount of time questioning witnesses about the conditions in which women worked at home and in factories. The commissioners were concerned, as the following excerpts suggest, about the entry of young women into work that was not "respectable" and the effects of that work on their future health.

Toronto, 1896
Evidence, Toronto, January 8 and 9, Report on the Sweating System in Canada, *Canada, Sessional Papers, 29, No. 11, 1896, No. 4: 23, 29, 42-43.*

MR JURY–"What the Commissioner should do to satisfy himself is to walk up and down Bay Street for a few hours any day in the week and see the great number of women staggering up and down with great bundles of clothing, some of the poor creatures hardly able to walk."...

MR GUROFSKY–"There are shops in which gas-irons are burning all the time. There are no attempts at proper ventilation morning and night, from twelve to fifteen gas-lights are burning for about two hours, and the stove is going all the time. I have not heard of any establishment being ordered to be properly ventilated. The inspectors look over the closets and do not see the establishments themselves."

MR STRACHAN–"There are 140 men and 50 women out on strike at this moment. Why are they there? Because the 19 employers—good men, too, apparently—told us that they wanted the power over the pant and vest hands to do as they like. They found it so convenient that instead of paying two dollars for custom made pants they were getting them for 68 cents or one dollar. Eight years ago I knew a shop where they paid two dollars per pair for pants. We have struck to support these people because the contractors are just grinding them down. We want as a union to control this labour, and to aid the girls in the pant and vest departments.

The employers said we will pay $1.50 and $1.25 for vests and you not interfere, but if we did not interfere these girls would soon be doing the work for 50 cents. We will fight this thing. The only way to prevent it is to make employers of labour do away with back shops and employ a—contract. This system of spreading the word all over the city and putting one human being against another is wrong."...

UNEMPLOYMENT IN WOMEN'S OCCUPATIONS

In contrast to most of the documents dealing with women's work prior to 1920, the Ontario Commission on Unemployment recognized "the economic and social importance of wage-earning employments among women in Ontario." The commission's concern, therefore, was not to alter this fact but to insure that women's wage work did not interfere with the interests of the community in their motherhood and domestic responsibilities.

Ontario, 1916
Report of the Ontario Commission on Unemployment *(Toronto, 1916) 59, 71-72.*

Extent and Character of Unemployment
No one can tell what being unemployed means, not even those whose food and clothing, comfort and happiness depend on paid work, unless the individual applies the meaning of unemployment to her own case. A personal enquiry undertaken by The Commission on Unemployment has shown that some thousands of women wage earners in Ontario suffered from unemployment last winter, and that a smaller number are unemployed every year, with much harm to themselves and others. The following facts have been collected with regard to unemployment in women's occupations.

In Domestic employment which numbers between 30,000 and 50,000 workers in Ontario, there is no unemployment.

Among Factory Workers, who were estimated in 1914 to number 53,729 in Ontario, there was unemployment amounting to 8 per cent or 4,759 workers, as compared with the number employed in 1913.

In the employment of Saleswomen, who are estimated to number between 12,000 and 15,000 or even 18,000 workers in Ontario, it has not been possible to arrive at any percentage of unemployment. Specific instances have been found which indicate a certain amount of widespread unemployment. Thirty-two saleswomen registered at the Employment Bureau of the Toronto Women's Patriotic League during the period of greatest unemployment, and twenty-four of these were classed as skilled. A number of saleswomen also applied to go to country positions as domestics.

In the employment of Stenographers, which number 24,632 in Ontario exclusive of the City of Ottawa, and which can be taken as employing over 26,000 women workers, the unemployment after the dislocation of business in August and September, amounted to about two per cent.

Among trained nurses, numbering between 2,000 and 3,000 women in private nursing in Ontario, the unemployment may be fairly indicated by waiting lists [for positions] of 160 in November, 1914, 107 in February 1915 and 120 in October 1915 from one nurses' registry with a registration of slightly over 500 nurses in 1914. These waiting lists showing unemployment should be compared with waiting lists of 50 in November 1910, and 80 in November 1913.

The more or less casual employment of Women who work by the day is greatly increased in numbers during times of depression. At a conservative estimate, it includes between 5,000 and 6,000 women workers in Ontario. Unemployment among women who work by the day was acute during the winter of 1914-15, and is likely to be somewhat extensive in the winter of 1915-16.

These six employments represent a total of 135,000 women workers in Ontario. Other employments bring the total to at least 175,000. The fact that we have this number of women workers has not been realized, and the meaning of the fact, even by those who were aware of it, has been imperfectly appreciated nor has it been understood that these workers form equally with men a part of the world's working force. Unemployment in 1914-15 was experienced by between 8,000 and 10,000 women workers, judging from the amount of unemployment found in the occupations studied....

Recommendations: Your Commissioners wish to emphasize:

1. The economic and social importance of wage-earning employments among women in Ontario. Investigation indicates that there are at least 175,000 women wage-earners in this Province. While it is true that many of these women marry after some years spent in paid work, their places are taken by others generally younger, women workers, and thus this great total remains undiminished and will increase as manufacturing and industries expand. The fact that such numbers of women are at work and the significance of this fact have not been sufficiently realized, and thus, adequate action has not been taken to make their employments conform to the interests of the community, the family and the individual worker.

2. That, since changes resulting from the development of many paid occupations are tending to interfere seriously with the position held by home-making occupations, recognition should be given by the educational authorities or the State to home-making and the care of children as womens' occupations which represent training, skill, and a high degree of efficiency. Your Commissioners believe that such recognition will be to the advantage of home-making and wage-earning occupations, and the community....

CHAPTER THREE:

FOUNDING A FAMILY

Not to marry: could a Victorian woman choose not to marry? Perhaps as the child of a farm family chosen to care for her aging parents, her duties as daughter might linger on so long that the time for marrying passed. Perhaps if she were a Québécoise she might wed the church, care for children of the church, make the church her family. The proportion of Quebec women who became nuns more than doubled in the fifty years following 1867. In some Ontario districts, female age at marriage rose in the years immediately after Confederation. Across the country, in the late nineteenth century there was a marginal increase in the proportion of women who remained single. Yet none of these changes was very large. In 1920 only two in a hundred Quebecoises over twenty were members of religious orders. The pattern of advancing rural marriage age may not have persisted. By 1911 the proportion of Canadian women in the married state had begun to rise again, and to levels higher than any that had existed since Confederation.[1]

Opportunities were opening for advanced education, and there were more places for women in teaching and medicine, and in new professions with a strong female identification such as nursing and social work. But the proportion of Canadian women who devoted their lives to child-bearing, child-rearing, and homemaking did not decline, despite a fall in the birth rate, a parallel decrease in the percentage of the population under fourteen (and in need of adult care), and the waning of household production. Rather, standards of mothering changed. "As men left the home to take wage labour jobs, leaving women behind to take responsibility for raising young children, motherhood began to take on an almost sacred quality."[2] Although between 1871 and 1921 the average size of a Canadian household declined, quality criteria in mothering rose. The more artificiality and danger were attributed to the world outside the home, the more frequently were fathers absent from home, the more nurturing and protecting was required of mothers, the more shame was attached to a woman who forsook the duties and obligations of wife.[3]

The choice of a husband was not a young woman's alone. Before the First

World War, when divorce was almost unheard of in Canada and separation exceedingly rare, courtships were usually long and prudently considered. Because the founding of a new branch of the family might strengthen the kin group's economic or social position, or alternatively dangerously impinge upon the welfare of a wide circle of relatives, parents exercised as much control as possible over a young woman's transition from maiden to wife. This control need not be obtrusive so long as it was effective. By carefully circumscribing their daughters' social circle, and restricting the domain of courtship to the family front parlour, parents were able to exclude broad classes of young men while rarely appearing to discriminate against individual suitors.[4]

Class and individual character sometimes provoked exceptions to this pattern. If the reports of their vexed mistresses are to be trusted, the servants who came to the prairies from Scandinavia and Great Britain under the sponsorship and guidance of the Dominion Department of the Interior often married within weeks of their arrival.[5] Working-class girls without strong family connections or without property to be husbanded in the family interest might decide quickly and be guided by their affections in the choice of a spouse. But a strong will and the willingness to risk ostracism and poverty were required in women from agricultural or commercial families who chose a marriage partner independently of or contrary to their parents' wishes, for in the ordinary course of events their husband would have become a member of the family enterprise.[6]

The duration of the engagement was, like the choice of potential suitors, strongly responsive to economic considerations. In agricultural communities, a sensible young woman whose father owned a farm married a man who possessed land, was certain to inherit his family's holdings, or was well established in a craft or profession. Before World War One in the North West Territories, Saskatchewan, and Alberta, these criteria might be quite speedily met, but in central and Atlantic Canada, barriers to entry into local agriculture were high and the wait while fiancés established themselves on farms outside the region or in distant city careers might be long.[7]

Girls from working-class homes hoped to be able to leave the paid labour force upon marriage, and although many knew about mechanical methods of birth control,[8] by preference they began families soon after their weddings.[9] Unheard of were marriages of two wage-earners who by intention remained childless. As male wages were often insufficient to support a family, and female wages always so, engaged couples had to save for their mutual goal for some time while living apart or had to compromise upon their domestic ideals and have the wife continue to work outside the home after marriage. The bride of an urban labouring man wanted lodgings independent of her parents although she and her husband probably chose accommodation nearby so that they could continue to enjoy the help and companionship of kin.

Upper-class urban wives maintained similar close association with family and supplemented these opportunities for sociability by regular visiting among friends—the ritualized "at homes"—and as the period wore on, by more frequent participation in voluntary organizations.[10] For rural women, especially prairie women, marriage occasioned a more radical change in social experience. A farm girl left her mother's crowded kitchen or the busy household in which she had been employed as the hired girl and went to her own home, where she and her husband were alone together; this was doubtless a pleasant sensation initially, especially for those whose courtship had been closely supervised, but after a time a lonely predicament for the young wife. City women who followed husbands to prairie homesteads wrote poignantly of their want of female companionship, and when their husbands were away following flocks or herds or opportunities for wage work, of any companionship at all.[11] In the prairies the rural telephone system, speeded to completion under provincial government sponsorship, was a welcome antidote to this disheartening and often dangerous problem of female isolation.[12] In central Canada the loneliness of the countryside combined with the high cost of beginning in agriculture continued to be a force impelling young couples to the cities.

Women particularly valued the help of other women in the weeks before and after child birth. In the years immediately after Confederation most women delivered their babies at home. The movement away from home births was not at all marked before World War One. In 1926 only 17.8% of births in Canada occurred in hospital.[13] It is likely that most women who obtained hospital care were still of the special categories specified at the founding of the Ottawa Maternity Hospital in 1894: women who had previously had difficult deliveries or women for whom a home birth was not possible because they were homeless, either as a continuing condition or as a result of their pregnancy.[14]

Medical attendance at home birth was, however, more frequent than it had been at mid-century. While it was not uncommon for women to be guided through childbirth by other women, (the *sages-femmes* of Quebec, the European midwives of the prairie provinces, or women from Ontario and the Maritimes experienced through birthing their own young) child birth was more often seen as the province of doctors assisted by nurses. Amateur helpers were useful to the family. They usually stayed on for a fortnight after attending at the birth to keep the household running smoothly until the mother was sufficiently recovered to reassume her role as domestic manager. But birthing itself was seen as requiring scientific rather than neighbourly oversight and midwives became sad vestiges of an unwholesome past.

The rates at which Canadian women died delivering children, 4.7 per thousand live births in 1921,[15] while lower than those in the United States, were high by comparison with most of Western Europe, and appear not to have declined significantly until the beginning of the Second World War. Perhaps the geographical isolation of many Canadian mothers deprived them of necessary attention at the birth of their babies. In this respect the lack of a trained cadre of midwives contributed to the high death rate associated with child birth in the Dominion in the late nineteenth and early twentieth centuries.[16]

In one sense, labour in reproduction appears to have been less dangerous to women than labour in production was for men. In 1901, in the 25 to 34 year old age group, 80 out of every 100,000 deaths among women were attributable to puerperal infections, 9.9 to accidents, whereas 106 of every 100,000 deaths among men in this age group were accidental.[17] Yet in the same year in Ontario the liabilities of the separate spheres seemed to have evened out in the end; the probability that women who had reached age 20 would survive until age 60 was the same, 67%, as for men.[18]

But many a Canadian died soon after birth. Of every thousand born in the Dominion in 1901, 157 boys and 128 girls did not survive their first year.[19] A child was more likely to die within a year of birth in a Canadian city than in urban centres in other Dominions of the Empire or the United States.[20] Infant death rates show strong seasonal summer maxima, most marked among French-Canadian populations, both farm and city, but significantly present in English-speaking communities across the country as well. Diarrhoea was particularly prominent among the causes of infant death. These gastro-intestinal disorders seem linked to hand and bottle feeding of food most vulnerable to contamination in warm weather. Such risks were greatest among working-class families with less adequate storage facilities for food and stronger economic pressures to wean their infants soon after birth so that mothers could return to employment outside the home.[21]

The plague of infant death stood as a stark affront to a culture more demanding of its mothers, and a nation insistent upon its future perpetuating a British imperial race. Infant health became a public matter around which the energies of the emerging public health movement were mobilized to provide mothers with purer milk, medical supervision, and advice on sanitation and nutrition. By the early twentieth century motherhood, now a burden of state, a sacred office, and a scientific practice could be none other than a full-time occupation.

NOTES

1 The statistics on nuns come from the work of Marta Danylewycz. Age at marriage must be calculated from individual church records and thus is extremely cumbersome to acquire. For some suggestions about trends in marriage age in Ontario see David Gagan, *Hopeful Travellers* (Toronto, 1981) and Beth Light, "Determinants of Age at Marriage in Erie and Wentworth Counties during the Mid-Nineteenth Century," unpublished paper, York University, 1975. The data on incidence of marriage are corrected for changes in age distribution over the period, "The Canadian Family," *Census of Canada* 1931, XII, 30.

2 This discussion follows Constance B. Backhouse, "Shifting Patterns in Nineteenth-Century Canadian Custody Law," in David H. Flaherty, *Essays in the History of Canadian Law* (Toronto, 1981) and Ann Douglas, *The Feminization of American Culture* (New York, 1977).

3 The estimated crude fertility rate for Canada, that is the average number of births per thousand population, was 37 in the decade 1871-81, 29 in the decade 1911-21. The youth dependency ratio, that is the number of persons aged 0-14 years relative to the number of persons aged 15-64 years, was 67.7 in 1881 and 56.6 in 1921. See

Warren E. Kalbach and Wayne W. McVey, *The Demographic Bases of Canadian Society* (Toronto 1971) 56, 128. The figures on household size are our recalculations from "The Canadian Family" (1931) 32.

4 On the social constraints on British courtship, see J. A. Banks and Olive Banks, *Feminism and Family Planning* (Liverpool, 1964) 76-84 and Leonore Davidoff, *The Best Circles: Society, Etiquette and the Season* (London, 1973) 49-58; note Canadian examples of this pattern in Veronica Strong-Boag, "Introduction" to Elizabeth Smith, *A Woman with a Purpose* (Toronto, 1980) xxix; Nellie McClung, *Clearing in the West* (Toronto, 1935), and by le collectif Clio, a discussion of Henriette Dessaulles, daughter of a prominent St Hyacinthe family, in *L'Histoire des femmes au Québec,* (Montreal, 1982) 166-67.

5 Linda Rasmussen *et al, A Harvest Yet to Reap, A History of Prairie Women* (Toronto, 1976) 13, 16, 20-26; Georgina Binnie-Clark, *Wheat and Woman* (Toronto, 1979); E.C. Sykes, *A Home Help in Canada* (London, 1915).

6 See 'I would Rather be in the Grave', in this chapter.

7 Note the linking of marriage age and agricultural opportunity in Chad Gaffield, "Canadian Families in Cultural Context: Hypotheses from the Mid-Nineteenth Century," *Historical Papers/Communications historiques* (1979) 55, 59; David Gagan, *Hopeful Travellers* (Toronto, 1981) 75-87; for the Maritime provinces see Alan A. Brookes, "Family, Youth and Leaving Home in Late Nineteenth Century Rural Nova Scotia," in Joy Parr, ed., *Childhood and Family in Canadian History* (Toronto, 1982) and Margaret Conrad, "Recording Angels: Private Chronicles of the Maritime Women: 1800-1950," Canadian Research Institute for the Advancement of Women, *Papers,* IV (1982).

8 Angus McLaren, "Birth Control and Abortion in Canada, 1879-1920," *Canadian Historical Review,* LIX (1978) 319-40.

9 On Montreal, see Bettina Bradbury, "The Family Economy and Work in an Industrializing City: Montreal in the 1870s," *Historical Papers/Communications historiques* (1979) 86-90; for this phenomenon in a later period, see Gail Cuthbert Brandt, "Weaving it Together: Life Cycle and Industrial Experience of Female Cotton Workers in Quebec, 1910-1950," *Labour/Le travailleur,* VII (1981) 119.

10 J. T. Saywell, ed., *Lady Aberdeen's Canadian Journal, 1893-1898* (Toronto, 1960); W. L. Morton, ed., *Monck Letters and Journals* (Toronto, 1971); J. K. Johnson, ed., *Affectionately Yours, the Letters of Sir John A. Macdonald and His Family* (Toronto, 1969).

11 Rasmussen *et al, A Harvest,* 22, 43, 64, 130; Margaret Anderson, *Mother Was Not a Person* (Montreal, 1972); Byrne Hope Saunders, *Emily Murphy, Crusader* (Toronto, 1945); K. Strange, *With the West in Her Eyes* (New York, 1937).

12 A. W. Cashman, *Singing Wires: The Telephone in Alberta* (Edmonton, 1972).

13 W. A. Buckley and M. Urquhart, *Historical Statistics of Canada* (Toronto, 1965) 38.

14 See 'Ottawa Maternity Hospital' and 'Unmarried Motherhood' in this chapter.

15 Buckley and Urquhart, 40.

16 Suzann Buckley, "Ladies or Midwives? Efforts to Reduce Infant Mortality," in Linda Kealey, ed., *A Not Unreasonable Claim* (Toronto, 1979) 131-150.

17 *Census of Canada,* 1901, vol. 4, Table 5, 56-72; Buckley and Urquhart, 39-40. We are grateful to Dr. R.M. McInnis and the Historical Atlas of Canada project for guidance in the preparation of this section.

18 *Census of Canada,* 1901, vol. 4, Table 5, 56-72; Buckley and Urquhart, 40; unpublished data from the Historical Atlas project.

19 Buckley and Urquhart, 41; *Census of Canada,* 1901, vol. 4, 68 as recalculated for the Historical Atlas of Canada.

20 Terry Copp, *The Anatomy of Poverty* (Toronto, 1974) 93; S. Buckley, "Ladies or Midwives," 131.

21 Copp, *Anatomy of Poverty,* chapter 6; Suzanne Cross, "The Neglected Majority: the Changing Role of Women in Nineteenth Century Montreal," in Susan Trofimenkoff and Alison Prentice, eds., *The Neglected Majority* (Toronto, 1977); Micheline Dumont-Johnson, "Des garderies au XIXe siècle: les salles d'asile des Soeurs Grises à Montréal," *Revue d'historie de l'amérique française* (Sept. 1978).

1. COURTSHIP AND MARRIAGE

I WOULD RATHER BE IN THE GRAVE

In April 1873, Margaret Thompson agreed to marry William Donnelly, asking him, however, to keep her acceptance a secret for a number of months and, for an unspecified reason, to request her hand of her parents only after the first of November, 1873. She suggested an engagement of five years but indicated her willingness to accept his wishes on that matter. By December of the same year, however, Margaret was prepared to defy her parents and marry William to escape a home situation which had become intolerable because of her parents' objections to the marriage.

It is not difficult to sympathize with her parents' point of view, for Mary had chosen as her husband a member of the 'Black Donnellys', a family deeply embroiled in feuds so virulent that they had persisted through emigration from Ireland to tear apart the New World community of Biddulph with murder and arson.

Biddulph, Ontario, 1873
M. Thompson to W. Donnelly, 1875, William Donnelly Papers,
MG 29 C72, Public Archives of Canada.

1873
Biddulph April 22
Dear William

I address you with those few lines hoping they will find you in good health as they leave me enjoying the same blessing at present. Dear William I was a long time about getting this picture for you you can keep it now in hopes you think as much of me as I do of you. At the beginning of another term of our future summer which we can look back upon with pleasure I desire to bear testimony to the faithfulness with which you have laboured for my benefit and the kindness which you have ever shown to me.

Yours truly
Maggie Thomson

April the 30th 1873
William Donnelly
Dear friend

I take the pleasure of writing you those few lines hoping they will find you in good health as they leave me enjoying the same blessing at present. I now wish to inform you that I have made up my mind to accept your kind offer as their is no person in this world I sencerly love but you. This is my last and only secret so I hope you will let no person know about it. But I cannot mention any certain time yet. You can acquaint my parents about it any time you wish after the first of November next any time it is convenient to you. it will please me if it is in five years after the time I mentioned. if it does not suit you to wait so long you can let me know about it and I will make it all right. Do not think that I would say you are soft for writing so often for their is nothing would give me greater pleasure than to hear from you and no matter how. I think soft turns in very scarce about you [sic] if you have ever herd anything of the kind after me I hope you will not attibute it to a desire on my part to give you pain but regard it as the thoughtless behaviour of Youth and the blessing of God may ever attend you this is the sincere wish of your affectionate friend,

Margaret Thompson

December 24th 1873
William Donnelly
Dear friend,
I adress you with those few lines to let you know I am well and hope you are enjoying the same blessing. I wish to let you know a little about the performance I had to go through sence I came up here. My friends herd all about me writing letters to you which caused an awfull storm so that I could not attempt to ask to go any where and on that account you will please excuse me for not writing to you. *Dear William I would rather be in the grave than home at preasant for the way my people abused me on your account hinders me of ever forgiving them.* I will never have anything like a chance of fullfilling my promise of marriage with you except you come and take me away by force and if you think as much of me now as you did always I trust you will relieve me before long and if not you will please send me my letters to Offa P.O. and I will try to put up with all. I burnt your letters when they commenced to abuse me about you for they would shurly get them if I did not do something with them. Excuse my bad writing for I am in an awful hurry as it is in the office I am writing it. No more at present from your loving friend.

Margaret Thompson

COMMUNITY MATCHMAKING

Tucking was a preindustrial method for fulling cloth, which served to mat the fibres of woven woolen material so that the garments made from it provided greater warmth. In England by this time waterpowered mills performed the tucking operation. However for at least one Nova Scotian family as we see below tucking remained a productive household activity and a source of supervised sociability or community matchmaking for the young people.

Port Morien, Nova Scotia, 1889
Edith Jessie Archibald, "The Tucking Frolic," Halifax, Evening Mail, *1889.*

We are bound this evening for a farm house, some five miles distant, where we shall receive a true Highland welcome from our dear old host and hostess and their worthy daughter. All through the early winter months the women have been busily preparing and spinning the wool from their flocks of Southdown sheep. Now, woven into cloth by the same skilful hands, it is ready for the last process of shrinking or 'milling in' as it is termed, and what more fitting than to celebrate this event with a real, old time 'tucking frolic?'...

Soon we are being warmed and refreshed by our kind hosts before a huge fire of mingled coal and driftwood; and after partaking of the cup of strong boiled tea which never fails to cheer the Cape Bretonian heart, and tasting some real old fashioned Scotch shortbread, we are permitted to adjourn to the scene of festivity in the adjoining kitchen.

The room is long and low, with a raftered ceiling and huge brick fire place. Cranes and pot hooks are here, and above the tall, narrow mantle shelf are several old flint lock muskets and fowling pieces of ancient make. There is a tall dresser full of quaint old china. Bunches of herbs and strings of onions descend from the ceiling. Round the fire, and occupying the chimney corners are several of the older guests: the men with hard, weather-beaten faces, the women brave in much be-frilled, closely fitting white caps. The men smoke, the women knit.

The fire light as it flickers in the broad chimney warms up their withered cheeks with something like the glow of youth, and casts fantastic shadows athwart the room. A sort of rude table of boards supported on barrels occupies the centre of the kitchen and some twelve or fourteen young people of both sexes are seated around it, chatting volubly in Gaelic, and much interested in the operations of a sour visaged elderly female who is manipulating in some wonderful manner the contents of a steaming wash tub....

Now she draws our attention to a young man who, with his chair tilted against the dresser, at the end of the long table, is apparently oppressed with the deepest gloom. He seems to be afflicted with toothache for his face is buried in his hands. The somewhat boisterous merriment of his companions appears to jar upon his feelings, and he is quite indifferent to their jokes and laughter. We look at him sympathizingly and feel much exercised on his account. Suddenly, his foot begins nervously to tap the floor; he writhes;— poor fellow! we know how it is—we can feel for you!

He sways backwards and forwards;—really, this is very distressing:—and at last utters a sound—a long, dismal melancholy wail —which goes to our very marrow. To our horror, the guests take it up and we are just considering whether we too must shriek, when the sour visaged female, with a seemingly superhuman effort, dumps down on the table before the company, about fifty yards of steaming hot, wringing wet flannel cloth. The wail passes into a recitative and from this into a rhythmic measure. And now begins the work of 'milling' or 'tucking' the cloth. Led by the gloomy young man, who never once lifts his hands from his face, and never ceases his footbeat, the young men and maidens commence a process, compounded by wringing, swaying and thumping. With measured beat they bend right and left: again they lean forward on the table, passing along with a sounding thump, the cloth now twisted into a long rope. Every muscle in the body is brought into play. The song rises and falls; now it is mournful and joyous; sometimes a solo in recitative, again a ringing chorus. There is no attempt at harmony, the singing is all in unison. The women's voices rise shrilly above the male chorus: the whole effect is wild and weird in the extreme.

The features of the sour faced female relax, her eye brightens; she paces majestically up and down, keeping time with her withered hand to the music, and urging the 'tuckers' to still greater exertions.

Suddenly the chorus ceases: the waving and clapping still go on; the soloist continues his mournful strain; it is indescribably pathetic. He droops—he falters—surely he must stop—we fairly suffer for him!—Whence this wild skreigh?* Can it be? Yes! It is! The sour-visaged damsel—and—what is this she is reciting? Mark the effect upon the company. The swaying and bending become more rhythmic, more languid, less boisterous: eyes brighten; many are the sly pokes and pushes given by the gallant swains to their fair neighbors. Even the clapping motion is changed; hands are crossed and recrossed; they fairly twinkle; one by one the lasses take up the strain, each singing at the highest possible pitch. The men chime in 'at libitum': the *primo tenore* chants with renewed vigor. Even the old people in the chimney corner nod their heads and feebly beat time to the music. What is it they are singing? what, but the old, old story, told in the Gaelic: a Highland love song....

Now the tune changes and we are listening delightedly to the soft rippling strains of 'Fhir a Bhata' the 'Boatman.' Surely never was any song so witching, at once tender and pathetic, yet full of hopefulness and joy.

The company, once roused by these Highland love songs, cannot be persuaded to cease, and so presently give us another favorite, 'Mo chailiun dillis doon' which is an ode in praise of a 'Nutbrown Maid,' the Sailor's Sweetheart. Our host assures us it is indeed old—older than the flood! He would have us believe that Adam wooed Eve in some such terms. We are incredulous on this point, although the sweet wild minor melody is charming!

At last the amorous ditty ceases, and there are signs of evident fatigue among the workers; and fresh volunteers, seizing hold of the cloth as tired fingers relinguish it, slip into their places, hardly losing a measure of the clapping and pushing which still goes on....

'From labour to refreshment' is now in order and the laughing girls, mopping their heated faces, and exchanging witticisms with each other and

*[a shriek, Scottish derivation]

their comrades in arms, file out into the 'living room,' where the table fairly groans under the load of substantial and inviting dainties. They fall to with an appetite well earned by their evening's work, and after the goodly number of dishes are duly appreciated, the table is pushed back and the company prepare to enjoy themselves and to make a night of it....

EXCHANGING LETTERS

Social custom in the Victorian era dictated a formal style of courtship and engagement. Visits to young women were pre-arranged and most were supervised by parents, older siblings, or a party of peers. Declarations of love and marriage requests might be made by formal correspondence rather than in person as we see in the case of Anna de Gonzaque and George Govin. Such formal courtship customs were also sometimes native to recent immigrants to Canada. Manuals, like the Armenian one excerpted below, set out a variety of example letters in the native tongue and with an English translation, requesting a marriage.

Quebec, 1893
Diary of Anna de Gonzaque, April 9, 1893. Acc. 216.1 Laval University Archives.

1893
April 9
   Today Sunday I had to stay at home. I received a letter from Mr George Govin. Papa and Mama went to supper at Mr Denis'.
[Letters copied in diary]

8 April 1893

St Michel des Saints
My much loved Anna,
   Not daring to take the pleasure to come to see you in person, I am going to compensate myself a bit for this great punishment by expressing to you on this paper what I don't have the pleasure of telling you out loud. Because I don't dare to present myself to your father, having heard that he doesn't want to receive me. What a pleasure it would be nevertheless for me to see you today to tell you how I love you and how sad for me is the time which I spend far away from you. The couple of days which I have spent without seeing you seemed to be a century. Nevertheless, I will not visit you again before I know by a few words in reply where your allegience is. As for you, my very dear Anna, may I hope that your feelings toward me are the same as what you made me hope.

That I may count on your love as you may count on mine. If this is the case then soon we will no longer fear that anything will come to separate us. I pray my very dear Friend that you will reply to me on the question which I have already asked you and that I repeat to you today with all my heart. It is whether you are decided to unite your destiny with mine forever. I want to know your decision all the more because, for my part, I would like it to be before the month of June. What happiness would be mind if you surrender yourself to my wishes and to my desires.

In hope of a few words in reply soon, I will live in great urgency. I pray you to excuse these few words written in haste and to depend for ever on the affection, the constancy and the loyalty of the one who wants nothing but your love and who lives for nothing but you.

George Govin

15 April 1893

St Michel des Saints
Dear Friend

In reply to your letter of last Sunday I will tell you that my decision is still the same and that I have not changed my mind since you came the last time. For me I have decided not to marry at present. Thus, if you are prepared (to marry) go to see a young woman who would be more deserving than I of your love. Consequently forget me. I will no longer receive you—fearing to take your precious time. If I had wanted to abuse your good favours I would have had many opportunities but I do not want to amuse myself in that way. I value you too much to have you wait perhaps a long time, without knowing what would result in the future, emotions changing with time. Believe me, dear friend, if I refuse all statements of love, whether written or otherwise, it depends absolutely on me. Act as if you had never known me and you will be happy. I hope that the frankness with which I have spoken to you will merit your esteem.

I remain your devoted friend
Anna de Gonzaque.....

•

H.H. Chakmakjian, Armeno-American Letter Writer, *(Boston, 1914) 263-64. Given by a St Catherines, Ontario donor to the Multicultural History Society of Ontario, Archives.*

To An Acquaintance of Long Standing.
My dear Miss _____:

I have so long enjoyed the happiness of being received as a welcome guest at your respected parents' house, that I write with more confidence on a subject of most serious importance to my welfare.

From constantly meeting with you and observing the thousand acts of amiability and kindness which adorn your daily life, I have gradually associated my hopes for future happiness with the chance of possessing you as the sharer. Believe me, my dear Miss _____, this is no outbreak of boyish passion, but the hearty and healthy result of a long and affectionate study of your disposition. It is love, founded on esteem; and I feel persuaded that your knowledge of my own character will lead you to trace my motives to their right source.

May I, then, implore you to consult your own heart, and, should I not have been mistaken in the happy belief that my feelings are in some measure reciprocated, to grant me permission to mention the matter to your parents.

Yours faithfully,

_____

_____

"IT SEEMS AS IF THE PREPARATIONS WERE ALL FOR SOMEONE ELSE"

Like many young educated women, twenty-year old Annie Burbidge worked as a school teacher. With her engagement to Jack D. Clark, however, she abandoned any thoughts of pursuing a teaching career and devoted herself to acquiring a trousseau, and the accoutrements appropriate to her new role as wife and household mistress. It is particularly interesting to note that Annie seems to have taken no part in the selection and rental of her large, furnished nuptial home, these business details being left to her fiancé.

Halifax, Nova Scotia, 1904
Annie Burbidge to Ella Lathrop, January 25, 1904. Burbidge Papers, MG 100, Vol. 115 #4, Public Archives of Nova Scotia.

to Ella Lathrop

Morris St. School
Halifax, N.S.
Jan. 25th 04

I know you are waiting to hear all about my preparations for the eleventh. I do wish you could be here for it, only two weeks and a few days more—I have to teach until the Friday before. Isn't that cruel?

Where shall I begin? With my "trousseau" I suppose. I haven't very much but want (sic) I have I think is pretty good.

Mother made all my underwear and I wouldn't exchange them for the best ready-made. There is a lot of work in everything and the material is all of best. Am I boasting? I don't mean to, I want you to have as correct an idea of everything as possible.

I will send you a sample of everything I have, in the dress line, except my tailor-made suit. I was not fortunate enough to be able to get any from the tailor.... My wedding dress is not finished; it is white silk with chiffon yoke and under sleeves. I have a pretty green dress, trimmed with reside silk yolk covered with lace; a broad silk girdle and long cuffs of silk and lace.... With this dress I have a grey hat, trimmed with silk the same shade and a egret (Is that correct?) My every day suit is blue (Norfolk style) and I have a dark grey hat trimmed with red velvet.

I wonder if you would care about seeing the plan, as Jack sent it, of our house. I will copy it exactly as he gave it to me. You knew that he had rented a house furnished.

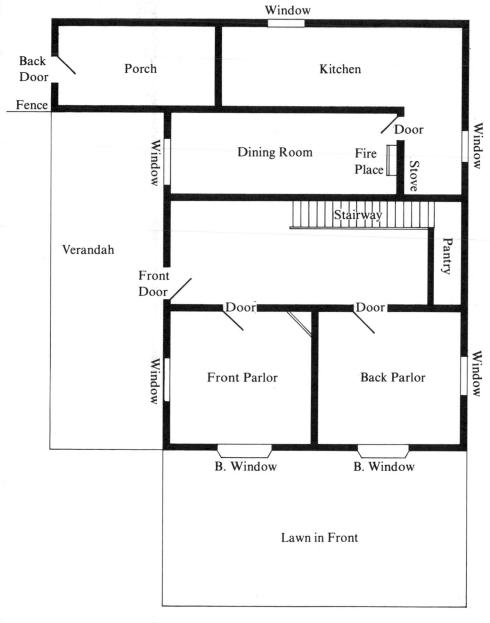

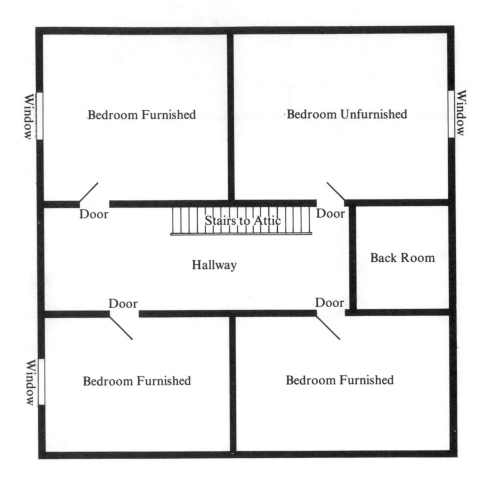

This is as Jack sent me. I expect this corner room has a window in it; but when you come to Kentville you can see for yourself. Of course I have no idea of the proportions.

Are you not tired of hearing all about wedding? My next letter will probably be written under different circumstances. I cannot realize it yet; it seems as if the preparations were all for somebody else.

Sincerely yours,

A. Winnifred Burbridge

Although some of the women documented in this volume did not marry by choice or circumstances, marriage was the norm for the vast majority of adult women throughout the period. According to the 1891 census, a third of the women aged between twenty and twenty-four were wives, while over sixty percent were spouses in the remaining age cohorts to age 44. Marriage defined a woman's social, economic, and legal identity.

Credit: Mr G.E.H. Binney's Bridal Party, Notman #25815, Photograph Collection, Public Archives of Nova Scotia.

A FOUR YEAR COURTSHIP

In searching for documents that indicate something about the emotional content of the relations between the sexes in the late nineteenth century, the historian frequently finds that only one side of personal correspondence between individuals has been preserved. The letters below were important enough to Edith Sauder that she retained them throughout her life. Certainly they must have represented a difficult period in her life. Engaged to Frank Dunham, she found that her wedding was postponed when he moved in 1908 to Edmonton finding a newspaper job, delayed until her fiancé had established his career and economic position, and, even after the date had been established, still uncertain because of Dunham's business and sport commitments. The couple finally married in 1911 and Edith Sauder moved to Camrose, Alberta, to establish her marital household.

Edmonton, Alberta, 1908-1911
Martin Frank Dunham Papers, Acc. 72.325, Provincial Archives of Alberta.

To Edith L. Sauder, Carstairs, Alta.   Edmonton September 10, 1908
My Dear Edith: —
Judging by your letter of yesterday your thoughts and feelings on these beautiful moonlight nights are the same as mine. As I look up and see the beautiful moon rising I think how happy I would be if I could be enjoying it with you. I am sure that the prospect must be even better on the wide open prairie where there is nothing to obstruct the view. The longings of the heart and soul seem never to be satisfied or realized to anywhere near the extent that we would like them to be so we must try to content ourselves for the present with things just as they are.

However, my dear girl, I want you to let me know as soon as you can, what is the latest date that you will remain at Carstairs. I do want to see you again before you leave and will try to manage it if I possibly can I would have been down to see you on Labor day but the office wanted me to keep track of some things that day and I did not like to refuse. Then I was not sure that you would be home and had no way of letting you know on short notice. After the day was over I felt sorry that I had not shoved all obstacles aside and gone down anyway.

I was greatly amused to hear of the way Elmer gets you girls to work. You will certainly have developed a great muscle by the time you turn eastward. I really think you ought to remain until he gets his harvesting done. There will be the threshers to cook for and I do not see how a bachelor is going to do it. At such a time two girls about the place would be invaluable and would result in Elmer getting twice as much work out of the men. They would work harder thinking that it would bring meal time all the closer.

I do not like to make suggestions to you that you might think foolish but I do wish you could stay until October 19 which is Thanksgiving day. I would certainly be able to spend two days with you then if I do not get down before. I can not help thinking that this suggestion sounds selfish but my dear I do wish you could arrange it. I really believe we are going to have a delightful fall and if so there will be very little chilly weather to bother you on the ranch. After all a four months trip is not so much when you are so far away from home. However if you think it any injustice to your father I will withdraw the idea at once...

Your loving Frank

Edmonton Jan. 27, 1909

My dearest Edythe: —

It is some time since I have heard from you so I suppose you are taking me at my word and writing when you feel like it. If so, I hope it will not be long before you again have the inclination. ha! ha!

The legislature is sitting every day now at three o'clock and this makes a busy day for me. This week has been a record for conventions of all kinds in addition to the regular work. Even the annual poultry show had to fall on this week...

On Tuesday next there will be a large reception at Government House to which several of the boys at the YMCA myself included have received invitations. On Friday evening there will be the annual banquet of the YMCA members which will be something along the line of the YMCA banquets which used to be held in Edmonton.

This residence in the YMCA is a great thing for us out here Edith. I have made friendships among some men here which I value, perhaps more than any I have made in the East. Western boys or rather Eastern boys after coming west seem to jump into the status of men more quickly than they do in the East. They certainly are not afraid to attempt big things and to carry them through with a dash and hustle.

This is another optimistic letter my dear which reflects my state of mind from week to week. I wish you were here so that we might enjoy this Western life together. This city and in fact the whole province is undergoing such a rapid change that you will hardly recognize it when you visit the west again or when you come to stay. ha! ha!

Yours lovingly and faithfully Frank.

Edmonton Nov. 25th 1909

Dearest Edythe:

How many times in life do we find Edith that the unexpected happens and just when it is least expected. The other day I heard of a third daily paper being started in Edmonton with excellent backing, and shortly after I found myself offered the job of news editor with a considerable increase in salary over what I receive at the Bulletin. I have accepted the offer and I believe that by so doing I have grasped an opportunity which does not come to every man nowadays. It is up to me to build up the paper and make it the best in the city... It was for a chance like this that I broke away from Toronto and now I see it fulfilled. I believe in a past letter I mentioned about the passing of CPR agreement for the entrance of the railway into the city. Well the voting turned out three to one in favour of it which means that the money bylaw on December 20 will carry all right and that after that property in Strathcona will take a very considerable increase in value. I find however, that I am not so anxious now to sell the lots as with my more responsible position in the journalistic world I am beginning to give more serious thought to a happy home of my own. That concerns you my dear girl doesn't it! I want you to realize Edith that my recent success means the near approach of the day when our nuptial knot will be tied. That means probably next summer but this is just an advance thought for you to think about. It means also that I intend to communicate to your father in a matter which hither to I have not felt that my humble position warranted me in doing. You will prepare the way for me wont you?

Yours as ever Frank.

Camrose
October 11, 1911

Dearest Edith

The big fair at Camrose is almost over now and has been a success in everyway. Great numbers of farmers and large entries in the various classes have been the rule so the fair directors as well as everybody else is well pleased....

Well Edith you know I expected to leave directly after the fair but find that the Winnipeg man who has been getting transportation for me has been out of the city on other business and the matter has been delayed. As soon as this matter is arranged I'll be off home without wasting a minute. I told you before that I'd be leaving on or before October 10th well this holds good all right....

How long are you to remain with your aunt on the farm? No doubt you have gone there partly to get away from the anxious inquirers in Berlin who wonder when we are to be married. If you were not the kind of a girl you are I'd feel truly sorry for you but I know you are strong minded enough to let talkers talk. We'll pull this through yet Edith to our entire mutual satisfaction and then what care we for the world at large.

I have been trying to get some duck and chicken shooting before I leave and no doubt that accounts for the cold I have contracted. If it were a little colder I'd have some stored away for the winter use but that is not feasible just yet. We'll have to draw on someone else's larder I suppose. Believe me Edith

Yours as ever Frank.

KEEPING A GIRL

The work required of a wife and mother on a ranch in early twentieth-century Alberta was tremendously demanding. Some families hired female servants, from local areas or from abroad, to meet their needs. Catherine Neil recalls below her experiences in "bringing a girl out" and attempting to keep her.

Grassy Lake, Alberta, early 1900s
Catherine Neil, "Pioneer Days", Acc. 74, 1/89, 67, Provincial Archives of Alberta.

My experiment of bringing a girl out here didn't work very well. The bachelors came after her right away, and by November we had her wedding at the ranch, with neighbours from all over the district being at it. I waited till next Spring and then got a local girl, but she could only wait a couple of months. I put an ad in an Old Country (Scotland) paper and managed to get another girl. She arrived in July. Again the bachelors came, and she was married at Burdett on New Year's Day. That was the first wedding at Burdett.

Acting on the belief that the old saying might come true, and the third time be lucky, I sent for number three. She stayed with me for eight months and then married a bachelor. I gave up after that and just carried on myself, with a little extra help at lambing time.

A WAR BRIDE

The end of World War I meant not only the return of surviving Canadian soldiers but also the immigration of a number of women who had married or become engaged to these men overseas. War brides, such as Esme Tuck who recalls her impressions of the ocean voyage and of her Canadian home below, faced the challenge of adapting to a new land and a new life situation in marriage.

Pouce Coup, Alberta, 1919
Esme Tuck, "A Homestead Saga of the Peace River Valley," 1, 4, 9-11, M1254, Glenbow-Alberta Institute Archives.

The 49th Edmonton Regiment left England in May 1919 for its homeland and with it went my husband who was a sergeant in that gallant corps. I was left behind to get to Canada as best I could. English brides of the rank and file of World War I did not get the preferential treatment accorded to those of World War II. I literally had to assail and importune the authorities to get a passage and finally, as a great favour was given one in what was then known as 'steerage,' in the S.S. Minnedosa.

It had been arranged for my younger sister, Olive, to accompany me, mother being somewhat suspicious of overseas bridegrooms. After many visits to London and much correspondence my father managed to secure a passage for her, too; third class....

...so we came to beautiful and historic Quebec.

Here we found ourselves in the large, cold Immigration Hall answering numerous questions. We felt very miserable till Olive spied the following paragraph in a folder issued by the C.N. Railway. 'The birth [sic] rate on the Pullman cars is very low.'

This piece of information cheered us considerably and we began to collect our wits.

"Why can't we go on our own now we're through with the immigration authorities," asked my sister.

Again we examined the family exchequer and found that we could just pay our way with enough over for meals.

"But," said she "If Spencer doesn't meet us at Edmonton.."

"Of course he will," I said hastily.

We slipped quietly away from the crowd and secured the necessary tickets. We did not realize that we were ticketed and numbered and were expected to answer the roll call in Edmonton.

Arrived there, I looked eagerly for my husband who had told me that he would make the journey from Pouce Coupe and be at the train to meet me. He was nowhere to be seen and I began to wish that we had not been so spendthrift with our money. For we had hardly enough to pay an hotel bill for the night. And worse still Spencer had not given me any address in the city.

"What did Mother say?" asked my sister mischievously. But I had no misgivings.

"Must be the roads," I said. "We must just sit here and wait." And wait we did. After some hours we realized that we were becoming objects of suspicion and noticed two women eyeing us curiously. We were feeling rather uneasy and lonesome so we were glad when they finally came across to us.

"Are you the girls who are lost?" asked one of them with a certain amount of asperity.

"You should have been on the train that came in early this morning," said the other one. "Your husband's nearly out of his mind. He thinks you're lost and has been 'phoning up every one he can think of to try and get track of you."

At this moment a harrassed looking man hove in sight.

"Here we are," I shouted, fearful that he might escape again he came hurrying across to us. He thanked the ladies for all the trouble they had taken and hustled us in to a taxi.

"What on earth have you two been up to, I've pretty well roused the town to find you."

We explained...he was too glad to see us to scold. We spent ten days in Edmonton meeting some of Spencer's friends and finding our feet in this new world....

"There she is," said my husband as he drew aside the branches of a small poplar tree. A shower of leaves, like little gold coins, fell all about us. I peered eagerly through the gap for a glimpse of my new home.

There she was. A log cabin attaining a degree of dignity by its simple lines and quiet brown colouring...

My husband unlocked the door of the cabin and we went in. Olive and I almost gasped at the bareness though we knew what to expect—more or less. As cabins went, at that time, it was quite a mansion. A living room 12 x 15 feet with two little bedrooms and a lean-to kitchen. The roof was ceiled and the walls were lined with planed lumber, a luxury we did not fully appreciate then....

The furniture in the shack was reduced to a minimum and had been made at night when he ought to have been sleeping. In the kitchen was a deal table, a little stove, a wash basin, bare necessities in the way of eating and cooking utensils and a board shelf. This was against the wall and did duty for a cupboard. Two little bags hung from the rafters. Dried beans were in one, dried apricots in the other. The living room was simple in the extreme. A deal table covered with a piece of oilcloth (a concession to our feminity) on which stood an oil lamp, a long shelf across the end and the pièce de resistance in the middle of the room—a prospector heater. This article struck us as being extraordinarily funny; we had never seen stove pipes before, and to find them in the middle of the living room! My husband was at a loss to understand the peals of laughter that fell on his ears as he brought in an armful of wood. It had the graceful steamlining of a dachshund dog; a bow round the bottom of the pipe would have set it off nicely.

"What's the bulge in the neck, Spencer?" asked my sister.

"That's a drum oven," proudly opening the little door to show the tiny tray inside. "It's a splendid place for anything that requires bottom heat."

We made a mental note of this for future reference.

In our bedroom was a homemade bed, a little table and space. My sister's room contained simply space.

"Well, anyway," I said as we peeped in. "You can arrange the bed we bought in Grande Prairie where you please."

All floors were bare. Each room had one little window 24 x 24 inches. Like everything else that had to be freighted in, this cost money (at 10¢ per pound) as we soon learned. But though the house was bare, the air was so clear that the sunshine streaming in through the small windows filled the room with golden light and turned the unpainted walls as creamy a yellow as a pot of spring butter.

The very bareness of the little home made a strange appeal to me and I loved it at once as one does an underprivileged child or a hurt animal.

_____

2. CHILDBIRTH

CHILDBIRTH AT FORT SIMPSON

Louise Camsell Mills' life as a white woman contrasted in many ways with the lives of the majority of native and Métis women who also lived at Fort Simpson in the late nineteenth century. She was educated in England and exposed to a variety of situations through travel. Although she shared with the other women of the fort the life-cycle experience of childbirth, her approach to that stage of life was quite different from theirs.

Late 19th Century
Louise Camsell Mills, "Seventy Years Ago in the North West Territories," Acc. 74.1/88, 6-7, Provincial Archives of Alberta.

The young Indian women were generally alone when their children were born. I remember one young girl going out in the bush in the depth of winter. About a mile from the Fort she made a little camp for herself, first clearing away the snow with her snow shoes, then cutting down some spruce boughs to sit on. She then built a small fire and there, all alone in 50° below zero weather, her baby was born. The next day she walked into the Fort with her infant strapped up in a moss bag on her back, neither suffering any ill effects after their trying experience.

Some of the old Indian men had "roots" which at times worked wonders. When my first baby was born, I really needed a doctor, but there was none nearer than 500 miles away. After a great deal of consultation between my mother, the Bishop's wife, and my Indian mid-wife, they decided to call in an old Indian, who said he could help me. He gave me some dried up root, which he cut up very carefully with his jack knife. This he put into a spoonful of water which he told me to drink. He then sat, smoking his pipe and after he was finished he got up and said, quite convincingly: "You'll be all right in a little while," and strange to say, I was. Years afterward, I asked his son what this medicine was, which undoubtedly had saved my life. He said he did not know and as his father was dead and gone, his secret died with him.

_____

BLUE DAYS

The Ontario-born Nellie Bailey married Albert Edward Bolton, M.D., and moved from Ontario with her husband to Port Simpson, B.C., where he served as a medical missionary. Her diaries of October 1890 until January 1891 are dominated by the birth of her daughter. They contain rare entries about the pain of childbirth and problems of breastfeeding and are especially interesting for their revealing frankness when this mother admits on January 2, 1891 "I indulged in the luxury of a little cry before breakfast...."

Port Simpson, British Columbia, 1890-91
Nellie Bailey Bolton Diaries, 1890-1891. Add. Mss. E/C/B631, Provincial Archives of British Columbia.

Tuesday Oct 14th (1890)
Awoke about two feeling very miserable & continued ill until half past three when our little daughter was born the last few hours I suffered very much Mrs Crosby and Martha Ryan were with me we got all settled down & I felt quite comfortable. Slept well.

Wed. Oct. 15th
Felt well baby good Miss Hart & Mrs Crosby in. Mrs Cover again in the afternoon & remained a while & got my tea. Albert busy.

Thursday Oct. 16th
    Baby still good & I felt well a quiet day I read a little Miss Ross in during morning. Also Miss Hart Mrs C came in a while in the afternoon.

Friday Oct. 17th
Did not feel so well. Milk came but impossible to get baby to nurse feel quite discouraged Miss Beavis in a very quiet day Miss Ross in.

Sat Oct. 18th
Felt better baby very cross during night wrote some on my letter had a few calls. Miss Beavis staid while Martha went for a walk.

Oct 19 Sunday
Another bad night. Albert up for prayer meeting....

Oct. 22nd Wed.
Rainy in showers another quiet day read some. Mrs Crosby in in the afternoon. Albert read to me in the evening a bad headache. Baby still troublesome night & refuses to nurse.

Oct. 23rd Thursday
I got up & dressed about ten it was such a relief to be out of bed wrote & read during the morning & sewed during the afternoon. Miss Beavis and Mrs Crosby in. Did not retire until about eight.

Oct 24 Friday
Baby good during the night I got up soon after breakfast crocheted during morning after watching Martha bathe baby. Read and wrote in the afternoon. A quiet evening all went to church but Martha.

Sat. Oct 25th
Baby still keeps good began to nurse with tube and nipple today. I went about quite a little....

Friday Nov. 14
Baby a month old today the little darling has walked right into our hearts & she is very precious may we have wisdom given us to bring her up wisely. I was out at prayer meeting and left her at home with Albert a fearful storm.

Wed. Dec. 3rd
A very busy day. Visit Mrs Crosby and Miss Ross here for tea. Baby was baptised about seven. Miss Hart up & the children were in retired late. Baby good all evening. May her life be pure and blameless....

Friday 2 January 1891
Up early, the boys very discouraging & I indulged in the luxury of a little cry before breakfast for what I don't know, only I was tired and worn with baby's restlessness & the boys do worry me so. A busy morning. Dinner was late I darned and took care of baby also read some spent the evening writing. A dark rainy day.

A HOSPITAL BIRTH

Although most homesteading women delivered their babies at home with the assistance of a midwife or local doctor, hospital care during childbirth began to be an alternative by 1900. In Eliza Jane (Brown) Wilson's case, she may have chosen hospital care away from her own community because she had previously lost a child. Her fears that this child would die and her longing for her husband's presence are evident in the excerpts from her diary.

Alberta, 1904
Mrs John Wilson Diaries and Correspondence, M1320, Glenbow — Alberta Institute Archives.

1904
June 18 Very warm all day — feeling somewhat tired and stiff; such talks Veenie and I are having. Wish I could hear from Johnnie.
    19 Nice cool breeze blowing, help to keep the flies down they are getting

troublesome. I have decided to go to the hospital on Friday I hope everything will be all right this time. Yesterday was the Anniversary of our Wedding....

24 Cloudy and raining all day and not very warm during the day. Windy. Rained heavy about 6:00. Going to the Hospital today, sorry to leave Veenie so soon.

25 Lovely cool day after the rain. Got in to the Hospital about 11:00, hope to have better luck this time. I am wearied to death already wrote to Veenie, Jack, Pa and Ma....

28 Nice cool day mercy how wearisome it all is. I will be glad when I am able to go home. Another kind of medicine tonight. I hope everything is all right — but it scares a body nearly to death.

29 A beautiful day, nice sitting out on the Veranda. Got a letter from Jack and 2 from Ma. Feeling better now since I heard from Johnnie wrote them both this afternoon.

30 Dreadfully warm all day not a breath of wind. Taken sick today. "Baby" was born at 7:00, a nice strong lassie. I am so glad it is all over and everything is all right — feeling quite strong myself.

July 1 How warm it is lying in bed. Baby cryed all night and morning. Something must have riled her. I am glad she is all right now — Veenie had a little son born at 1:00 tonight great!!

Sat. 2 The days are pretty sultry. I was shifted into the nurses room this afternoon, stifling warm too. Jack came down tonight-so glad to see him again. He is quite pleased with his little lassie I think.

4 How wearisome it gets lying in bed. I am so glad that Baby is so strong and well....

8 Cool day for a change, going to sit up tomorrow or next day.

9 A warm day. Baby sleeps all day and keeps awake all night she is growing fine and has good healthy lungs.

11 Up today Hurrah! I did feel sick at first I had to lie down several times, felt better toward the afternoon. Dont get much sleep at night with "Dorothy".

12 Feeling fine and getting stronger, had a lesson in bathing the bairn.

14 Nice day I get along pretty good bathing the bairne. Jack came down on the evening train, we stayed at the Hotel all night. Baby pretty good....

THE NATURALNESS OF PREGNANCY

For Catholic women, the practice of birth control contravened the teachings of the Church. In most rural parishes in Quebec at this time, pregnancy and childbirth were regular occurrences and approached by women as they were approached by Madame Brassard, in the following description expecting her fourth child. Although the author of these comments, Jessie Sime, did not specify the differences between rural and urban pregnancy, one can speculate that she was referring to increasing medical intervention in urban centres and the effects of prescriptive literature.

St Aniel, Quebec, circa 1915
Jessie Sime, In a Canadian Shack *(Toronto, 1937), 112-14.*

I have spoken of the naturalness of pregnancy among these hills and among these people. The baby was already a citizen of this New France which, while it differed so profoundly from the thing it had set out from, yet shared its characteristics. We all accepted the baby. He was coming into a hard life, but it was a life. He had brothers, and a sister (who fervently hoped "he would be a girl"); he had a father who would acknowledge his parenthood. These seem ridiculous things to say, or perhaps, rather impossible things to say. Hasn't nearly every baby most of, and often all, these things? Well, in that place which seemed so remote, where there were so many quite real discomforts to face, there seemed in the coming of this baby a naturalness that has been lost in the towns. He was not so much expected, perhaps, as taken for granted—as "Father" is expected home after his day's work. Each thing round about was reproducing its kind, and this human reproduction varied from the rest only by the fact of humanity's possession—or should one say by the great gift that has been bestowed upon humanity?—of consciousness. Madame Brassard went about her work as usual, and doubtless much of it was a burden to her. The child itself would be a burden. She was an overworked woman and often looked dreadfully tired. Yet—how is one to say this?—behind all that, behind the ill-adjusted framework of her life (for I will dare anyone to maintain that the conditions of a St Aniel are ideal) there was something that not only sustained her but made her happy. No one could doubt it who regarded the sweetness of that contemplative face of hers. She not only believed that God has sent the child, and so accepted it; in spite of all the drawbacks and the increased work the child must bring, she wanted it, boy or girl, to press to her breast and feel. The instinctive joy in bearing children—that kind of joy that we can neither master nor control, no, nor increase or make other than it is, when it takes possession of us—had not lapsed among those wilds, as it has often lapsed in cities now.

OTTAWA MATERNITY HOSPITAL

The Ottawa Maternity Hospital was founded in 1894 by members of Ottawa upper-class society concerned with the provision of obstetric and "reclaiming" care to mothers who they judged to be either morally or medically at risk—the homeless, the unmarried, and the poor woman.

Ontario, 1894
Ottawa Maternity Hospital File, 1894, Bronson Co. Papers, Public Archives of Canada.

On Friday, the 9th, of February last, a public meeting was held in the City Hall, at which Her Excellency the Countess of Aberdeen graciously presided, and the following resolutions were unanimously passed.

"That it is desirable to establish in the City of Ottawa a Maternity Hospital for the following special objects: —

(a) To afford to married women for a small remuneration or free, if necessary, proper accommodation, medical attendance and experienced nursing during their confinement.

(b) To give to unfortunates a home where they will receive medical attendance and proper care, and be brought within the reach of kind friends who will endeavour to exercise a reclaiming influence over them.

(c) To afford aid and experienced nursing to poor women during their confinement at their own houses."

Her Excellency in moving the above resolution delivered the following address: —

The object which is defined in the resolution, and on behalf of which we are met this afternoon, is one which it would seem only necessary to mention in order to ensure support, especially from women, and more especially still from women to whom has been granted the blessing of motherhood. When we who live in sheltered homes think how in our hour of trial we look for and expect all the comfort and consideration and love that those homes can give us, and how even then, with all the advantages of skilful medical attendance and nursing, with seclusion from the noise and bustle and turmoil of the world, recovery is tedious, and often beset with many difficulties and dangers; and when we compare our lot with that of women who live in narrow homes, all whose suffering and trouble is gone through in the midst of the noise and the occupations of daily life, and consider the anxieties which the mothers in those homes must feel as to whether their husbands and their children will be properly cared for, and the temptation which must come to them to get about again before they should—when we think of all these things, surely we must see at once the necessity for such a hospital as is now proposed, even were it only for the poor married women. But when we think of yet another class, the expectant mother who has no home at all to go to, who must look forward to her hour of suffering as one which will brand both her and her child, who must often be too apt to look upon that child as a disgrace, and therefore as something that she would be glad to be quit of, we can but wonder that in Ottawa, which, as Sheriff Sweetland has told us, abounds in all good works, such provision has not already been made....

As to the third object which has been kept in view by those who desire to start this institution, namely the opportunity that it gives for the training of nurses in this necessary department. I think the advantage to be obtained by the public at large is too self-evident that I need not dwell upon it.

UNMARRIED MOTHERHOOD

The risks of childbirth and infant mortality in Canada were relatively high in urban centres. For unmarried mothers they were probably even greater, deprived as these women often were of family, moral, and financial support. The following report on unwed motherhood presents a picture of the childbirth situation faced by some 108 patients in Toronto licensed homes and those outside such care.

Toronto, 1901
Dr. Harley Smith, Third Annual Report of the Toronto Inspector of Maternity Boarding Houses and Baby Homes. *In* Nineth Report of the Superintendent of Neglected and Dependent Children of Ontario, *Ontario Sessional Papers, No. 43, 1901, 17.*

During the past year there have been in the ten Maternity Homes of this city 108 patients, of whom thirteen left before confinement, eighty-six were confined, and nine await confinement. Of these patients three died (3.5 per cent.), one in January of diphtheria, one in April of peritonitis, and one in June of septicaemia. The other patients made a good convalesence. One of the patients was sixteen years old and another fifteen. Nine of the infants were still-born (10.5 per cent.). Four were premature and lived three days or less. Two went to the House of Providence, twenty-five to licensed Baby Homes; thirty-nine went home with their mothers. Four went to the Infants Home. There was but one miscarriage in the twelve months. The fact there have been only three miscarriages in three years seems to indicate that criminal medical work in our Homes is unknown. Two patients were married; one before the birth of her baby and one after her confinement. Two others, who were confined last year, were married this year.

The largest number of patients in the Homes in any single week was in the week ending April 13th, when in nine Homes there were twenty-nine patients and ten infants. There have been 112 babies in the thirty-four Baby Homes during the year. Three of these, after being placed in the homes, were deserted by their mothers. Of these, one was adopted; one went to the House of Providence, the third went to the Infants' Home. Thirteen babes were adopted into good homes (making a total of 32 in three years). Four babes went to the Children's Aid Society Shelter. The deaths were as follows: — November, one; December, one; January, one; April, one; May, one; June, one; July, three; August, ten; September, two; October, one. Total, twenty-two. Last year there were thirty-four deaths. The death rate was for the whole year 19.6 per cent. Omitting the month of August it was 10.7 per cent. It is a fact worthy of note that during the months of February and March, a most trying time for children, we had not a single death....

During the year four new licenses for Maternity Homes were issued, four were renewed. Eight new licenses for Baby Homes were issued; seventeen were renewed; three were cancelled. Twenty-nine houses were examined as to sanitary condition and general fitness for homes. Seventeen other investigations were made in accordance with instructions from the office.

Four of the thirteen babes adopted were taken by women in whose homes they had been living as boarders. This is proof of the attachment that springs up in many cases between the foster mothers and the children.

A few other interesting cases may be noted. A.H. nursed her child for some months and then placed it in a baby home. Through the efforts of the person for whom she worked, the father of the child married her and took her to his mother's home. The baby, some time later, went to live with his parents.

G.M., a pretty mulatto baby, was boarded by Mrs J. for four months, when his mother died. The baby remained in the home, without pay, for three months longer, when Mrs J. adopted it.

G.D. was boarded by Mrs E. for two years. The mother then went to New York to be married and took her baby to her new home.

E.M. remained in a Maternity Home for ten months, nursing her baby. She was then married to the child's father and took her baby home with her.

The care taken of unfortunate girls in our Toronto Homes is in marked contrast to that in places where the Act is not in force. Statistics were lately published in our daily papers, showing the great mortality of infants in a Maternity Home outside of the city. A judicial enquiry in Christiania in May last, in connection with a baby-farming sensation, led to a charge being made against three women of having killed twenty-seven children in less than twelve months. Many of the children were suffocated, while others were starved to death.

This photograph carried with it the caption "A Madonna of the Tenements" when it appeared in the *Annual Report of the Superintendent of Neglected Children for the Province of Manitoba* in 1912. Its message was clear. A working class mother's place was in the home, nurturing her children and not in the public workforce.

Credit: Public Archives of Canada, C 30948.

DEPT OF HEALTH No 243 OCT 29 1911

The sweating system and poor housing conditions took a toll on the health of female home workers. The picture also documents the positive aspects of these conditions. While the woman in the background cuts material for sewing, perhaps on piecework to provide family income, she is also able to provide supervision for children and the nursing mother in the foreground need not abandon breastfeeding to work outside the home. Secondly, while their living conditions are crowded, the women enjoy the companionship and support of each other and do not face the isolation of frontier or suburban life.

Credit: Department of Health Collection, No. 243, City of Toronto Archives.

3. INFANT CARE:
THE GROWING PERCEPTION OF A PROBLEM

"MY LITTLE EDITH"

A rare look at the relationship between a mother and her infant daughter is provided in the Merkley diary excerpted below. Concerned to record the almost daily physical and emotional development of her daughter, Isabel Merkley also illuminated her hopes and concerns as a mother and parent.

Morrisburg, Ontario, 1886-1887
Isabel Merkley Diary, 1886-1896, Merkley Family Papers, Public Archives of Canada.

Nov. 2/86 My little Edith is eight months old to day and what a little treasure she is; she is bright and happy and smiling always. She does not walk or creep yet and has no teeth. She takes one good sleep in the forenoon and very often does not sleep anymore until I put her to bed at seven or half past. Her first present was a brush from her uncle James Jarvis, Her Aunt Minnie gives her very many little things and Hugh and Harry are very good to her. Her first plaything was a little rubber doll from Aunt Maggie which she enjoyed very much. Her first visit was made to Mrs R.H. Bradfield's when she was about six weeks old on a very stormy day. When she was five months Helen Maxwell who calls her her baby and Dr Rutherford took her away and had her photo taken with them.

The Dr brought her a very handsome high chair from Montreal in Sept.

Her Aunt Nellie gave her a pretty hood for winter. She got it in Montreal. It is white.

Nov. 3rd/86 Helen found baby's first tooth today and she was delighted. She has been good as usual and I did not know it was coming but Helen has been watching for it and was so glad she happened to be the one to find it, she is real well all the time and has only had one sick spell when she was two months old, she got cold and had a sore throat we supposed as she could not swallow and once she choked so that we thought she would never get her breath she was purple. Her father went right away and got Mr Horrell and she was christened in her nightdress, all over goose-oil and we did not think of her christening dress I was trying to get done to have her christened in. She was received into the Church about two weeks after when Eva Jarvis was baptised, her Aunt Minnie, Aunt Stuart and Dr Rutherford stood for her.

Nov. 19/86 We went to the dinner party last night and had a very nice time and baby was as good as *could* be, but she either took *cold* or her teeth are troubling her for she cried all tonight and has been so cross today and feverish.

Nov. 20/86 Baby is all right to day and so full of fun we can hardly hold her. It seems good to have her all right for the house seemed so lonesome when she did not feel well, her father did not think it seemed like the same house to come into.

Nov. 21/86 Baby has gone out for a ride with her father the first time he ever took her out unless I was with them.

I hope she will be good.

Dec 2/86 Baby is nine months old *today*. She has only two teeth and cannot creep or walk yet but she is a dear little girl though and I do not know how we could live without her.

Dec. 31/86 The last day of Edith's first year. God grant she may remain as pure and sinless as she is to night is the prayer of Her Mother.

Jan 2nd 1887 Edith is ten months old to day. We commenced to wean her yesterday *she* is not one bit of trouble and not at all cross. She can get all round the floor now but does not creep.

Jan 17/87 Edith is weaned without any trouble. The first night she wakened up once or twice but would not take a drink and the second night she slept from seven in the eve until seven next a.m. without waking and we have only had to light the lamp once or twice for her since.

———

NURSE WILSON'S SOOTHING SYRUP

Nurse Wilson's Soothing Syrup for children was only one of a number of non-prescription medicines that had proliferated by the end of the century. Alcohol was a common ingredient in these elixirs. Its presence served, as the ad suggests, to calm fretful children, possibly while their mothers worked either inside the home or away at a factory. The advertisements for such products usually were included in medical almanacs or health pamphlets for families, which, like *Brayley's Family Medical Almanac,* were published by the product's maker. The message to the mother in these booklets was a simple one: people who care about their families will read and follow these directions and buy these products.

Quebec, 1883
Brayley's Family Medical Almanac *(Montreal, 1883) 34.*

NURSE WILSON'S SOOTHING SYRUP

This Soothing Syrup has been so long before the public, and has been so thoroughly and satisfactorily tried, that it has become an indispensible article in every well-ordered nursery. Its inventor, Nurse Wilson, enjoyed during a long lifetime a large practice as nurse and lady physician, and profiting by the advice of the numerous able physicians, under whom she was employed, and after an extensive trial of many articles of the Materia Medica, for the relief of the little ones under her charge, at length hit upon the prescription, upon which this Soothing Syrup is compounded, and finding it to be exactly the thing wanted, at length gave to the public the benefit of her experience. Nurse Wilson's Soothing Syrup differs in composition from all the other Soothing Syrups and Carminatives in the market, and is proportionally safer, more certain, and more efficacious.... Wind colic affects many infants from birth; their mother's milk does not seem to agree with and nourish them as it ought; they vomit it almost as soon as it is taken, or pass it through them in curds unaltered, or mixed up with greenish slimy discharges, passed with much pain and distress. As a consequence, instead of being plump and hearty, they look wizened and shrivelled, their skin loose and wrinkled; they do not gain flesh, their limbs are cold and drawn up, and their whole system is disordered, because their stomach and bowels being so irritated, their food does not nourish the body while the constant pain and loss of sleep worry and weaken them so that they cannot gain strength. The constant worry and loss of sleep also affects the mother's health, so that she cannot grow strong after her confinement, and if she is not in good health herself she cannot furnish good nourishing milk, such as would be suited to give strength to her offspring. From this cause many children die young, and with many others the foundation of life-long disease is surely laid. In such cases as this, Nurse Wilson's Soothing Syrup acts like a charm.... The vomiting and curdy, slimy, greenish discharges will cease; the child will sleep quietly and wake up bright and refreshed; the pitiful wailing will be replaced by smiles, and the child will soon assume a plump and healthy aspect, while the mother will have the needed opportunity for rest, will gain in health and strength and her milk will become more nourishing, and digestive in proportion....

INFANTS' HOME

The Toronto Infant's House and Infirmary was established in 1876 to provide care for deserted or destitute infants and children under the age of two years. Like most urban charities of the time, the Home's philosophy included a strong dose of moral training for the working-class mother and the requirement that the mother's care be paid for in kind through work at the Home. It was particularly interesting to note the special reference to wet nurses in this document. At this time, some middle- and upper-class urban women continued to judge it unseemly or inconvenient to breast feed their infants and might hire a wet nurse for this task. The recently delivered child of the wet nurse may well have been deprived of this nourishment or receive less milk than required.

Toronto, 1895
"Infants' Home, Toronto," Proceedings of the Ontario Conference on Child-Saving, *Ontario Sessional Papers, No. 29, 1895, 59.*

INFANT'S HOME TORONTO

The following paper explaining the work of the Infants' Home and Infirmary, of Toronto, was presented by Mrs E.M. Williamson on behalf of the board:

The Infants' House and Infirmary was established nineteen years ago. Before that time there was no single refuge in Toronto for a destitute or deserted infant. During this period the managers of the Home have sheltered 1,367 mothers and admitted 2,659 infants and small children under two years of age.

The primary object of this Home, as set forth in its constitution, is "to receive and tenderly care for destitute children under two years of age."

Early in the days of the Home it was found that if infant life was to be properly cared for a rule must be adopted, and strictly adhered to, that when possible the mother must enter with her infant; therefore, it will be seen that, although an infants' home, a large proportion of our work lies among the mother nurses, and here our rule is firm, that "no unmarried women may enter the Home, except with her first born," medical certificates to this effect being given by the hospital or private physicians to the authorities of the Home each woman admitted, when pronounced fit do to so by our attending physician, taking charge of one infant beside her own, the nourishing diet of both mothers and infants being carefully watched over by the medical staff of the Home. We have also a special nurse for the infirmary and general oversight of the health of the children.

The primary objects of the charity are to provide: 1st, a home for the children of wet nurses, among which class there was great suffering and mortality; 2nd, a home for infants deprived by death of a mother's care; 3rd, a free refuge for children accompanied by their mothers, the latter being expected to give her services to the Home in return for board, clothing and medical attendance.

MOTHERHOOD

Advertisers were quick to assume the ideals of Victorian motherhood. While promoting their medicines for mothers and their children, the British Chemists Company in its Canadian advertising also saw fit to promote the virtues of holiness, purity, and nationalism as keynotes in its education campaign. In this message are presented ideals that few mothers could meet. One can only wonder, without documentary evidence, what psychological effects such literature may have had on the mothers of infants.

1900
Motherhood *(Toronto, 1900) 11-12.*

PHYSIOLOGY OF MOTHERHOOD

The relations of mother and child are the highest, holiest, most important in existence. The duties and responsibilities of motherhood are of most vital consideration. "The hand that rocks the cradle, is the hand that rules the world." Considering the duties and responsibilities devolving upon the mother, as the moulder of nations, how vastly important it becomes that she be able to govern and develop her own progeny, that they grow in physical, moral and intellectual strength, and become fitted to bear the duties and burdens of life, as well as to share in its pleasures and prosperity.

Motherhood then is the permanent function, its magnitude no mortal mind can conceive. Every mother should not only *desire to know* but *should know* how to mould the plastic nature of her infant, so as to maintain a healthy mind in a healthy body. To possess both herself, is the first essential.

During the few months prior to birth, the child in embryo lives, grows, and is nourished solely from her vitality, until the period arrives when it is severed from the parent, and breathes the breath of life from the outer atmosphere, becoming a living, independent personality. "As the twig is bent the tree is inclined." Hereditary influence, as well as environment, have much to do with the new born child. Some children lack vitality from birth, and are puny and sickly, "born tired," expresses it in a brief sentence. Even when blessed with healthy parentage, the trials and struggles of the little stranger with physical influences, are fearful to contemplate, and demand the most watchful care on the part of the mother, to protect, and to prevent the encroachments of disease. Many ailments and evil influences are founded during pregnancy—it is doubly important that prospective mother be not only physically well, but tranquil in mind—if she would beware of a progeny of degenerates and weaklings. Ignorance on the part of parents may not be an intentional fault, but is often from thoughtlessness, and again the conventional false ideas—such as false modesty—the leaving of everything to the doctor, or hired nurse, the lack of interest in studying nature and natural laws—especially those pertaining to sex nature, are blamable for serious consequences....

The most beautiful and healthful women in the world are found in the realms of the British Queen. They have raised a progeny that rules o'er land and sea. Many American women grow old before their time, and their infants are proverbially puny. The influence of the emotions on the secretions of the mother's breasts—the milk that should nourish and sustain—becomes but little better than a slow poison, implanting the germs of physical and mental weakness—degeneracy, disease and death. To make the race beautiful, pure, strong and good, is the high and holy mission of MOTHERHOOD....

ONLY A BABY GONE

More than one of every ten babies born in Canada before 1901 did not survive twelve months. For some reformers, these deaths were statistical evidence supporting pure milk campaigns, the public health movement, or school domestic science education for the working-class girl. For the mothers involved, like the author of the following poem, a baby's death might be viewed quite differently—with resignation for this fact of life, with grief, and with a renewed religious understanding.

Canada, 1876
M.E. Muchall, "Only a Baby Gone!" Canadian Monthly, *X (October 1876) 310.*

ONLY A BABY GONE!

Only a little empty cot
Where baby was laid to sleep;
But sore is my heart when I see it now,
And what can I do but weep?

Only a soiled and broken toy,
She used in her baby play;
I cannot bear to see it now,
Let it be hidden away.

And here lies another thing,
Recalling the sunny past;
Only a scarlet coral chain,
Her hands have so often claspt.

Only a baby's smile
Is missed in our home to-day;
And the sound of her pattering feet,
And her rippling laugh at play.

Only a baby gone?
Only the loss of these?
But when will our home seem bright again?
Oh, when will our hearts find ease?

Just when faith can behold
Our baby from sin set free;
Forever safe in the far off fold,
On the shores of the crystal sea.

M.E. Muchall

————————

WHAT WE CAN DO TO PREVENT INFANT MORTALITY

If the urban newborn and mother survived labour and childbirth, they faced the continued possibility of infant mortality. A 1910 Report by Dr Helen MacMurchy argued that breast-feeding might significantly reduce infant mortality by eliminating the risks of milk contamination. Some of her recommendations to reduce infant death are reprinted below.

Ontario, 1910
Dr. H. MacMurchy, Report on Infant Mortality, *Ontario Sessional Papers No. 66, 1910, 30, 35-6.*

WHY DOES A MOTHER NOT NURSE HER CHILD?

1. Ignorance—She does not know that it makes all the difference to the child. When she does know, she nurses it. Most mothers think cow's milk is just as good. We must tell her that is not so.

2. Because the mother-in-law, or the sister-in-law, or the nurse, or the neighbour, or some other meddling busybody, has told her not to, etc. Many people ignorantly give this advice. We must give her skilled medical advice.

3. Because, in a very small proportion of cases (not more than 1 in 100, or 1 in 1,000) she cannot nurse her child, or, (rarer still) the milk does not agree with the child. Here again she needs skilled medical advice.

4. Because she has to work and she cannot take the child with her or come back to it. This is something we must set our faces against as a public danger. Everything possible must be done to avert this calamity to the child, and prevent the community making the blunder of allowing it. It should not be allowed to happen. The mother should have a pension, if necessary, to take care of the family. She is the one to save the baby, and the only one. Later on, if the baby is bigger, a few months old, and the mother must work, everything should be done to improve conditions for her. A nursing mother, if she has to work, should have short hours, and lunch early, and generally good conditions. If sanitary conditions were good—light, air, and cleanliness—it would be much better....

MILK

At about nine months of age, the baby should begin to use clean cow's milk. Sometimes babies have to use it sooner. Improvement in the milk supply alone has been known to cut the infant mortality rate in two. We urgently need legislation defining clean milk, giving a legal standard, both chemical and bacteriological, and requiring a nourishing milk with a low bacterial count and clean. The provision of free ice in summer is very important for poor mothers. Milk Depots are good, but Consultations are better, and their success is measured by the small quantity of milk they sell and the large number of nursing babies and mothers that come to them....

FOODS AND DRUGS FOR BABIES

Foods sold for babies should be labelled in accordance with facts, and not described as "a perfect substitute for mother's milk." These foods should not be used till the baby is nine months old at least, and then only by the advice of a physician.

Mrs Winslow's Soothing Syrup should be marked in accordance with its contents. It contains opium.

Steedman's Powders should be marked as containing calomel and starch, and so with similar preparations.

CONCLUSION

Looking back only three years, it will be seen how great has been the progress in Britain about Infant Mortality. It is far ahead of Ontario. England, with an infant mortality rate of 132 per 1,000, is far ahead of Ontario; and Scotland and Ireland are farther ahead still. We have not even the figures for 1908 published, and in 1907, Ontario had an infant death rate of 150. London itself has an infant death rate of 113, and England is a country where the conditions of life are not easy, "where industries flourish, where mothers labour, and where babies decay."

"MISTRESS IN MY OWN."

It remains for those who proudly say,

"Daughter am I in my Mother's house,
But Mistress in my own,"

to set that house in order.

The lines are fallen unto us in pleasant places, but our goodly heritage will go to the sons of the stranger, unless we put our hands and our minds in earnest to the work of rearing an Imperial race. The Jews have discovered the secret of National Immortality, and what is it? It is very simple. "Take care of your children." The future of our Province, the future of our country, the future of our Empire, the future of our race, is signified by the same sign, and that sign is a child.

Before the babe this year newly-born, or yet unborn, takes his first step and speaks his first word, the question of vigour or degeneracy is almost settled for him. The keys that unlock the problem of Infant Mortality, are the keys of National and Imperial hope and power.

———————

CHAPTER FOUR

MANAGING THE FAMILY

Having married and borne her first child, a Canadian woman of the late nineteenth or early twentieth century found herself in a position of considerable complexity. Families always have been difficult social institutions to keep running smoothly, so intricate are their webs of economic and emotional dependence, so uncompromising the demands of shared domestic space and so complicated the power relationships of intimate life.[1] In the cultures from which late Victorian and Edwardian Canada sprang, maintaining a delicate balance at the hearth was a female responsibility.[2] And this was the case still in the years when wives and mothers from the old settlements of British North America and Europe first moved in large numbers into the cities and the west. Of course the nature of that frail domestic balance was changing, as it had changed for each preceding generation.[3]

The patterns by which couples made decisions were various. Alice Johnson, "Alys the Hermit," bore total domination with a passivity broken only by the bitter outpourings in her diary and the furtive act of recording distant news of men hanged, perhaps regretting that the husbands dying did not come from closer to home.[4] Some marriages allowed partners considerable independence, wife and husband running separate businesses and keeping separate books. Some men responded to wives who were independent not by dominating them, but like the old shantyman observed by Joshua Fraser, by simply moving away. There were wives who did the same, like Sarah Drinkwater's sister, Mary, although for them the burdens of leave-taking must have been considerably greater. The ledgers of philanthropic institutions and the archive letterboxes of politicians reveal how precarious was the predicament of a wife alone in the days before mothers' allowances or even nominal provisions for child support.[5]

Couples who remained together found new uncertainties being introduced into their lives. Hannah Kern's problems were part of an old story, a husband incautious in his investments, a proud wife taking in boarders and bemoaning her lost gentility. But there are new elements in the dilemmas of Jane Curran and Harriet Neville. Among all classes in urban Canada, families had become more dependent upon the male head of household for their material support, at a time when many husbands' job security was diminished. Working-class families, having moved to town, needed cash to buy the food and fuel in which they had formerly been self-sufficient and found the range of family members who could undertake wage work restricted by legislation or by the industrial mix of their community.[6] In commercial firms the older patterns of business life and the long bond between patron and client were replaced by an efficiency-minded personnel policy, and in the flurry of late nineteenth-century consolidations and rationalizations in Canadian business,[7] many managers and semi-professionals were made redundant. As the couple contemplated career changes for the husband or unemployment, the wife's role as stabilizer became more demanding. She planned and provisioned for the family's move to a new place, put her labour and acumen toward the founding of a new family business, or found wage work to provide the cash to tide the household over the crisis. The wife who lived in one locality from first child born to last child leaving home, gradually perfecting one set of domestic arrangements, was gone—if she had ever existed. More frequent was the experience of a marriage possessing several segments, each requiring different financial and residential arrangements, all demanding flexibility from the mistress of the house.

The uncertainty of urban household management was amplified by the fact that as married men became more dependent upon the fluctuating labour market, married women became more dependent upon their husbands. Some wives worked away from home for wages in the late nineteenth century: in some particular settings, for example, textile towns in the twentieth century, substantial numbers of them did. But in general the transition away from the family work force and household production created an uncomfortable hierarchy in family labour, distinguishing the paid work of men and teenagers away from home from the unpaid home work of wives and mothers. It was not only to add to the family coffers but also to affirm their autonomy that city women late into the nineteenth century kept cows and chickens and market gardens, took in laundry and lodgers. The cabbages, the unfamiliar linen, and the strangers lounging under foot were signs of a wife's productivity that could be compared, through their market value, with the productivity of wage earners; they were her resistance to adolescents' teasing, to husband's condescension, to the coin of dependence.

Still the wife's principal obligation remained accommodation. For a woman with children the pressures were extreme to excel as facilitator, compromiser, and support. By comparison with the most unhappy marriage, life without a male bread-winner was a meagre and unwelcome alternative. Even leaving aside material and social considerations, in a culture in which serenity and nurturing were a "good" woman's essence, a wife who turned from the responsibility to keep domestic harmony, whatever the costs, and appeared to hazard her children's futures by either fueling or fleeing discord in the home, cut herself away from the primary sources of her own self-esteem. Therefore women made their marriages work, and measured themselves by their capacities to be good mothers.

Most were mothers of young children for almost all of their adult lives. David Gagan has calculated that the average number of years between first conception and last birth was fifteen years in Peel County, Ontario in 1871, so that for a married woman, illness, the onset of menopause, and early death were the only real checks in this perfectly natural regime, referred to by Frances Stewart, a farm woman from the Otonobee region in Ontario, as "the everlasting nursing business".[8] Jane Curran of Orillia, Ontario, listing her blessings in her diary on 26 November 1881 noted both the survival of her nineteen-month-old baby and the recent marriage of her daughter May. In that year Jane Curran was nearing the mid-way point in the forty year period of a late Victorian marriage between first child born and last child independent.

By the early twentieth century, a change in this pattern was noticeable. Both household size and crude fertility rates were declining, which suggests that couples were planning for smaller completed families. Later marriage would have helped achieve this end by decreasing the proportion of her child-bearing years that a woman spent in wedlock. Still, after her first pregnancies, a wife would have needed to look for other means to limit family size. The search had costs. Under section 179c of the criminal code the dissemination of birth control information was punishable by two years in prison. Men used condoms, women homemade diaphragms and various concoctions purchased from mail order catalogues. However, because abstinence and abortion, the first unpleasant for both, the second potentially lethal for the wife, were the only reliable methods of birth control, the desire for family limitation must have led to a marked increase in domestic tension after the first years of marriage passed.[9]

In these days before either Doctor Spock or the Gerber baby were ubiquitous, it is likely that large cultural differences existed in the practice of mothering. Upper-class women sometimes farmed out their children to the wet nurse and nursemaid, and reluctantly observed that these members of the household staff knew their child, and the changes in its growing, best. Working-class women probably faced the problem of paid child care with additional ambivalence because to secure outside help with their children they often had to take their youngsters outside the home to institutions. Some working women continued to nurse their children after they returned to the factory, paying a young person to bring their infant to the plant gate at the noon whistle.[10] Isabel Merkley, a Morrisburg, Ontario, matron, in 1887 weaned her daughter at 10 months. Bas, a woman of similar class background, though a recent immigrant, took her son from the breast at 5½ months in 1914, proudly declaring him "absolutely a bottle baby and....a great credit to the cows." Bas may have been responding to a forming ideal of the modern woman who placed more faith in sterile bottles and scientific formula preparations for her baby than in the vagaries of nature.[11] But the cultural dimensions of this problem must be complex. In Quebec agricultural communities in the pre-industrial period, women also weaned their children early. In Europe

Terry Copp, *The Anatomy of Poverty* (Toronto, 1974) chapter 3; more generally see Lise Vogel, "The Contested Domain: The Family, Early Capitalism and Industrialization," *Marxist Perspectives*, I (1978); Hans Medick, "The Protoindustrial Family Economy: the Structure and Function of Household and Family during the Transition from Peasant Society to Industrial Capitalism," *Social History*, III (1976) 291-315; Wanda Minge-Kalman, "The Industrial Revolution and the European Family: the Institutionalization of Childhood as a Market for Family Labour," *Comparative Studies in Society and History*, XX (1978) 454-68.

7 A.E. Epp, *Co-operation among Capitalists: the Canadian Merger Movement 1909-13* (Baltimore, 1973); Michael Bliss, *A Living Profit* (Toronto, 1974); Carol Christ, "Victorian Masculinity and the Angel of the House," in Martha Vicinus, ed., *A Widening Sphere: Changing Roles of Victorian Women* (Bloomington, Ind., 1977); Alan Smith, "The Myth of the Self-Made Man in English Canada, 1850-1914," *Canadian Historical Review*, LIX (1978) 189-218.

8 David Gagan, *Hopeful Travellers* (Toronto, 1981) 87.

9 Angus McLaren, "Birth Control and Abortion in Canada, 1870-1920," *Canadian Historical Review*, LIX (1978) 319-40.

10 Bettina Bradbury, "The Fragmented Family: Family Strategies in the Face of Death, Illness and Poverty, Montreal 1860-1885," in Joy Parr, ed., *Childhood and Family in Canadian History* (Toronto, 1982); Suzanne Cross, "The Neglected Majority: the Changing Role of Women in Nineteenth Century Montreal," in Susan Trofimenkoff and Alison Prentice, eds., *The Neglected Majority* (Toronto, 1977).

11 Nancy Pottishman Weiss, "The Mother-Child Dyad Revisited: Perceptions of Mothers and Children in 20th Century Child Rearing Manuals," *Journal of Social Issues* (1978) 28-43; Chistopher Lasch, *Haven in a Heartless World* (New York, 1977) 107-110; Veronica Strong-Boag, "Intruders in the Nursery: Childcare Professionals Reshape the Years One to Five," in J. Parr, ed., *Childhood and Family*.

12 The finding that among European rural agricultural populations, wide regional variations existed in the proportion of children who were breast-fed was first published by John Knodel and Etienne van de Walle, "Breast Feeding, Fertility and Infant Mortality: an Analysis of Some Early German Data," *Population Studies* XX (1967); additionally see John Knodel and Hallie Kinter, "The Impact of Breast Feeding Patterns on the Biometric Analysis of Infant Mortality," *Demography* XIV (1977) and John Knodel, *The Fertility Decline in Germany* (Princeton, 1973).

13 Rosemary Ball, "A Perfect Farmer's Wife," *Canada, A Historical Magazine*, III (1975) 2-21; Rasmussen and Rasmussen, *A Harvest Yet to Reap* (Toronto, 1976) 42; "Feeding a Family," *infra;* Edith Rowles, "Bannock, Beans and Bacon," *Saskatchewan History* V (1952) 1-14.

14 Bettina Bradbury, "The Family Economy and Work in an Industrializing City: Montreal in the 1870s," Canadian Historical Association, *Historical Papers* (1979); Elizabeth H. Pleck, "Two Worlds in One: Work and Family," *Journal of Social History*, X (1976) 178-95; Joan M. Jensen, "Cloth, Butter and Boarders: Women's Household Production for the Market," *Radical Review of Political Economics*, XII (1980); Annette Kuhn and Anne-Marie Wolpe, *Feminism and Materialism: Women and the Mode of Production* (London, 1978); Shelia B. Kamerman, "Work and Family in Industrialized Societies," *Signs*, IV (1979) 632-50.

1. THE MARITAL RELATIONSHIP

"INSTEAD OF SERVANTS..."

Raised as a gentlewoman, Hannah Kern expected when she married to be mistress of a household, overseeing servants and children and engaging in the voluntary works that were befitting the wife of a prominent man. Her husband's financial woes, however, brought this ideal into sharp conflict with the reality of her life as she explains in her diary entry for October 15, 1873.

Wentworth County, Ontario, 1873
J.H. Holbrook and M.H. Farmer, eds., "Diary of Hannah Aikman (Hammill)
Kern of Dundas and Ancaster, Wentworth County, Ontario, 9 April 1870-1
January 1885," Western Ontario History Nuggets, *XXVI (1958) 12.*

October 15, 1873...Instead of servants to come at my call, I am and have long been, my own. Instead of using money already my own and spending my time in works of charity as well as pleasure, I must now work hard for my living.

...My husband, ah, my husband is now almost my only thought; by endorsing and losing his money he has put himself in such a position that he can never own anything, and the consciousness of that joined to a naturally irritable temper makes him at times almost ungovernable either by himself or anyone else,...

I have had a gentlemen boarder almost six weeks.

"ALYS THE HERMIT"

First born in 1857, Alice Jane Johnson spent her entire life in Missiquoi County, St Armand West, Quebec. She attended school on an irregular basis until she was fourteen years old. Her father's ill-health required Alice's mother, her sister, Lucy, and Alice herself to devote themselves to maintaining their 14 acre farm. Her mother died in 1889 and her sister in 1892, leaving Alice to meet the constraining demands of her father and, after 1896, her husband, Alva. One cannot help but sympathize with her, a woman of forty-one at the time of these excerpts, who felt so remote from any human contact that she dubbed herself "Alys the Hermit."

Quebec, 1898
Excerpts from the diary of Alice Jane Johnson, Property of H.C. Yates,
Stanbridge East, Quebec. From Randoff Yates, A Critical Analysis of the
Diary of Alice Jane Johnson. *MA Thesis, Bishop's University, 1975.*

July 21st, 1898: Father has gone to Bedford with Alva this afternoon. Alva went to Len's this morning at four o'clock to work in haying but was sick and came home he has gone to get a truss. Jack and Len and the Englishman are all sick. Alva has been changing works with Len's folks in haying and has worked six days to Len's. I have not been well myself since I came home from Farnham the fifth of July. Alva's stomach troubles him a great deal. It scares me since mother died of a cancer in the stomach. Alys the Hermit.

It is a terrible thing to have a Hermit's life, as I am compelled to live, not allowed but one holiday in a year to go to Farnham but not allowed to go to any other place unless it is to Anson Seagel's or Alva's brothers for an hour or so. As soon as my school days were over I was not allowed to go to see anything and all that I know about the world is just what I have learned from books and Newspapers. How I have longed to see what it could be like to behold with the eye and not pictured from imagination. My husband came here to buy eggs the way I happened to get married but he don't like to take me out to see anything nor father would not allow us to go if he did. I thought if I got married maybe I could get out or maybe my husband would take me out a day once in a while but father won't allow but one day in a year to go to Farnham. When I was a child going to school there was some Highlanders came and showed in the schoolhouse some Magic lantern views. I thought it wonderful. I supposed when I was a child going to school that father was going to bring his children up like othrs but as soon as our school days were ended we were compelled to live like hermits. My mother was sick three or four years and when she died father was stricter than ever and did not allow but very few people to visit us and my sister died three years after my mother. I have seen Franklin Bend and when we went to school the teacher that boarded here wanted to go to Pinnicle Mountain. We had a cousin lived at the foot of the mountain and we went to our cousin's one Sunday and he guided us up on the mountain I saw more of the world that day than I ever have since. I have been to a fair a few times in my life and have see Yankey Robinsons Show and Adam Fourpaughs show and I have been to a picnic to Mystic twice and once to a school Picnic in the grove by the schoolhouse. Before mother died father complained of ill health. My mother, sister, and myself worked outdoors hard as we could and mother said we should have a holiday once a year, so once we went to a celebration to Stanbridge the 24th of May and twice went to Frelighsburg to a celebration on Dominion Day. After my sister died father and I went to a Lime light show in the schoolhouse but that has been the last. It is now six years since my husband took me to a fair to Redford the fall before we were married and he took me to a campmeeting at Eccles Hill once since we were married and twenty years ago I went to a Campmeeting one Sunday in the grove by the school house. When I was a little girl father took my sister and myself to the Pike River Springs after spring water. I am now fourty one years old and a married woman and am not allowed to go anywhere without fathers permission. If I get one day in a year it is a mirricle. I have worked hard as I could at home all my life and father dont...

Aug 1st 1898 Oh how I wish for relief which I cannot be allowed until death sets me free. I dont see why I was brought up and compelled to live a Hermit I am sure my health would be better if I was allowed to go out and get fresh air but father will not allow it and Alva ain't much better so between them both I am as secluded as a cloistered nun but the Lord knowns what is best. Alys the Hermit.

September 1st, 1898: Mrs Burley commenced doctoring Alva's side.

September 19th, 1898: Tom bit father's hand.

September 20th, 1898: Mr LaGrange came to see Alva's side.

September 21st, 1898: Finished husking the corn.

September 21st, 1898. Ed Guthrie lost a horse.

Eccles Hill Sep 21st 1898: Charley Yates had an accident by falling from a butternut tree.

September 22, 1898: Jack Stapleton moved to St Armand Station last week.

Oct 5th 1898: Susie Catchepaw's house taken down. Oren Barlow left Dr Cruthers and went to Gages Oct 1st 98. Poor me I am not allowed one holiday only to go to Farnham once a year on a visit. I am ashamed of my bringing up. I have proved the truth of the old proverb that all work and no play Makes Jack a dull boy. Mother used to tell father it want to be wondered at that the children did not know anything he kept them to home so, I believe if I was allowed to go out once in a while my health would be better but I am kept at home and lame with rhumatism the most of my time father is different from other men and keeps up the old tin lantern style I am fourty one years old now and don't have the privlige of children that I know that are but four years old but I must continue to live a Hermit's life if I murmer father tells me it is in vain. After my sister died, for four years I only went out when I was obliged to go to a store. Oh how I wish I could live like other folk how ashamed I am, buried alive as it were just as secluded as a cloistered nun. How I wonder what it must be like to live as others do. Alys the Hermit.

A PLEA FOR SUPPORT

The desperate plea of Mrs A. Chapman reveals one side of an unhappy marriage. Faced with a husband who was unable to support her and her children and who carried patriarchal authority to its most extreme bounds, Mrs Chapman did not, however, consider separation. Rather, she sought assistance so that she might take on the role of family provider through the only skills she possessed.

Sudbury, Ontario, 1905
Letter Mrs A. Chapman to Hon. J.P. Whitney, April 24, 1905, Whitney Papers, MU 3116, Archives of Ontario.

Confidential   Sudbury April 24, 1905
Hon. J.P. Whitney

Dear Sir;

Don't let this letter surprise you although perhaps you have never received one like it. Trouble makes me write to you & I hope you will sympathize with me & the children and help me out. I am a staunch conservative & worked for you. I am sorry to say that I have a very cruel & lazy husband. We are behind about $40.00 with rent & I am going to loose my furniture, and now what I would like you to do is to help me out with the rent & purchase a lot (not for my sake but the childrens) and I will get a house built in the Building Coy and take a lot of boarders, as this is a good town & I can make lots of money keeping boarders. I will then pay you back all you have lent me & pay my house also, through time, this is what I have been advised to do & I have considered every way myself & find that this is the only way that will bring me & the children peace & provisions. I have been told that if I could get my husband under control so that I would be boss myself, I would get lots of help.

I have two very promising boys & able now to help me quite a bit. The baby is a girl. The little boys cant go to school, he will not even let them out in the yard to play. Just keeps them in to abuse them. He won't let them go to school nor let them study at home. in fact I cannot describe the miserable life we have, we would be better dead. And now Mr Whitney do help me out or see that I am helped & you will never loose by it. I will be able to pay you back easily & God will bless you more abundantly. But above all things keep this to yourself as my husband would be very angry if he knew I told on him & it would also be a bad blow on you as we are living in a Grits house. We will likely be put out of this house in May & our furniture taken besides, the only thing I have to make a living by. I think what I have said here will be sufficient as you are a man of broad views & good intellect & you can readily see that my life is one of misery & torture. Please answer by return as I am very uneasy. Let me know what you can & how soon, for if any person ever needed a friend I do now & I think I am asking one who will help me out of punishment. Hoping to hear from you by return I am, believe me

Yours very obediently
Mrs A. Chapman
Sudbury

"MARY HAS RETURNED TO FATHER"

Until 1968, when the federal government passed divorce laws for all the country, legal divorce and separation were governed by provincial laws. Nova Scotia and New Brunswick (and later Prince Edward Island) brought divorce laws to Confederation, while Ontario and Quebec joined the union without laws for dissolving a marriage. In those provinces, divorce had to be granted through a Private Member's bill passed by the federal parliament. Separation, however, was considered to be a private contract between the couple. It was usually the case, when the wife left her husband, as did Mary in the brief document below, that she lost her children, shelter, and financial security.

Ontario, 1875-1876
Sarah Hallen Drinkwater Diary. Diaries Collection. Public Archives of Ontario.

1875
April 5th.
Mary was married to Dr Gilmour. Tom drove me up to the wedding; it took place on Jan. 13th. Dr. Gilmour is a widower with 2 girls and 5 sons.
Extract of a letter by Summer:—"The Dr found her very hard to spark, her heart seemed impervious to cupid's bow, for it took two years to accomplish it; 999 men out of 1000 would have thrown up the sponge in despair long before that time, but I suppose he kept the saying fresh in his memory, 'faint heart never won fair lady'...."

1876
September 9th.
My father has left Penetang. I forgot to mention Mary has returned to father as no longer living with Dr Gilmour.

OLD SAINT-SAINT'S MARRIAGE

In his descriptions of shanty life among the lumbering men of the Ottawa River Valley, Joshua Fraser rarely found occasion to mention women. In the case of the former lumberman hermit, "Old Saint-Saint," our observer was clearly curious about the marital relationship which had been abandoned.

Quebec and Ontario, 1883
Joshua Fraser, Shanty, Forest and River Life (Montreal, 1883) 69-70.

His history is one of the most singularly unromantic you ever heard in your life. He has a wife and large family living on a comfortable farm near Montreal. The former he has not seen for twenty-five years, and the reason he left her was not because she was unfaithful, or extravagant, or unkind, or any other of the common-place frailties of womankind, but because she was too saving of his hard-earned wages. When he would give her money on his return from the shanty, or send it to her, she was in the habit of putting it out at interest, on good security, without telling him anything about it. Whatever was her motive in this, it was, as far as I could learn, the only ground of disturbance between them,—otherwise she was, even according to Saint-Saint's account, an exemplary wife and mother in all respects. He is, however, very reticent about this, and all other personal matters.

Be the cause what it may, the old fellow left wife, and children, and home, and, burying himself in this isolated retreat, refused to have any further intercourse with them. His wife has made repeated overtures for reconciliation, but in vain; and though one of his sons came to see him a few years ago, and brought clothes and money, yet he told him never to come back, and not to "bother" him any more. He lays no claim to his property, but allows his wife and children to do as they please with it. Altogether his mode of existence is a strange freak of human nature, and quite unaccountable on any of the grounds from which people generally take enjoyment and satisfaction out of life; but that is his business, and, if he likes it better than any other, let him by all means enjoy it.

"GIVE ME THE ENERGY"

Although the social image of wife as a non-income earner, supporting her husband by maintaining his household and family in an appropriate manner survived, for some women, the image did not always mirror reality. Jane Curran faced this dilemma of stabilizing her household and working in the family business. At the same time, she faced a second challenge: the roles of mother to a newborn baby and mother of a newly-wed daughter.

Orillia, Ontario, 1879-82
Diaries of Mrs. Jane Curran, J.E.G. Curran Papers, MG 30, C85 Vol. 4.
Public Archives of Canada.

Sept. 29 1879 My baby was born on 18 Feb. I was ill for a long time but am mercifully restored to my usual health. baby is a very pink little girl and *so* good.

Nov. 27 Was interupted on my last entry. It seemed impossible to get time to write. I have felt so hopeful lately. John had a situation as editor of the Times Newspaper for some months now it seemed so good to have something to depend on outside the business but they have made some changes in the management of the paper and he is again left in the cold. God help me to keep up & try to see a bright side. I feel it pretty bad right now but perhaps it is all for the best....

Nov. 26 81 Just about a year has passed since I last wrote a year of blessing. I believe I have every cause for thankfulness. baby is now 19 months old and our daughter May has been married on 1st Nov to Mr. King I do trust it will be for her own good he seems a very nice young man and seems to love her very much I do trust she will make him a wife. *She can* if *She will*.. [prayer]

Our business has been very good for which I am thankful. I pray God to help us pay our debts and to give me the energy & luck & perservence necessary to make our business a success. I trust to be able to spend a little time now and then to chronicle my thoughts I believe it does me so much good...

Jan 1st 82 Another year is numbered with the past & still I am spared.... I feel my responsibility very much in regard to my children. O God help me to set a worthy example before them. George went to Toronto last week and may it be for his good. I think my health is better than for a long time although I have been in the work room steadily for over three months from morning to night it does not seem to affect me.

Feb 19th 82 My baby was two years old yesterday a big health girl she is.

TWO DIFFERENT PEOPLE

After 1870, a Mrs Thomson ran a millinery story in a lean-to next to the Elora Oddfellows Hall. Her husband operated a butcher's shop in the same town. From an incident related to Mrs Charles Allan and reported below, one is introduced to the relationship between two spouses involved in separate businesses.

Elora, Ontario, late 19th century
Mrs. Charles Allan, "Some Businesses in Elora," 9. Wellington County Archives, Wellington County Museum, Fergus, Ontario.

Two Lowe women (Robert Lowe's family) bought spring hats from Mrs Thomson. When it came time to pay, they said, "Mr Lowe has delivered a beef into your husband's butcher shop up the street, and you may get your money from him." Mrs Thomson replied, "Mr Thomson and I are two different people."

———————

SOLVING ECONOMIC PROBLEMS BY MOVING

Harriet Maria and Anthony Neville and their children were perhaps typical of the Ontario families who sought a new economic security and life in the farm lands of the Canadian prairies in the 1880s. In 1882, Anthony Neville joined a surveying party bound for the west where he claimed a homestead in the Cottonwood district of Assiniboia. Harriet and her children left for their new home almost a year later in July 1883. In the following excerpt from her memoirs, Harriet Neville recalls their momentous decision and plans to move west to solve their problems.

Assiniboia, 1882-1885
Harriet Purdy and David Gagan, ed., "Pioneering in the North-West Territories 1882-1905", Canada: An Historical Magazine, *II, 4, June 1975, 11-17, 30.*

We moved to the city of Hamilton, Ont. where for eight years my husband was Secretary and Treasurer of a large Fire Insurance Company.

One night Anthony came home and at our six o'clock dinner did not have much to say and seemed absent-minded. That was unusual for him, but as we had two nieces and a nephew and his boy friend boarding with us for college and other work, I asked no questions till we were alone, then it was not necessary for he told me without. He said his company and another were going to unite. It would be some time yet. But when it was done only one staff of officers would be required. They had given him notice but asked him to stay till the final arrangements were made, perhaps longer. However, he knew that new ways would be adopted, typewriters and copying machines, etc. and younger men would apply for situations. What would I think about going away out west and taking up land? "How would you like to think about living here all your life in a rented house, never having a home of your own and only going perhaps once every year to your father's or mine? Our girls leaving school to stand behind counters for a living even as I growing older would probably not be able to earn as large a salary as now." I said, "You are the oldest of your family and I the youngest of mine. We both like a home of our own. We are not likely ever to have one unless we earn it. Let us go." So we wrote to our parents who thought it a wise plan if we had the grit to face it.

Father said my husband should go first and see the country and I could come near the old home and live in one of his small houses till we found out just how things must be done. So we sold part of our furniture and my husband settled me in the house where my aunt, whose son had died, lived and was paralyzed with no one who would live with her and take care of her, and I took care of her till she died, a few months after.

My husband went to Winnipeg and from there taking field notes for a surveying party who went away west of the Saskatchewan river.... In the fall they came back to where the construction train had come as far as Moose Jaw. All this time I had only two letters and he had none, though I had written every week. No mails could get to them as they were constantly on the move. He could not hear how we were, whether dead or alive and I did not know whether I was a grass widow or a real one. However we were in a measure prepared for that so neither of us worried much. I had been getting plans made, and when I got the letter that my husband had come to a station called Regina which might be the capital of Assiniboia, and was going to stay there that winter building houses, and he said he would take a homestead ready for me to come out in the spring, I felt then that I could make ready for the flitting.

I had to think of the journey when the railroad was not yet complete, what would be most useful to take, and what to leave behind. Anthony could not write these things to help me, because all the conditions were different from when he went. I could talk to my family but not one of them knew as much about it as I. I had a little money but wanted to make it go as far as possible, for we would have a great venture to supply what was needed to start a new farm in a strange country. Clothing was first. I could go to Toronto, do shopping and return any day. So I bought material and sewed. Fortunately my mother had me well-trained to always have plenty of good bedding so that was not on my mind. I made rugs for bare floors. The material for these I got by taking rags from a good friend, the minister's wife, on shares. Making all the rugs for half of the rags. It was hard work, but paid well, for well-made hooked rugs last almost indefinitely. Books. I knew there would be no schools and our children must be taught. My piano I traded with Mason & Risch for a good organ. They gave me some value over and came out took my piano to Toronto, packing and sending my organ two weeks before I was ready to go. They did so and it was all that had arrived before I did, though my things were sent from home about the same time. They were very good paying all expenses.

Health and education, comfort and pleasure, all had to be taken into consideration. I was a pretty good nurse though not by any means strong. I could use all the common sense with which I was endowed and must take remedies and outfit for emergencies. I sold all my china and good dishes. Saved all the cutlery and necessary cooking utensils, bought granite plates cups and saucers and all small table dishes of the same that I thought useful.

My fruit sealers I traded for good butter packed in pails made specially for travelling and keeping good. Some of my Dutch cousins gave me two large bags of old-fashioned dried applies. My father and brother belonged to the Grange so took me to their store in Toronto where I bought common groceries and some canned fruit, they packing and sending these for me. I took no furniture but what was useful for packing cases for clothing and bedding. Bureaus, a cupboard, fall leaf table and trunks.

Now here was something in which I was deficient. I was something like an English lady who told me that all she was taught about Canada was that it was a country of extreme heat and cold. I knew about the extreme cold but did not know just when to expect the extreme heat. So I started from Toronto on the 3rd of July (1883) thinking there would be a long cold spring and I would miss that. But for fear, I did not change the children's winter underwear....

After leaving Chicago we passed through Dakota and Minnesota along to Emerson to Winnipeg. I had as clear ideas as to the dimensions of the North West Territory as, after a few years, a new homesteader, an Englishman (who) told me, when he mentioned having a letter from his mother in London, England, who said he might run down to Toronto some week-end and spend it with a cousin there. For as my husband had written he would be sure to meet me, I half expected he might run down to Winnipeg, or if not there to Brandon. So every station I told the children, we would soon see Papa. We were not travelling on the "Through Limited," so it was some time before we reached Regina....

It was three o'clock on Saturday morning when the train pulled in to Regina Station. A dingy small room and dingier lanterns here and there. Men on the platform calling "This way to the Victoria," "This way to the 'Royal George'" and shouting all the names of the large hotels in Eastern Cities. I asked one man, "Where's your cab?" You should have heard the laugh all along the platform! These westerners had no sympathy for my sensitive feelings at all. Well, I said "Take us to the Victoria." He started ahead with his smoky lantern across a plank each side of which was water, never even mentioning that it was not a bottomless quagmire, but only a mud hole. Mr Urquhart carried the baby while I kept tight hold of the hands of my two little girls fearing to lose them in the deep water. We were led to a small shanty of boards (a shack is the proper name now) lighted by another smoky lantern (I supposed they had no newspapers with which to clean them). ...A short bench beside a shorter sheet iron stove. There was a fire in it for the morning was cool.

My husband [was] not there. My friend said he would not leave me till he came, but I told him to go as he would surely be there. And while we were talking he arrived over-joyed to have us once more. He said the carriage was just across the rail-track. I had my doubts about that carriage, but we started over and found a fine yoke of oxen hitched to a lumber wagon with hay for seats. We had not to go far, for his house was near. There were no better ones in the city except maybe the Methodist parsonage. It was a city of tents, almost surrounded by Indian tepees....

Papa tethered his oxen and I put the sleepy children on his bed of hay on the floor, covered with grey blankets. As far as I could see the rest of the floor was covered with clothes. Either he had no nails or had forgotten to hang up his clothing. When he came in, I said I would like a cup of tea if there was any place to make it. "Yes of course, come this way" and he started up what was intended for a stairs. I followed and there was a camp tin stove, with two holes and an oven, boxes and packages of food all around it on the floor, and he started the fire and set a small tin pail of water on top to heat for the tea. I said "What on earth did you put your stove up here for." "Just because I could not get pipe enough to reach farther." One phase of pioneer strategy.... My husband informed me that he had everything ready for an early start to our homestead.

He had a shack out there, had bought a cow which [would] go beside our oxen, as the Indians from whom he bought her had trained her that way. He had a mowing-machine, rake, plow and harrows on the land all ready for work. He had hired ten acres broken and planted potatoes, a bushel for which he had paid five dollars. His idea for risking this was taken from the pamphlet issued for guidance to homesteaders. They were just to cut potatoes as usual and lay each piece under the sod and they would therefrom reap a good crop, a lot of bushels per acre—I just forget how many. He had planted them in April. Not a drop of rain came in June as was promised, and hot weather instead, so our potatoes laid there just as they were planted. As five dollars were not to be picked up readily we wished they had been saved to buy rolled bacon, or some other food. Pioneer life calls for some disappointments even re potatoes....

"I AM VERY SORRY FOR THE WOMEN AND CHILDREN"

Husbands' decisions to relocate to the Canadian prairies or to remain in pioneer conditions despite the lack of social amenities for their families called for accommodation on the part of their wives, despite their preferences. Such was the case for the women observed by E.O.S. Scholfield, a British Columbia archivist.

British Columbia, 1913
Ethelbert Olaf Stuart Scholfield Diary, 1913. Add. Mss. 491 Provincial Archives of British Columbia.

Friday September 5th....
Made Sucher Creek in time for dinner with Mr and Mrs Powers who keep a "road-house" consisting of a one-roomed log cabin. Mr and Mrs P live in tent, while guests lay their blankets on a bedstead in corner of cabin or on the floor—I took the floor. Terrible dinner of boiled potatoes, boiled turnips, stewed raisins and hot bread. After sleeping in open found cabin insufferably hot and stuffy but it was too wet to sleep outside. Grand hail storm just after we got in. Could hear the hail stones smashing into the trees a long way off as it swept over the hills and valleys: then with a roar burst upon us.

Lunch at Rasmussen's place at government meadows. Fine butter. R. a Dane brought up to dairy farming.

Saturday September 6....
Got up betimes; dressed while Mrs Powers prepared breakfast of fried turnips, and potatoes tea, bread, butter and marmalade. Mrs P a very cheerful young body, said she liked Sucher Creek and enjoyed her life there. Her husband, seems to be a good natured individual, but not much life about him. Although he must be a good worker because he has done a lot in the few months he has been on the place. Both Mr & Mrs Powers are Americans. I find that a good many Americans are finding their way into this country. They will never make good British subjects—in my opinion—the leopard cannot change his spots, but their children may become loyal citizens. It would be better, I think to have our country filled with our own people.

Left Sucher Creek about eight thirty o'clock. Felt quite ill after that breakfast dinner—must have got a chill also, for which our wet camp at Mud River may be responsible. Lunch at a poor little cabin opposite a place owned by one named Mapes. Such a home—in one corner Mrs Mapes ill in bed, in another a poor little girl—both of them feverish and requiring attention. Mrs Ferrall, the mother of the little girl, was nursing the invalids, she herself looked very ill. The house, or rather shanty was full of flies, while outside the black flies drove one to distraction. Certainly the pioneer, especially the pioneer woman, has a terrible time of it. Mrs. Ferrall came into BC from Spokane, Washington, trekking the whole distance—seven hundred miles or more—in their own wagon, taking about seven months to make the journey. Mrs F says she does not like the life, but her husband likes the country, so she must stay in this out of the way outpost and cook meals, look after children, and work day in and day out until the end. This is a very sad and all too common picture of pioneer life in the vast wilderness of the western interior. I am very sorry for the women and children more especially for the women to whom the little amenities of social intercourse mean so much. Every cloud has a silver lining, however and just as soon as the Grand Trunk Pacific and the Pacific Great Eastern Railway lines are running, settlers will pour into this rich country and schools and other evidences of civilization will follow. In time the district will be covered with prosperous communities for no country is so better adapted for dairying. Reached Mrs McAllen's for dinner, felt hot and feverish. Stomach upset all day. Mrs McAllan gave me some hot milk which made me feel a little better.

———————

"CRYING AND SAYING NO"

The decision to move to improve a family's economic opportunities was a difficult one. From the brief case of the Carmichaels, recalled below by a daughter of that union, we can identify emotional and economic aspects of the marital relationship that emerge from making that decision. Although the mother was obviously reluctant to leave her home and her dream of settled life, she trusted in her husband's judgement and signed the deed of sale. Under the New Brunswick law at that time, derived from England, Mrs Carmichael had the right to dower; that is, the right to one-third of her husband's property on his death. The husband, during his lifetime, might not sell his property unless his wife voluntarily signed away her dower interest allowing him to sell that property.

Sunnyside, New Brunswick, c. 1915
Helen Carmichael Dodge, My Childhood in the Canadian Wilderness *(New York, 1961) 34-35.*

We noticed a great change in our father. He seemed more unsettled and dissatisfied with the McMillan Company for which he had worked all these years. He didn't seem to be making enough money any more to provide a decent living. Each spring he would have to sell one of his teams to pay the men their wages. That left very little for his family to live on. The good lumber was being cut off, so it meant going farther and farther in the woods.

He now got the urge to move farther up north. This was a great decision to make. Our parents talked late in the night, trying to decide if it would be a wise move. If we did move, the home would have to be sold, and that Mother didn't want to do. She always felt that someday, perhaps, he would give up lumbering; and as we children got older, we might be able to farm and stay in the settlement.

After all was said and done, they decided to sell. I can see Mother now, crying and saying no, she wouldn't sign the deed. All the children had been born there, the only real home we had ever known. She would go anyplace for the winter, but she insisted we must maintain some place to call "home."

My father said he couldn't see any other way out; the place would have to go. Mother finally consented and signèd the papers; she felt he ought to know what was best. Again we were heading for a new outpost.

―――――――

2. TRADITIONAL MARRIED WORK

A BUFFALO HUNT

In the following excerpt from an unpublished essay written when she was 87, Victoria Callihoo recalls community preparations for an 1874 buffalo hunt and the roles of wives and young women.

Alberta, 1874
Victoria Callihoo, "Our Buffalo Hunts—1874" (1948) Acc. 74.1/45, Provincial Archives of Alberta.

I was thirteen years old when I first joined in a buffalo hunt. We left here (Lac Ste Anne) after the leaves were out on the poplar trees. We had our small fields and gardens seeded or planted. Before making the journey, there would be a meeting among the leading men as to the exact day of leaving. After this was decided on all the families who wanted to join the hunt would prepare for the trip. Our main transportation, the Red River Cart would be overhauled....

 I used to accompany my mother always on these trips. She was a medicine woman. She set broken bones and knew how to use medicinal herbs....

 When the kill is over, the women folks go out to help bring the meat in, then the slicing of meat begins. We girls would then keep a little smoke going all day to keep the flies away from the meat. The meat would be hung on rails that rested on two tripods at each end of the rails....

 We made pemmican out on the plain, as the dried meat was too bulky to take home. A large green hide would be hung on six posts, three on each side, the hide would form a V-shape; when it was dry the dried slabs of meat would be dumped in the V-shaped hide and two men on each end with flags would then pound the dry meat into pulp. Then sun-dried Saskatoons would be mixed, grease would then be poured on and stirred to have an even mixture.

―――――――

FEEDING A FAMILY

When Mrs John Irwin Jameson completed the following questionnaire in 1951 she was 73 years old. Her memories of the woman's means and methods of feeding her family in late nineteenth-century Alberta are interesting evidence of the balance between home production and commercial preparation prevalent among homesteading pioneers.

Near Lacombe, Alberta, 1895
Mrs John Irwin Jameson Papers, "What did Western Canadian Pioneers Eat?" Acc. 75.182, Provincial Archives of Alberta.

Name   Mrs John Irwin Jameson.
Address   Byemoor, Alberta.
Birthplace E. Manchester, England. Age 73 years old.

1. INTRODUCTORY QUESTIONS

What year did you start housekeeping in Western Canada? *June 1895.*
Where did you set up housekeeping? *Near Lacombe Alberta.*
Where had you been living before that? *In England and United States.*
For how many people did you prepare meals? *Four and callers and visitors.*
How far was it to your nearest store? *Eight miles.*
How often could a visit be made to the store? *Rarely in winter and monthly in summer.*
What groceries did you usually buy in those earliest years? *Flour, tea, sugar, salt in the late nineties. Dried applies and prunes, rice, small quantity of spice for flavoring, little sage for dressing, toilet soap and laundry soap at first, coal oil, salt, pepper, vinegar, oatmeal, beef pearl barley, flour, shorts and bran, rolled oats and pearl barley.*

2. FLOUR AND OTHER GRAIN PRODUCTS

What brand of white flour did you use in the early years? *Ogilvie Strong Bakers—3rd grade also Ogilvie's Glenora 2nd grade and then Hungarian and Royal Household—1st grade.*
In what quantities did you buy it? *100 pounds later in larger quantities of 500 lbs.*
What was the usual price per hundred pounds of white flour? *Best $2.25. 2nd grade was $1.75 and 3rd—$1.25 per 100 lbs.*
How much did you use graham flour? *Very little. We mixed shorts with flour.*
Whole wheat flour? *For porridge only.*
Was flour milled locally? *No.* How far away? *Brandon, Manitoba.* What year? *1895.*
What was the price for a twenty pound bag of rolled oats? *About 35 cents.*
What other grain products did you use? *Later we used some Corn meal and pearl barley.*
Cornmeal? *Yes years after.* Whole wheat? *Yes.* Farina? *Yes years after.*
Other? *Rolled oats.*
Did you grind your own wheat for porridge? *No.*
How did you grind it? *We did not have a small mill even an old fashioned*

coffee mill some of the neighbors used. We used ours for grinding the barley for coffee....

8. PRESERVING
In the early years did you preserve any foods by drying? *No.* peas? *Yes.* corn? *No.* beans? *No.* Saskatoons? *Yes.*
Other foods? *Gooseberries, strawberries, rhubarb, currants, raspberries and cranberries (wild fruit).*
What year did you first preserve fruit by canning? *1896.*
What year did you first preserve vegetables by canning? *1915.*
Do you still preserve foods by canning or drying? Canning and making preserves and jellies. *Yes.*
To what extent? *Bought cases of fruit of all kinds and baskets of grapes.*
Did you make your own vinegar? *Yes for many years from vinegar Mother brought from Ireland by a neighbour in 1895 also from dried apples and sugar by an American Settler in 1896.*

10. BAKING
What type of yeast did you use? *Royal Dried Yeast Cakes.*
Did you make yeast for your own use? *Yes.* Salt rising? *No sour dough sometimes.*
Did you buy baking powder? *Yes.* Baking soda? *Yes.*
Cream of tartar? *Yes.* Did you make your own baking powder? *At first I made it of Cream of Tartar and one teaspoonful of Bicarbonate of Soda mixed well together. We also used sour milk or buttermilk and soda for making pancakes, bannocks, scones and biscuits. I also made Bachelor biscuits out of flour, salt, little soda and water. Spoon biscuits were very good....*

12. WATER SUPPLY
Where did you get water for drinking and for cooking? (Well, river, slough, dugout) *Well 39 feet deep in 1895.*
How far was this water from your home? *A few feet.*
How was it brought to the home? (pail, barrel, tank) *Pail.*
Regarding water supply, mention any changes which have taken place since you first started housekeeping, giving dates where possible. *Where I live at Byemoor, S.E. of Stettler, we still use well water....*

17. Give a typical day's menu (breakfast, dinner & supper) for the earliest year you can remember. Give the year and list the members of the family with their ages at the time. State approximately the month, e.g. winter or summer.

Breakfast
Oatmeal or wheatlet porridge up to 1900.

Cracked wheat was also much used but took a long time to cook.
Warmed over potatoes, bacon and eggs.
Sometimes eggs and toast.
Buttered toast, jam or marmalade. Tea for beverage.

Dinner
Roast meat, stewed meat, or fried meat, sometimes fish.
Potatoes, vegetables with gravy.
A milk pudding, bread, no butter. Water for beverage.

Supper
Cold meat or eggs or perhaps fish.
Warmed up potatoes.
Fruit, if possible, or scones, jam, or cake. Black tea for beverage.
This was our menu all the year round with more cold meats in the summer and
hotter dishes in the winter varied with pork and beans, head cheese, scrambled
eggs and salads.

18. What year did you serve your first Christmas dinner in western Canada?
.... Give the menu. List those present and give their approximate ages at that
time.
Our first Christmas as a family was in 1895. There was my father aged 51 years.
My brother aged 21 years. Myself aged 17 years. My sister aged 14 years. We
had two guests. An elderly gentleman aged 50 years and a younger one aged 22
years. Our dinner was roast beef, potatoes, carrots and turnips boiled and
mashed together, gravy, Christmas pudding and white sauce with apples, nuts
and homemade candy and a little Port wine. I was the housekeeper and
cooked the dinner myself.

19. Were you ever reduced to almost starvation level living on one or two
locally produced foods? Give details.
No we were never in that condition but a good many of our neighbours were as
we afterwards found out. One family in 1895 existed that winter on rabbits,
turnips, potatoes, black bread made from 4X flour (that the Indians used),
coffee made from roasted barley. They had no milk, butter, sugar or fruit of
any kind. Some fish had been caught early in December and some of the
neighbors gave them beef fat to fry them in. Of course everyone had salt. One
family, I heard of far to the south of us, lived on rabbits and turnips for weeks
having neither potatoes or bread and barley coffee which was a favorite drink
with all of us. The new settlers suffered great hardships in the early days and
would have starved but for the rabbits. In 1896 all the gardens were frozen. We
had no vegetables of any kind. Grain was only fit for cattle feed and poor at
that. The winter of 1896-1897 rabbits had a disease and were unfit for food.

There was great hardship as well among the Indians on the reservation north of Lacombe....

21. When did you begin to rely on purchased foods and prepared foods instead of homegrown and home prepared foods? (Give as many details and dates as possible).

As we were not fond of canned foods except salmon, corn, tomatoes and sardines we did not buy any others. I always canned at least a hundred quarts of fruit, vegetables, meat, chicken, etc. Made lots of jars of various kinds of pickles. A farmer's wife was a very busy person in the old days. Money was too scarce to spend on food in cans that we could and did cure and preserve ourselves.

22. Please add other details from your early experiences of buying and securing foods in other ways during pioneer days in western Canada. Include items not mentioned above, quality, methods of merchandizing, prices, problems of storage, shortages and other details. (Use back of page if extra space is needed).

When I left the settlements around Lacombe in 1903 we went seventy miles south and east and built up a ranch. A fairly large log house, lots of other buildings and corrals. We had to take enough provisions to last for six months so bought everything in bulk. Of course our first year was the hardest for we could not tell exactly how much we needed. However, we started with 1,000 pounds of flour, 2-80 pound sacks of Rolled Oats, 10 pounds black tea, 5 pounds coffee, 10 pounds cocoa, 25 pounds rice, 25 pounds beans, cases of dried apples, peaches, apricots, pears and prunes, cases of canned corn, tomatoes and salmon, 2 barrels salt, 20 gallons of coal oil, 8 cans of lye for soap making, 20 bars of soap (laundry), 20 cakes of toilet soap, 5 lbs. currants, 10 pounds raisins, 3 lbs. candied peel, 5 pounds cocoanut and other smaller items. Winter clothing, towels, etc. In February we ran short of coal oil, cattle salt and sugar (we had taken 200 pounds) and he (my husband) had to make a trip out to the nearest trading post 25 miles away. A bad blizzard came on. There were no trails in those days as the country was not settled until two years later. It was travelling as the crow flies and hard on for anyone who was caught in a blizzard. A good many people owed their lives to the sagacity of their horses on trips like that one. My husband's favorite mare brought him safely home. How she picked out the way he never knew.

In the early years of the "nineties" there were very few cattle among the early settlers and very few pigs and chickens. Eggs were scarce and considered a luxury so was beef and pork products. The American settlers came in covered wagons and perhaps had a cow and calf and sometimes a sow. The horses were not acclimatized and many of them died the first winter. The sufferings of some of the settlers was intense owing to the lack of proper food and severe cold. Wood was plentiful and so were the rabbits which were a Godsend to many. It was late in the fall when the settlers finished the long trek from Iowa, Kansas and Nebraska to Alberta and winter was upon them. Some went back to the United States to work there a while and came back. The settlers who came later on from the United States came by train shipping horses, cattle, pigs, chickens and machinery in box cars. They also brought money with them and bought up the homesteads from the earlier settlers. They and their descendants are some of our best citizens today. There are still some of the real old timers from the United States here and their families. Great praise is due to the women of the early pioneer days for the privations they suffered, the hardships they endured and the fine families they raised.

The way we canned fruit in 1896 (if we had plenty of jars) was to put hay in the bottom of a wash boiler we had. On this we put our jars filled with fruit, sugar and water. We used Mason jars and old rubbers and metal caps. We filled up the boiler with water to the caps and then boiled them for two hours. Let cool and stored in cellar. We canned wild gooseberries, saskatoons, raspberries, made preserves of strawberries, currants, and blueberries. Jelly and jam of cranberries. Preserved rhubarb out of our own garden. All the fruit we canned and otherwise preserved was wild fruit we picked around and in the vicinity of our house.

I am sorry I can not remember the exact prices. Ten or 15 years ago I could have filled it out better.

It is to the amazing courage and endurance of the early United States settlers that Alberta owes so much. They were wonderful pioneers taking their experiences as a matter of course without complaining, as so many of the later settlers did, who came ten to fifteen years later. This small tribute I pay to them. Many of the children and grandchildren of the early United States pioneers are some of our most prosperous and enterprising pioneers of today.

We also burned grease lights made of any kind of grease but mostly beef tallows. This we melted and put in a saucer with a piece of cotton an inch wide. We lit the cotton which hung over the side and the grease would burn for hours. One of our neighbours from Ontario had a mould and could make a proper wick. Sometimes the roads were very heavily drifted and our coal oil done so we kept a few wax candles and burned grease lights.

The men, when out of tobacco, smoked kinnikineck leaves dried, also the inner bark of the Red Willow dried. An old Indian told my father about this.

Mrs. John Irwin Jameson
Byemoor Alberta

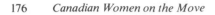

Labour-saving gadgets and devices to mechanize household tasks such as washing, cooking, and cleaning had invaded the department stores of Canada by the twentieth century. Their advertisements addressed female consumers in their roles as household scientists and managers. The photograph above taken in Eaton's Toronto store in 1912 shows a demonstration of the Soyer "Kookera" Bag, a paper bag used in the oven for roasting.

Credit: Eaton's Toronto store, March 26, 1912, Archives of Eaton's of Canada.

Prairie homestead women faced an endless round of household chores which they normally undertook without the aid of expensive labour-saving devices. Mending, baking, gardening, laundering, soap-making, and other tasks were daily combined with childcare responsibilities. Because farm servants were scarce and expensive for a homesteading family, the typical prairie woman also did field work, especially in times of intensive work or when the men of the homestead were absent on business or at war. The 1916 photograph above shows two women haying in Souris, Manitoba.

Credit: Jessop Collection No. 199, N3230, Manitoba Archives.

ADVICE TO A SON

Although a child left the family household that fact did not necessarily end parental control or responsibility. For example, in the following letters by a Quebec mother to her son, we find that Marie-Anne Lemine-Duguay played the roles of moral and financial advisor, found her son, Rodolphe, a job through her contacts, and acted as liaison/moderator between the son and his father.

Quebec, 1908-1909
Jeanne L'Archevêque-Duguay, ed. Lettres d'une paysanne à son fils. *(Montréal, 1977) 48, 52-53. Translated from French original. Punctuation added.*

25 November 1908

I am replying to you immediately. You have given us all the details of your expenses. That is very good. That is the best way you can take to be frugal but I think my dear Rodolphe that you misunderstood what I wanted to say to you with regard to small expenses. I did not explain myself clearly enough. It was not reproaches that I wanted to make to you, it was very simply advice that I wanted to give you. You know that a mother does not thwart her children. It seemed to me that you appeared a bit irritated with me in your last letter. If you have not spent uselessly for those things that is very good, continue, but do not take offence. You ask my permission to buy boots. We are very happy with your request. As always we will never refuse what is useful. You may buy yourself a pair. For the money, don't wait until you are given a written receipt [but ask us] several days earlier so that we have time to send it to you so you are not lacking....

9 December 1909

I have just seen Mr L _____ he told me that he does not know the priest at Sherbrooke but that he knows the priest of Richmond he says. Even though it is more English than Sherbrooke, I told him to write to Richmond that he should write tonight since that will send you right away to Richmond and you will see the priest Mr Q _____ who will give you the required references. Even though that is not exactly what you wanted, go at the request of Mr L _____ who is interested in you.

20 December 1909

At last you have succeeded in finding yourself a job. You can say thank you to Mr L _____. Don't forget to thank him. How do you find it to be at work? Try to be obliging to them and be honest and courageous....

Now let us talk about other things. We are sending you a bit of money. You will find that the amount is not very much, only four dollars. You know that money is always scarce here and your father does not want to borrow. We are sending it to you in the expectation that you pay one week of your lodging. That's all that there is in the house. We have 25 cents left. We will have difficulty buying New Year gifts if we don't receive some more. That makes 46 dollars that we have sent you since the 11th of November. As you see that's a large allowance. You will permit us to tell you that we think that you were a little extravagant in Montreal....

A STEPMOTHER AND A NEW MOTHER

"Bas" is the nickname of a British woman who travelled with a friend, Cathie, to Alberta in the first decade of the twentieth century to work briefly and to see the nation. However, Bas did not follow her plan to return to England. After her marriage to George, Bas continued for at least four years her sporadic correspondence with her friends in England. No longer a novice British woman, Bas adapted easily to marriage, motherhood, and farm work.

Stoppington, Alberta, 1911-14
"Bas" Papers, Acc. 78.79, Provincial Archives of Alberta.

October 17 - 1911
A week since I started & I hope it won't be another week before I have finished—we are awfully busy as usual & every afternoon I have been driving four horses on the disc—an implement with 16 revolving circular discs that cut the sod. It is most important to get the land prepared as far as possible (for next year's crop) before the spring comes. The season then is so short that there is no time to work the land before cropping it....

While in Calgary in July we bought a couple of ponies, one for Marvin [her stepson] & one for myself.... We have had some dandy rides & Marvin is a first-rate companion. He is eight years old, & seems to have taken a great fancy to his new mother. He is very easy to get on with, tractable, and bright, yet full of fun & he tells me I'm "just like a girl & real sport for play." He walks 2½ miles to school every day now but will not be going regularly much longer. Up to the present we have had ideal autumn weather; however it is time we expect the winter & then Marvin thinks I'll be as good a teacher as Dr Lonergan!...

28.1.12.
My dear Girls!
...What with preparing for Xmas, (which we spent at home, instead of with my brother as planned,) & preparing for a gang of threshers & a Box Social all

at the same time we were kept pretty busy. The threshers arrived just the Wednesday before Xmas & were here until Friday. I had about 18 men to feed, 7 meals in all & breakfast at 5:30 am!! Gee why! We had to go some to get the cooking done, & who said baking bread!! They were an awfully decent set of men & on the Thursday eve they worked by lamplight & early again next morning so that we could get away to a Box Social in aid of Mr Cruikshanks, our visiting minister. For the Social the ladies had to take decorated boxes or baskets with enough supper for two. The gentlemen bid at an auction & the lady had to eat supper with the buyer of her basket... Sarah's was red (crimbled paper) & silver & fetched the most £1 — mine was white muslin & pale blue & sold next highest at 10/6.... Mine was bought by a bachelor called "Slattenhaus" — an excellent young fellow, typical of our neighbours. I had taken an extra supply for the lone bachelors, so we invited a crew that couldn't buy boxes and had a great time....

Dec. 4, 1912

...We have been as busy as usual this year — all the summer I was occupied with my poultry business & had bad luck. Everybody did this year, so the season was at fault, not me! Cathie gave me five turkeys and two duck's eggs & 3 turkeys & both ducks hatched out. I have two turkey hens, & one gobler which we shall use for Xmas & I'm buying another to take his place. We have 27 young roosters ready for killing, & our own home grown pork & that with beef & fish (frozen whitefish, herring & halibut) we shall fare better than the first winter when it was beef, beef, beef, few potatoes & no garden truck. This year I put down about 10 dozen cabbages & savoys in the celler, also cauliflowers, all from my own raising & tending — & a quantity of roots... I made green tomato pickle & marrow jam from home grown stuff, so we are doing better, but as for cherries, currants, plums, pears, I forget the look of them....

Marvin grows & is the dearest fellow — always willing & a thoughtful helper. We get on well together & he is "tickled to death" to be doing his lessons at home. He attends to the chickens & the two ponies every morning, then he wipes the breakfast dishes, then he gets his lessons and does very well. Last week I made hir. a blouse & some winter knickers, which pleased him immensely....

June 14th 1913

To Lily Anna

...You ask how I am!!!!!!!! Guess!!!!! as busy as usual & more so preparing a layette for a little stranger due to arrive at the end of next month. The first three or four months I was too horribly sick to care about anything & didn't do as much sewing as I would have wished.... Sarah had a most beautiful baby boy on Sunday, March 16th — a nine-pounder — & tell Mrs Clement from me that this prairie air or life or something has a most wonderful effect on women in that condition. "Ralph Slater Ringdahl" came in less than half an hour, & though that is the quickest I know of, yet other women are never ill many hours, & I'm hoping for an easy time too. My nurse was down to see me last Sunday—Mrs Kopp, Mrs Stopp's mother, & we have been quite intimate with them ever since we had been here. Mrs Kopp is getting elderly & giving up the work as much as possible, but awfully good at such times & is in fact a fully qualified doctor....

Jan 9th 1914

...Alvin Jocelyn is the name of the marvel & we call him Alvin. He is a proper little John Bull, so fat and rosy-cheeked, saucy blue eyes & a real little eater. He is absolutely a bottle baby & is a great credit to the cows. He is 5½ month old now, & weighs 17 lbs—was 7½ at first. His morning bath is the happiest hour of the day—Marvin gave him a dear little bath tub & he just loves to disport himself in the water. He is a fine specimen of health & content & is always so happy & merry that I have to forgive him for not being a girl....

WEEKLY WORK SCHEDULE

Reading the following excerpt it is clear that the rural Ontario woman of the late nineteenth century played a crucial role in the maintenance and management of the family economy.

Ontario, 1880s-1920s
A.W. Currie, "Growing Up in Rural Ontario," 10-14, Queen's University Archives.

My grandmother, like many women of the time, organized her housework according to a strict schedule. "What would they ever think of me," she would say, "if I were to die before morning and the neighbours, coming in tomorrow, would find out that some of my work was not done or the house was dirty." Each day had its special task in addition to the normal jobs of cooking three big meals, setting and clearing the table, washing the dishes, keeping the fires going, making beds, getting the children off to school on time, cleaning the lamps and periodically filling them with coal-oil (kerosene), having a chinwag over the back fence or the telephone, and so on. How much time, thought and energy a woman devoted to her work varied widely. Some women kept their places spotless: you could eat off the floor, people said. Others were less particular. This prompted such comments as "did you ever see such a cluttered kitchen?" or "upon my soul, she hasn't dusted for the last six months," or possibly "her house looks worse than any pigpen but when they came to church, you'd think they had stepped out of a band-box."

Traditionally, Monday was washday. Just before or after breakfast, two or three big kettles and a large copper boiler 30 inches high and with a base or bottom 24 by 12 inches would be placed on the hot stove and immediately filled with water that had to be carried in from the well. Extra wood also had to be brought in and the fire stoked to the limit. Clothes were sorted into three or four piles, one for white shirts, dresses and other so-called fancy wear, another for wollens, still another for towels, dish cloths, overalls, and denim shirts which men wore about the farm. A good supply of soap—but not a wasteful amount, mark you—was added to the hot water and stirred round to make good suds. Then the pile of dainty clothes was added and, if necessary, pushed beneath the surface of the water with a stick. After the water with its load of laundry had boiled for what the housewife considered the proper length of time, she lifted the clothes out with a wooden rod, an old broom handle as a rule, and dumped them into a wooden or zinc tub. Partly filling the tub with water that was as hot as her hand could stand, she grabbed some of the clothing, wrapped it round the back of her hands, that is, across her knuckles, and then rubbed it with almost all her strength up and down the rough sheet of zinc that covered one side of the wooden washboard that she had stood in the tub. The smell of the soapy steam and the sound of mother's hands as she rubbed, indeed virtually scoured, the laundry over the corrugations of the zinc used to fascinate me. When she had scrubbed all the clothes in the tub, she would swish them round, use her hands to wring all the water she possible could from them, carry pails of dirty water outside to empty since we lacked an inside sink or drain, fill the tub again with hot, clear water, rinse the clothes, squeeze the water out of them, fluff them out before placing them in a clothes basket, and repeat the process with the other piles of clothes that had meanwhile and one after the other, been placed in vigorously boiling water on the stove. Finally, she hung the clothes on wires strung across the yard. Since pulley clothes lines were unusual in my youth, hanging out the clothes meant walking the length of the line, sometimes in deep snow, hanging the clothes, and lifting or dragging the basket containing clean but unhung clothes along behind.

A housewife might vary the process slightly if pressed for time or if, by chance, one kind of clothes was markedly larger than the others. Women with infants would have to wash almost every day and take special care that the clothes were spotless, otherwise her baby would develop diaper rash. In that event she would be put to extra expense for baby powder or be kept awake at night by a fretful child. By glancing at the clothes upon anyone's line, a smart housewife could soon judge how many people lived there, the ages of the children, the cleanliness of the house, the skill of the homemaker, and the income of the family. Thus, the contents and length of the clothes line would reveal either an extensive wardrobe or the short and simple flannels of the poor. Invariably, on laundry day a housewife would be in a rush to hustle or, as she would probably say in my youth, rustle up a meal for her hungry brood. Though I do not recollect that we ever shared in the sort of experience recorded by Samuel Pepys in his diary—today being washday, we dined on cold meat—we were not surprised to get a warmed-over dinner on Mondays.

If all went well, the clothes hanging on the line would quickly dry in the wind and sun. If the weather were unfavourable, they might get caught in a rainstorm and have to remain over-night, brought into the house while still wet and dried on lines strung up in the kitchen, or even hung out again when the weather had improved. Worse still, the clothes might be frozen on the line and have to be pulled away by half-frozen hands, care being taken, of course, not to tear the clothes. In very cold weather, however, clothes would freeze dry. In brief, doing the laundry in the days before power-driven washing machines and spin-dryers was decidedly not a job for weaklings. On the other hand, the old-fashioned method gave the clothes a fresh, clean smell that modern detergents and machinery cannot duplicate.

The special task for Tuesday was ironing. Wash and wear or no-iron fabrics were far in the future during my childhood. No man considered himself well-dressed unless he was wearing a white shirt with a detachable, stiffly starched collar and perhaps cuffs. Dickies or false shirt-fronts had gone out of fashion by 1914 or thereabouts, though one chap of roughly my age wore one to church until he was teased so much that he declared he would never be found dead in it. Collars were usually taken to a Chinese laundry in the nearby town for expert attention but the shirts as such, women's blouses, table cloths, table napkins, and even handkerchiefs had to be washed and starched at home. The amount of starch going into each article was a matter of personal preference and many a housewife declared that if the members of her family complained any more they could jolly well do their own laundry.

Electric irons were unknown on farms in my childhood since almost no rural areas were served by power lines. So a flat iron about the size of a man's hand was heated on the stove. Then it was picked up by a wooden handle with an iron base. The curved wooden grip was supposed to protect the user's hand from the heat. The metal fitted under a small cross-bar on the flat or smoothing iron and the spring was designed to hold it securely until released by pressing a knob just below the handle.

Once she had the iron off the stove, the housewife usually tested its temperature with the tip of one finger which she had previously wet in her mouth. If the temperature were too high, the iron would stick to the starch or even scorch the cloth. If it were too cold to start with or as a result of the normal cooling of a previously hot iron, the cloth would be wrinkled unless the housewife pressed down with all her strength or even hammered the cloth. Before many minutes had elapsed she would have to carry the flat iron back to the stove, disconnect the handle, and then re-fit it into another smoothing iron that had, meanwhile, become heated. Unless she were careful, the iron might become detached from the handle and land on the floor, on someone's toes, or even on the head of any small boy who had forgotten to obey his mother's order to keep well away from the ironing board and the stove. Only a few housewives had ironing boards that stood on their own legs, so to speak. Most used a board that lay on the table during use or from the table to the top of the back of a chair.

Ironing required all a woman's attention if she were to avoid burning the clothing. Besides, it was a tiring job on account of the walking, the hard pressing, and the heat. To make things worse, girls often wore pleated skirts, curtains were flimsy, table cloths were large, and dry cleaning was unknown.

Commonly all day Wednesday and frequently every evening during the week (except Sunday) were devoted to sewing, patching, knitting, darning, and crocheting. This involved more than appears on the surface. Most farmers' wives made dresses for themselves and their daughters, shirts for the males in their families, and pillow cases, cushions, and the like for the house. They also adjusted a lot of clothing, making it larger for children as they grew in size, reducing the measurements in order to fit a younger member of the family, or tearing apart the dress or suit of an adult and then remaking it to fit a youngster. Neither parent nor child was ashamed to see or wear a patch on a child's clothes, as is the case today. To save money, a thrifty housewife would darn mittens and stockings until, so it seemed, scarcely enough sound material remained to hold the darn in place. On occasion, knitted material would be unravelled and reworked. Add to all this, the crochet work on doilies and on sets for the tops of bureaus, dressers and vanities, add the needlework on pillow slips and bedspreads, on dresser scarves and cushion covers, add the work on fancy homemade baby clothes, include work on things to go into a girl's hope chest, take account of some arts like tatting and raffia work which seemed to have disappeared, put these things together and one begins to wonder where even the most industrious housewife ever found time to spend on cooking, baking, etc. Perhaps conditions were quite different in cities and in farm homes that were less providently run than ours. I do not know: but I do know what unremitting toil went on in the homes of my parents, our relatives, and our neighbours.

In my childhood, conscientious housewives set aside one day a week to give the house a "real good going over." This did not mean that cleanliness was neglected on other days of the week. Every morning the living room and kitchen were given at least "a lick and a promise." In a few homes fastidious wives swept the floor around the dining room table after every meal. A thorough going over meant sweeping out every cranny, scrubbing every square inch of floor that was scrubbable, dusting every picture, the top of every dresser, every chair, and the clock that stood on the shelf in the dining room. But cleaning did not involve applying wax which was reserved for covering the tops of jars or bottles of jam and jelly and for chipping on the floor before a neighbourly square dance or hoe-down. The parlour and the spare room needed attention only occasionally. After all, they were used but rarely and any child who by special permission was allowed in such rooms was so closely watched that he never displaced anything. Sometimes I wondered if it were safe to breathe in those rooms. Spring housecleaning took roughly a week every April or May. Before it was over I shared my father's view that we should live in tents and move elsewhere when they got dirty.

On at least one day a week, commonly on Saturday, baking was the housewife's primary occupation. Preparations often began late Friday when the dough for the week's supply of bread was prepared and left wrapped in a clean cloth and a blanket over-night, in our house usually on the corner of the settee nearest the stove. If bread-making started in the morning, small children were either sent outside or sternly warned not to jump up and down on the floor because if they did, the bread would either fail to rise at all or, having risen, would fall flat. If we behaved ourselves, we could watch our mother knead the dough, fill the pans, place them in the hot oven, and best of all, smell the hot bread as it came from the oven and was turned out from the pans on the table to cool. But bread was only part of the week's baking—at least one cake, two or three pies, a couple of dozen cookies, as well as muffins and tarts were included too. After the cakes were iced, we enjoyed cleaning out the dish. Farm families have big appetites and children needed at least one tasty tid bit for their lunch at school.

Though nearly sixty years have gone, I have vivid recollection of one bake day, November 9, 1913. A tremendous storm, the worst in history, occurred in the region of the Great Lakes and several ships with their crews were lost. My main concern—I was then only a little more than five and a half years old—was that my father who was of small build would be literally blown off the face of the earth as he walked between our house and barn, and that a nearby apple tree would be uprooted by the wind and wreck our house. As it happened, mother was baking bread and the howling wind came down the chimney with such force that it blew the damper in the stove into the "open" position. As a result the fire burnt furiously but most of the heat went up the chimney. Had this situation continued for any length of time, the oven would have cooled off and the batch of bread would have been ruined. So my sister had to sit beside the stove with one hand in a rag and hold the damper closed, that is, in such a position that the oven would heat up again. For a time she thought her job was rather funny and sang Coming through the Rye and Red

Wing, My Pretty Red Wing. By the time she had finished the second song, the oven was heating up nicely. Soon it became so hot that she herself became uncomfortable for she could not move more than a few inches away from the stove without losing control of the damper. At last, she started to cry but mother kept her on the job until the bread was done.

———————

INGENUITY

Overland travel to western homesteads limited the personal belongings, implements, and animals that could be imported. In the brief account below, George Robinson recalls the means Alberta women used to expand their poultry flocks from the few laying hens they could bring west.

Pruden's Crossing, Alberta, c. 1915
George Robinson, "Reminiscences of the South Peace River Country, 1915,"
7A, M1061, Glenbow-Alberta Institute Archives.

Another rather interesting item is how the pioneer women increased their flocks of hens. Naturally they could not bring many in over the trail and when it came time to set hens to raise chicks few had hens to spare for this chore. Well the crows were laying about that time too and so some of the women, taking careful note of the date they did it, would put chickens eggs in crows nests after removing the crows eggs and the crows would not know the difference and would hatch out chicks. Of course they would have to be retrieved the day they hatched but as they hatch in just three weeks and the farm wife knew the date she put the eggs in the nest there was no difficulty there.

———————

SUPPORTING A SOLDIER'S FAMILY

Despite government financial support to the families of World War I soldiers, many women found it difficult to make ends meet. A Mrs Farquharson from Kamloops, B.C. outlined her circumstances in the following letter of 1917 to the Prime Minister.

Kamloops, British Columbia, 1917
Mrs R.E. Farquharson to R.L. Borden, Nov. 27, 1917, Robert Laird Borden
Papers, MG 26 H, Vol. 61, 30683, Public Archives of Canada.

Kamloops, B.C.
Nov. 27th, 1917

Dear Sir—

I write to ask your opinion on which way a Soldier's wife with a family of seven should vote. As far back as I can remember we have upheld the Borden Gov. This year my husband is in France. When he enlisted (Feb. 1916) it was with the understanding that the C.P.F. [Canadian Patriotic Fund] were to make up what the Gov. lacked in providing us a living, since that time the price cost of living has gone up at least double and our allowance remains the same as it was when the C.P.F. was started. My oldest child is a girl eleven years old my youngest 15 months, the price of fuel and clothing is awful as well as the price of the plainest food-stuffs. It is impossible to keep the family on $75.00 per month. I have asked the C.P. Society also the City for help and can't even get an investigation. I am ashamed to ask from the returned men who have done so much for us. Where there is being so much money wasted and spent on Election and such, surely it is not necessary that any little one's should suffer when a small cheque of perhaps 75.00 would meet extra expenses for winter and make us comfortable....

I remain yours,
to Win-the-War
Mrs R.D. Farquharson
460 Columbia

COMMUNITY BUILDER

Pioneer western women, while engaged in the time-consuming tasks of managing families and households, also often contributed to the development of communities. One such woman, Mrs McNeil of Leslieville, Alberta, approached the problem of constructing a church with enthusiasm and considerable ingenuity.

Leslieville, Alberta, 1907
Mary C. Bailey, "Reminiscences of a Pioneer", Alberta Historical Review, XV (1967) 22.

During the ensuing months this lady [Mrs McNeil] played an important part in the lives and doings of the Leslieville community. It was she who first saw the need of a church building, and promptly started to do something about it. The McNeils were Methodists, but the country was fast filling up with people of different beliefs, and little attention was paid to denomination. Mrs McNeil evolved a plan whereby a building could be built by the settlers themselves all working together. Meetings were called and plans were made to decide the size of the building. The site was already settled as Mr Bureau had generously donated a square plot of land measuring half an acre. As most of the homesteaders were interested in the project, they went to work promptly and in a short time the required number of logs were hauled and piled at the building site. They were of spruce, cut from tall, straight timber which abounded in this western district, but had to be "dressed" or shaped for building by being hewed on opposite sides to a uniform thickness of about six inches.

To get this accomplished, Mrs McNeil called on all the settlers for a "hewing bee". Not every man who could chop wood was an expert at hewing, but all who were able turned out, and the hewing began. Some of the women of the district, led by Mrs McNeil, brought lunch at noon for the workmen, and a good start was made. The first few bees were well attended, but gradually homestead duties and other important matters made it increasingly difficult for Mrs McNeil to get a bee together. Once she sent penny postal cards around; another effort was an announcement in the post office reading; "WANTED—1,000 men for a worthy cause! Payment—Virtue is its own reward."

The hewing of the logs was finally completed, and everyone helped in the erection of the building. This job of chinking was undertaken by the women. The men fashioned paddles from poplar wood for putting on the mortar, and it was a gala day for all concerned. In those days any occasion that brought people together was a social affair, a time for fun and good-natured jollity, generally with something to eat, which was always a treat to those who happened to be bachelors. Afterwards a nephew of Mrs McNeil cleaned the paddles and decorated them, finishing them with the date of the occasion; I still have my paddle....

A DOCTOR'S HELP

Mrs B.R. Arends and her husband settled near Jasper, Alberta in December 1915 and worked on a dairy farm. The next year they moved into the town and Mrs Arends was asked to assist the doctor. We cannot tell from Mrs Arends' reminiscences whether she was a paid assistant or not, but we can identify her voluntary role as a protector of community mores in her quest for the father of the baby from McBride.

Jasper, Alberta, 1916
"Reminiscences of Mrs B.R. Arends," 1-2, Acc. 67.92/7, Provincial Archives of Alberta.

We hadn't been in Jasper long when Dr Gow called and asked if I would help him. There was no hospital here and no one to help him with the sick. I told him I had no experience whatever with sick people so didn't think I'd be much help. He said:—come and help me and I'll teach you as we go along,—and he did just that. We got along fine and we never lost a patient,—many babies were born that year, all at home under the most primitive circumstances,—no running water, no electric lights, no plumbing,—just prayers and hard work.

One day a young woman came from McBride. She said she was pregnant and didn't want to disgrace her people by staying in McBride, so would I please keep her until it was all over. She had not told the baby's father. I took her in, and then proceeded to find that father. Time was passing and her time very near. Finally I found him, sent him a wire and he came, after a few days. They talked it over and decided to marry,—but—he had to go back to Edson for the license and the trains only ran every third day,—which meant waiting for the train to go east, and then a wait for the return trip. Besides that, the preacher came only once in two weeks. Oh! Those day of anxious waiting! Finally on Christmas eve the preacher came. Her pains started! We couldn't find the doctor! However, the preacher started the wedding ceremony with them using my wedding ring which was big enough to fit two of her fingers! The pains were real by this time, and the bridegroom was kneeling beside the bed saying his "I do's." The baby was born just as the doctor walked in and the preacher and the bridegroom were going out the door. We didn't have nerves in those days and in an hour's time the house had quieted and we were all fast asleep.

NO OCCUPATION

The following brief poem satirizing the occupational classification of wives and mothers outlines poignantly the work of farm wives.

1910
"No Occupation," Farmer's Advocate and Home Journal, *June 10, 1910.*

NO OCCUPATION
She rose before daylight made crimson the east
For duties that never diminished

And never the sun when it sank in the west
Looked down upon work that was finished.
She cooked unending processions of meals,
Preserving and canning and baking.
She swept and she dusted
She washed and she scrubbed,
With never a rest for the taking.
A family of children she brought in the world
Raised them and trained them and taught them.
She made all the clothes and patched, mended and darned
Till miracles seemed to have wrought them.
She watched by the bedside of sickness and pain
Her hand cooled the raging of fever.
Carpentered, painted, upholstered and scraped
And worked just as hard as a beaver.
And yet as a lady-of-leisure, it seems,
The government looks on her station
For now, by the rules of the census report
It enters her—No Occupation.

---

3. THE PAID WORK OF MARRIED WOMEN

DAY CARE

For poor women in the late nineteenth century, work outside the home was often necessary to supplement the family income. For such women who had young children, some form of child care was required during their working hours. At times other women or elder children of the family or the community might perform these functions. In other cases, charitable day care centres were available under the auspices of religious orders or, as was the case in St Henri, of laywomen.

St Henri, Quebec, 1881
Petition, 1881, Commissioners of Catholic Schools of Montreal, Archives of the Catholic School Board of Montreal.

Messieurs the Commissioners of Schools for the City of St Henri.
Messieurs
The undersigned have the great honour to humbly [petition] you:
    That for almost two years Miss Sophie Olivier has devoted all her time to the teaching of young childen in the district of St Augustin. —

That the services rendered by this admirable devotion are of the most obvious use: in that poor families or women without resources who live on outside work, would have been obliged to stay at home if they did not have this charitable school to entrust with all safety the care of their children.

That nothing has ever been done by the public, or by the authorities to come to relieve and in aid of this devoted person—

That, without any doubt a moderate assistance would be a great good and would assure the existence of this charitable school, destined without a doubt, we repeat with confidence, to render immense service to our young children.

That in confidence, a certain sum will be voted by the schools corporation to this noble end (five dollars per month plus rent).

And the undersigned will not cease to pray.

Felise Borduas and 35 others

St Henri, 19 June 1881

To Mr A. Deseve
Secretary-Treasurer of Schools
for the Municipality of St Henri,
Sir,

I acknowledge receiving your letter by which you make me party to the deliberations of the meeting of the School Commissioners for the Municipality of St Henri at the session of 27 May 1881.

I accept...in submitting myself to the regulations of Messieurs the Commissioners, the 50 dollars which you have accorded to the *asile,* because the needs of this establishment which are always growing make it necessary to hire an assistant mistress, and with this allocation, it will be possible for me to provide for these expenses.

But as it may be the case that this is not enough, therefore I reserve the right to discontinue when I judge it necessary....

Sophie Olivier

———————

PIECE-WORK AT HOME

While propertied women expected not to work for wages, many working-class women continued to contribute to the family income after their marriages by factory work, taking in boarders, or sewing on piece-work at home. The piece-work system had a particular advantage for mothers because it allowed them to combine child care with paid work. Because such work was in demand, however, women received poor wages and strict penalties for tardiness or imperfect sewing.

1896
Royal Commission on the Sweating System in Canada, Report, *1896, 45.*

Mr.O. Donoghue
"You say that in the custom trade it is nearly all by piece work. Do the men and women get the same pay for like work?" (The Commissioner had asked whether the piece-work system obtained more generally among male or female employees).
Mr. Sims (replying to Mr. O. Donoghue)
"Far from it"
Mr. O.D.—"In other words I might understand that if I were getting a particular style of suit made to order, a man working on it could get one price but if a woman made that suit for the same employer and the two articles being equally well made she would not get as much for her work but I would pay the same price for the suit to the master tailor. I would not get any advantage from the lower price of the woman's labour. I understand you to say that she would not get as much."
Mr. Sims—"Not by one-half."
The Commissioner—"That is a mean kind of sweating."
Mr. Sims—"You must understand that these women deal directly with the master tailors. They take the garment out, agreeing upon the price they are to get for them and that is generally one-half less than a man could get for the same garment."
Mr. O.D.—"The only inference to be drawn from this—an employer would scarcely miss an opportunity of sending as much as possible of any work into the woman's hands.".
Mr. Sims—"Exactly."

A TEACHER IN COBALT

With the discovery of silver in the northern Ontario area around Cobalt, male fortune-seekers created makeshift towns of tents and shacks. To this male society, Elizabeth MacEwen came to join her husband and eventually teach school, thus belying the assumption, which was increasingly held by the turn of the century, that married women could not or should not continue to teach.

Ontario, 1906
Elizabeth MacEwen, "Early Days in Cobalt," 21-22, Elizabeth MacEwen Papers, MG 31 H7, Public Archives of Canada.

...into this picture [of Cobalt] I stepped about the time of changing from tents to shacks. My adventures began early, on the way from North Bay part of the road-bed had been washed out and the track had fallen away for quite a distance—We all had to leave our train, walk across the trestle over the dizzy ravine and then board another train which had come this far to meet us.

It was highly exciting as you may imagine but as I was the only "girl" I had plenty of assistance—"men to the right of me—men to the left of me" and so I was borne safely across—

When we arrived at Cobalt station I looked out on the biggest crowd of all men I had ever seen in my life....

Not a month before this my husband had come to live, care for and do some prospecting on a claim my brother owned next to the Hudson Bay claims.

The men who had been working this claim had built a log cabin and *Pete* plastered papered and made this cabin into a pretty cosy little place for me.

...I can still see that inside room so clean and white as I stepped in that first night—I though those shiny nails all placed in neat rows up and down the walls just about the loveliest decoration I had ever seen and it thrilled me more than any fine house I have looked at since because I felt at once the love and high hopes back of it all. It was this crude little home we set out [to] that night over that rough narrow wet trail.

One of the first to see that the camp would develop into a permanent town was Dr McDougal, who was then a school inspector living in North Bay.

He began agitating for a school but no one paid much attention as the population was mostly men whose only thought was finding a silver mine and going back home.

However, it soon became evident that it would take years to mine all the available ore and so men began to bring their wives and families and to build more permanent homes known as tar-paper shacks, many of which we still have.

Then it was that men were eager for a school.

This school was one of the first little buildings of any size to be erected. the next difficulty was to get a teacher which seemed almost impossible.

Dr McDougal who had been an old friend of ours finally persuaded me to take charge, so in the early spring of 1906, we gathered our belongings on a crude sleigh & the driver hauled them over stumps and rocks. Altho they were pitched hither & yon they were patiently gathered up again till we got them safely into a little house near the school, owned by Wilfred Donaldson, who asked and got $35.00 for the one room which we thought extortion then.

I opened the school in March with an attendance of 12, this rapidly grew to over 100 pupils by the end of June—

They were wonderful boys and girls in those early days of making and building the town of Cobalt—they seemed to sense it was their job as well as mine to keep peace and order so that all could [get] the most out of this opportunity opened for them....

I finally divided the number took the older ones in the morning and the little ones in the afternoon. By the way I received $50 per month for this work of teaching!!

We at first had no blackboards—a big wood stove in the centre, some seats but the little ones sat on a platform which ran along the front....

We had many children from Poland, Finland Sweden United States and so on....

CLEANERS TO PARLIAMENT

The paid work of married women often has been viewed as secondary, supplementing the family's income. This position was not shared by the charwomen on Parliament Hill, some of whom were household heads. They argued in their petition to the Civil Service Commission that they required a wage increase because they were the principal support of their families.

Ottawa, 1908
Minutes of Evidence, Royal Commission on the Civil Service, Canada, Sessional Papers, No. 29a, 1908, 225-26.

To the Royal Commission.
The humble petition of the charwomen in the employment of the Dominion Government, showeth.
We the charwomen in the employment of the Dominion Government respectfully solicit the attention of your honourable body to our application for consideration in the matter of an increase of salary. The present remuneration for services rendered by charwomen is at the rate of seventy-five cents per day, for six days in the week only, notwithstanding that we are obliged to be at the service of our employers for the remaining day without additional pay, whenever they find it necessary to call upon us. Many of our number are obliged to maintain families on the small wages so earned. Aside from the argument of the increased cost of living during recent years—and the difficulty of obtaining a reasonable livelihood from such salary, we submit that considering the arduous character of the work alone we are entitled to more substantial remuneration than the amount we receive.
We would also direct your honourable committee's attention to the fact that the charwomen of the Senate (who are not parties to this petition) are now

receiving the sum of one dollar per day for work of an exactly similar character to that which we are called upon to perform for smaller remuneration. For the reasons aforementioned, we would respectfully request your honourable committee to take into your consideration the substance of this petition—which we will be pleased to supplement with such further information as may be required—and to make such report thereon as may be in accordance with the justice of our demands.

And your petitioners will ever pray.

> Mrs Lizzie Walsh
> President of Committee
> Josephine Ouimet
> Secretary

"THE PREPAREDNESS OF HER WOMEN"

The wives of fishermen on the coasts of Nova Scotia, New Brunswick and the Gulf of the St Lawrence had traditionally worked cleaning and drying the catches of their husbands. However, with the absence of men during the war and increased prices and demand for foodstuff, their work became not only recognized but also paid and lauded. From the following patriotic account of the "preparedness" of fishing women, one is left to wonder whether their efforts were motivated by nationalism as the writer believes or more by the cash that they could earn for their families.

Nova Scotia and Quebec, 1917-18
Victoria Hayward, "Women Workers of Canada," The Canadian Magazine, *L (1917-18) 390-91.*

The preparedness of her women is one of the most marvellous things about Canada in the eyes of the people of the United States. A visitor cannot help being struck by the utter lack of self-consciousness in the strong hardy women encountered in the fishing districts, at work, in all sorts of weather, on the fish. Their greeting is as direct and cordial as that of any hostess in our best homes. Strong, fine women with frank, honest, gentle manners that bid you welcome. Rugged figures that stand out boldly against the gray tones of the drying fish and the up-creeping fog. A people themselves full of trust and confidence, they inspire you with the same. The whole-heartedness with which they go about the task of washing, salting and spreading fish, morning, noon and night, week in and week out, in order that the worlds' supply of fish—a war-food if there ever was one—may measure up to the greater requirements of these times, is in itself inspiring. A group of them at work upon the great fish stages, against a background of gray sea roughening into white combers under a fresh breeze blowing out from dew clouds overhead, makes a dramatic scene the like of which one would expect to find only in the old world; yet here it is, equal in character to Breton coast scenes depicted by the best French artists. And why not? Are not these fisher folk of our Cape Breton shores of the same hardy, courageous stock? All along the Nova Scotia shores remnants of scattered Acadians work side by side with English Royalist and Highland Gael. Even in the far-away Magdalen Islands, in the Gulf of St Lawrence, ice-bound and cut off from communication with the mainland during all the winter months, the French *habitant* women work in the fish unceasingly, going a step farther than their sisters on the mainland, in that they dig the clams which are used as bait for cod and mackerel, in order that the men may spend longer hours at the actual work of fishing, the Canadian Government having sent out a plea at the beginning of this last fishing season to the fifty thousand fishermen of upper Atlantic coast to fish just two hours longer each day in order that the country might meet the war requirements for fish.

The lassie with the Breton cap, standing ankle-deep in water, is one of these women farmers-of-the-sea. With the home-made fork in her hand, which may be taken as the trident of victory, she turns the mud of the ocean bed when the tide is out, working as long as it is safe, unearthing the buried treasures, of which she holds a full basket in her right hand.

When not working at the fish and the clams, as at this time, the Islander betakes herself to the loom.... Many of these women are doing work formerly done by men now at the Front, so that in addition to an actual increase in the production of the farms they have also volunteered, in the language of the knitter, to pick up "the dropped stiches." Of course, the great thing about these women is they have all recognized and grasped their opportunity! They have all welcomed the stress of the times. They have all given and are giving unstintingly of their life's blood in their men; and they are rising to heights of record-breaking endeavour to fill the depleted ranks on the farm and the fishing at home. It does the heart good to hear the woman of Grande Pré tell you her record this year for apple-picking....

CHAPTER FIVE

BREAKING THE MOULD

The lives of Canadian women changed from generation to generation in the half century after Confederation. The young girls who went in such extraordinary numbers from the countryside into the cities,[1] the young wives who stayed on at their waged work after marriage, and the young mothers who decided to plan for small families all broke from established patterns, both those lived by their female relatives and those their communities idealized in women. It would be wrong to characterize these private decisions of rural and working-class women as passive accommodations, actions that pressed them into the mould rather than broke the conventions set for them by their culture. All of these decisions challenged past practice, involved risk and the conscious calculation of how to turn changing circumstances to personal advantage.

There were, however, other women more self-consciously involved in social change. These predominantly middle-class female reformers were not necessarily more courageous or more selfless than the girls and women who exercised their choices predominantly in the spheres of the family or working-class employment. In their assaults upon the universities, the professions, and the state, they took no greater chances, ventured no further from the sources of community support, were no more altruistic than their less propertied or less publicized sisters. Yet their struggles deserve some special attention. Because they were self-conscious, they were more likely to leave behind in their reminiscences clues about why they were innovators and how their demands for change emerged from the contradictions in their culture. They acted from self-interest. Yet because their own needs led them to challenge formal institutions of education and government, they established precedents that helped their female descendents and forced changes that percolated down to influence other less privileged women.

In comfortable urban homes, and some rural ones, in late nineteenth-century Canada, female education had gained a certain measure of acceptability, in some quarters had even become fashionable. The daughters of such families left private academies, convent schools, collegiate institutes, or high schools in their late teens with more than a genteel introduction to literature and embroidery. Their training probably did not include Latin and did not prepare them for other university subjects.[2] Still, teachers in both the private academies and the public schools imbued their students with a sense of self-worth and class obligation that led some young women to view medicine or teaching as the logical extension of their earlier schooling. Reason awakened, Agnodice[3] rejected the possibility that "the aim of my education was only to be accomplished by a constant round of garden-parties, balls and receptions" and set her sights upon the university.

Sometimes the influence of school mistresses was less subliminal. The teacher who prepared Maude Abbott for university entrance, eager that the prestige of her school be enhanced, prevailed upon the Abbott family to allow Maude to take up a McGill scholarship.[4] Women who followed careers in public school teaching turned to the suffrage movement as an elaboration of their work in the classroom and also, in at least two Canadian provinces, founded women teachers' associations to further their professional interests.[5] Female physicians played a prominent role in the campaign for women's rights.[6] More informally, networks of educated ladies "of rather advanced views" intervened with professional men from their own social circles to advance the cause of worthy young women. Maude Abbott was admitted to medical school through the intercession of such a group. Mount Allison opened its doors to women students in 1862; Queen's granted its first degree to a woman in 1878, Dalhousie in 1881, McMaster and University College, Toronto in 1884.[7] Gradually the number of female baccalaureates increased[8] and the tradition of helpfulness among peers grew stronger, formalized with the founding of the Canadian Federation of University Women in 1919.

As university women drew support from others of their class, women of strong religious conviction embarked upon unconventional work and championed unconventional causes guided and sustained by others among the faithful. Canadians remained devout. Revivalist movements were popular. Overseas evangelical work and the home missions demanded a wide-ranging competence of women who accepted the call.[9] Late in the nineteenth century the social gospel movement led Canadian Protestants to a broader definition of their spiritual responsibilities in the temporal world. This change drew Christian women to reconsider the appropriate boundaries between the private and the public sphere. Rather than being impediments, the specialized domestic skills of wives and mothers became qualifications for their more full participation in public life. Women who came together in farm institutes, temperance clubs, and patriotic societies learned the fine points of public speaking, debating, and Roberts' rules and examined contemporary policy issues from a woman's point of view confident that their political concern arose naturally from Christian conscience.[10]

The nuns of Quebec had long formed the backbone of that province's social welfare system. Female religious staffed hospitals, schools, orphanages, and refuges. In the late nineteenth century their helping role expanded to meet the needs of a larger and more urbanized population. Convent schools incorporated typing, bookkeeping and domestic science into their courses of study. City convents offered shelter and guidance to young women recently arrived in the city. The day nurseries and children's homes run by female religious offered relief to mothers in distress, helped fragmenting families to weather troubled periods, and allowed couples to sustain larger families knowing that emergency support was near to hand. Internally, religious orders were highly self-sufficient communities governed by democratically elected officers. Externally they owed absolute obedience to the male hierarchy of the church.[11]

The upper class Catholic lay women who became interested in educational, social, and political reform at the turn of the century found after a period of experimentation that this same model of internal democracy and external deference was the only one tenable in contemporary Quebec. Laywomen and nuns worked together to found an advanced studies institute for women, later called Le Collège Marguerite Bourgeoys, and a school of household science, to inform senior students about women's rights and disabilities under the civil law and to organize study circles on issues of social welfare and Catholic doctrine. Much of this work was conducted by groups loosely affiliated under the Fédération Nationale St-Jean-Baptiste, a group formed in 1907 by Catholic Québécoises unhappy with the assertive British Protestantism of the National Council of Women. An alliance of lay people and Catholic religious was more attractive to Quebec women. This choice did, however, bind all women active in public life to the limits fixed by the church.[12]

Education and religious conviction made women more confident participants in public life. With the granting of female suffrage, an obvious barrier to their full political rights was removed. By 1920, Canadian women could vote in all jurisdictions except Prince Edward Island and Quebec,[13] where suffrage agitation was limited by church injunction.

The franchise had traditionally been closely associated in law with property ownership and some individual female landholders had cast ballots in British North America sustained by this qualification. Under English law, however, married women could not hold property: "By marriage, the husband and wife are one person in law: that is, the very being or legal existence of the woman is suspended during the marriage."[14] Quebec wives thus were disenfranchised by the application of English law to Lower Canadian land transfers in 1831 and between 1820 and 1860 similar criteria were used to determine that women could not vote in various British North American colonies.[15] From mid-century British women had agitated for female property rights in marriage[16] and in the years immediately after Confederation their success spilled over into Canada. The Married Women's Property Act of 1872 (35 Vic. c. 16) allowed married women in Ontario to hold and dispose of property as if they were unmarried, and to enter into contracts.[17] By the end of the century similar provisions applied in most other provinces.

Property stipulations were most significant for the municipal franchise and it was in these jurisdictions that women first regained the vote, initially unmarried women and widows in Ontario in 1884 (47 Vic. c. 32). This grant left open the way for natural rights and equal rights arguments for the extension of the suffrage. As Letitia Youmans wrote in 1893, "'It is a poor rule that won't work both ways.' If only widows and spinsters are allowed to vote, then surely bachelors and widowers should be the only men eligible to the same privilege."[18] Christian reformers joined urban professionals in the suffrage campaign, hoping to increase the proportion of sober and morally upright voters. Radical women in Toronto, Vancouver, and Montreal published compelling philosophical arguments for broadening the franchise. The provincial vote came first, however, to women in western Canada, a region in which reform and natural rights considerations were buttressed by a recognition among the wider population of women's productive role in agriculture.[19]

Access to higher education, the professions, the franchise, and political office, none of these was a small accomplishment. With them came another change, liberation in the most literal sense, reform in female fashions. In the 1840s and '50s some American women active in temperance and anti-slavery campaigns abandoned the stays, corsets, and hooped skirts that hindered them in their political work for a looser costume. Upstate New York temperance advocates designed an outfit which by combining long loose-fitting pantaloons, the bloomers, with a shortened skirt allowed a woman comfort, modesty and freedom of movement. The costume gained favour with only a minority—the suggestion that both women and men should wear pants could not thrive in a culture that increasingly emphasized the differences in female and male natures. By 1890 fashionable urban women "wore an average of 37 pounds of street costume in the winter months, of which 19 pounds was suspended from the waist."[20] This clothing made women sick, most characteristically induced pain, torpor, hysteria, convulsions, and prolapsed uteri,[21] and so thoroughly limited their physical activity as to be unwearable in the performance of philanthropic, social, and political work. By the early twentieth century women had begun to trade their corsets for less confining waist belts and to experiment with two-piece costumes, narrower sleeves, and less full skirts, searching for a style of dress which would protect and cover the body but not restrict movement.

Still, women's activities were constrained by their isolated domestic workplaces, their sole responsibility for child care, and an ever greater emphasis upon the distinctiveness of male and female labour. Women had acquired political rights, education, and social services without challenging the doctrine of separate spheres. This final battle, to establish that love, work, and nurture were male or female by culture not by nature, and thus were susceptible to change, was the most difficult of all. Some English-Canadian women (following Charlotte Perkins Gilman and the American material feminists, and Edward Carpenter and the British sex radicals) broached these questions, advocating communal or mobile kitchens, cooperative housekeeping, collective child-rearing, and androgynous expectations in intimate life. But these calls sounded so far from the mainstream that they could not be heard, let alone heeded.[22]

The final section of this chapter deals with women who deviated from the expected roles of their culture, among them the solitaries, the prostitutes, and those who had committed or were accused of committing capital offences. With the exception of Carrie Best's mother,[23] they are all single women, and their situations illustrate the stark dilemmas of women without men in an economic system in which subsistence was supremely difficult for a woman alone.[24] Most of them were women who by the fact of living outside family seemed threatening. By the standards of our time, their eccentricities are almost undetectable. It was principally their independence that made them seem unnatural. They became the butts of children's jokes and neighbours' suspicion by wearing men's clothes even with the justification that they were more sturdy and unrestricting, by travelling alone even if the journeys were also missions of mercy, by doing men's field work even if the circumstances that brought them to this predicament were common community knowledge. And after a time they no longer appear to have worried what the world thought of them.

NOTES

1 The European discussion of this phenomenon is extremely interesting. See for example Abel Chatelain, "Les usines internats et les migrations féminines dans la région lyonnaise," *Revue d'histoire économique et sociale,* XLVIII (1970) 373-94 and Louise A. Tilly, Joan W. Scott, and Miriam Cohen, "Women's Work and European Fertility Patterns," *Journal of Interdisciplinary History,* VI (1976) 447-76. See the discussion of rural/urban migration among young women in Joy Parr, *Labouring Children* (Montreal, 1980) chapter 7. There is an interesting analysis of similar choices among Maritime women and men in A.A. Brookes, "Family, Youth and Leaving Home in Late Nineteenth Century Rural Nova Scotia: Canning and the Exodus, 1868-1893," in Joy Parr, *Childhood and Family in Canadian History* (Toronto, 1982).
2 Veronica Strong-Boag, "Canada's Women Doctors: Feminism Contrained," in Linda Kealey, ed., *A Not Unreasonable Claim* (Toronto, 1979) 111.
3 See "Letters on the Education and Employment of Women," in this chapter.
4 See Maude Abbott's 'Autobiographical Sketch' in this chapter titled "Struggles for Higher Education".
5 Wendy Bryans, "'Virtuous Women at Half the Price': the Feminization of Teaching and Women's Teachers' Organizations, 1875-1900," unpublished MA thesis, University of Toronto, 1974, and Apolonja Kojder, "The Saskatoon Women Teachers' Association: A Demand for Recognition," *Saskatchewan History,* XXX (1977).
6 Strong-Boag, "Canada's Women Doctors;" Carlotta Hacker, *The Indomitable Lady Doctors* (Toronto, 1974); Joanne L. Thompson, "The Influence of Dr. Emily Howard Stowe on the Woman Suffrage Movement in Canada," *Ontario History* LIV (1962) 253-66.
7 Ramsay Cook and Wendy Mitchinson, eds., *The Proper Sphere: Women's Place in Canadian Society* (Toronto, 1976) chapter 3; John Squair, "Admission of Women to the University of Toronto," *University of Toronto Monthly* (Feb.-Mar. 1924).
8 Robin S. Harris, *A History of Higher Education in Canada 1663-1960* (Toronto, 1976) 625-27; Statistics Canada, *Historical Compendium of Education Statistics* (Ottawa, 1978) 216-17.

9   Mrs John McDougall, "Incidents of Mission Life, 1874," *Alberta Historical Review* XIV (1966) 26-29; Mrs Robert Holmes, "Experiences of a Missionary's Wife," *Alberta Historical Review* XII (1964) 18-25; S.A. Archer, comp., *A Heroine of the North* (Toronto, 1929); Rosalind Gosforth, *Climbing* (Toronto, 1940); "A Mission" and "A VON in Labrador" in this chapter; Wendy Mitchinson, "Canadian Women and Church Missionary Societies in the Nineteenth Century: a Step toward Independence," *Atlantis* II (1977) 57-75. The educational and religious predispositions to broaden women's sphere often reinforced one another. See for example V. Strong-Boag, "Canada's Women Doctors," 121-23.

10 The standard treatment of the social gospel is Richard Allen, *The Social Passion* (Toronto, 1973). The earlier period, when this transformation was taking place is discussed in his "The Social Gospel and the Reform Tradition in Canada, 1890-1928," *Canadian Historical Review*, XLIX (1968). Veronica Strong-Boag deals with the influence of this theological change upon Nellie McClung in her introduction to *In Times Like These* (Toronto, 1972); Beatrice Brigden describes her own work in the social gospel movement in "One Woman's Campaign for Social Purity and Social Reform," in Richard Allen, ed., *The Social Gospel in Canada* (Ottawa, 1975) 36-62 and excerpted in this chapter. See also Wendy Mitchinson, "The WCTU: For God, Home, and Native Land," in Kealey, *A Not Unreasonable Claim*, 161-67 and her "The YWCA and Reform in the Nineteenth Century," *Histoire sociale/Social History* XII (1979) 368-84.

11 Bettina Bradbury, "The Fragmented Family: Family Strategies in the Face of Death, Illness and Poverty, Montreal 1860-1885," in J. Parr, ed., *Childhood and Family in Canadian History,* (Toronto, 1982); Marta Danylewycz, "Taking the Veil in Montreal, 1840-1920: An Alternative to Marriage, Motherhood and Spinsterhood," unpublished Ph.D Thesis, University of Toronto, 1981; Micheline Dumont-Johnson, "Des garderies au XIXᵉ siècle: les salles d'asile des Soeurs Grises à Montréal," *Revue d'histoire de l'amérique française,* (September, 1978).

12 Marie Lavigne, Yoland Pinard and Jennifer Stoddart, "La Fédération Nationale St-Jean-Baptiste," in Linda Kealey, ed., *A Not Unreasonable Claim;* Marta Danylewycz, "Changing Relationships: Nuns and Feminists in Montreal, 1890-1925," *Histoire sociale/Social History* (November, 1981); Micheline Dumont-Johnson, "Les communautés religieuses et la condition féminine," *Recherches sociographiques* (janvier-avril, 1978); Susan Mann Trofimenkoff, *The Dream of Nation* (Toronto, 1982) chapter 12.

13 In 1916 women received the right to vote in provincial elections in Alberta, Manitoba, and Saskatchewan. Ontario and British Columbia followed in 1917. The federal franchise was granted to women in 1918. The provincial franchise was extended in Nova Scotia in 1918 and in New Brunswick in 1920. Prince Edward Island gave women the vote in 1922. Quebec women waited until 1940 to receive the vote.

14 This discussion is based largely upon the carefully prepared note by Susan Altschul and Christine Carron, "Chronology of Some Legal Landmarks in the History of Canadian Women," *McGill Law Journal* XXI (1975) 476-94.

15 John Garner, *The Franchise and Politics in British North America, 1755-1867* (Toronto, 1969).

16 Lee Holcombe, "Victorian Wives and Property: Reform of the Married Women's Property Law, 1857-1882," in Martha Vicinus, *A Widening Sphere* (Bloomington, 1977) 3-28; H. Lesser, "Acquisition of *Inter Vivos* Matrimonial Property Rights in English Law, a Doctrinal Melting Pot," *University of Toronto Law Journal,* XXIII (1973) 145-214.

17 Altschul and Carron, "Chronology," 477.

18 Letitia Youmans, "Campaign Echos," in this chapter.

19 June Menzies, "Votes for Women in Saskatchewan," in Norman Ward and Duff Spafford, eds., *Politics in Saskatchewan* (Don Mills, 1968) 78-92; Carol Bacchi, "Divided Allegiances: The Response of Farm and Labour Women to Suffrage," and *Liberation Deferred? The Ideas of the English-Canadian Suffragists, 1877-1918* (Toronto, 1982); Deborah Gorham, "Flora MacDonald Denison: Canadian Feminist," in Kealey, *A Not Unreasonable Claim;* Barbara Latham and Cathy Kess, *In Her Own Right* (Victoria, 1980).

20 John S. Haller and Robin M. Haller, *The Physician and Sexuality in Victorian America* (Urbana, 1974) 31.

21 William Leach, *True Love and Perfect Union, The Feminist Reform of Sex and Society* (New York, 1980) Chapter Nine.

22 Deborah Gorham, "Flora Macdonald Denison," in Linda Kealey, *A Not Unreasonable Claim;* Jennifer Stoddart and Veronica Strong-Boag, "...And Things were Going Wrong at Home,", *Atlantis* (Fall, 1975) 42; Dolores Hayden, *The Grand Domestic Revolution* (Cambridge, Mass., 1981); Ramsay Cook, "Francis Marion Beynon and the Crisis of Christian Reformism," in Carl Berger and Ramsay Cook, eds., *The West and the Nation* (Toronto, 1976).

23 See "Like a Lioness With her Cubs", in this chapter.

24 See "Charged with Manslaughter", in this chapter.

1. EDUCATION AND NEW APPROACHES TO WORK

LETTERS ON THE EDUCATION AND EMPLOYMENT OF WOMEN

The anonymous "Agnodice" published a series of letters passionately advocating women's rights to public activity, education, and remunerative employment in *The Canadian Educational Monthly* in 1879. The first of these, excerpted below, argued strongly for woman's right to pursue a useful profession and against marriage as the sole vocation in a woman's life.

1879
Agnodice, "Letters on the Education and Employment of Women: Letter I,"
The Canada Educational Monthly, *(1879) 202-203.*

Dear Clyte,

I HAVE not forgotten my promise to commence a correspondence with you on my return from abroad. Yes! your Agnodice (for I still keep the old name you gave me at school) is at home again with her brother and sister. My brother has already settled down to his books and his studies, and his good, kind wife is immersed once more in her housekeeping affairs. To him, whether or no his last work will be favourably reviewed, is the most important consideration in the world; to her, the rise and fall of eggs or butter is the topic of the utmost importance. As for myself, I am still, dear Clyte, revolving in my mind the idea of following some profession. I know you are orthodox enough to be shocked at this, even in the face of the advanced views of the present day, but I shall meet your arguments, and I hope conquer them.

I am young, strong and determined. No one has a claim on my time as your delicate mother has on yours. Why should I be obliged to give up to Society, to whom, as yet, I owe nothing, the most active and vigorous part of my life? Is the aim of my education only to be accomplished by a constant round of garden-parties, balls, and receptions, — if so, why have I been taught anything else, but to read, write, dance, enter a room gracefully, and chirp a feeble song to a wandering and uncertain accompaniment? These acquirements would have been enough to have given me a footing in what is called Society. No! I cannot submit to that kind of thing; I must have a purpose, a life-work, a determined end in what I undertake. Such a purpose my sister sets before me in marriage! It is no wonder marriages are so unhappy, when they are put before girls as the end, the thing to be achieved, "the one thing needful" in their lives. When we struggle for a thing, when we fight for a prize, at least we expect, with reason, that the thing shall be worth the winning. If, in archery, we gain a golden arrow, we have a right to be disgusted if the prize turn out to be of counterfeit metal, and the arrow cannot expect to be treated with the admiration and respect that would be given it if it were genuine. This is truly the way our future husbands are held up to us, and the result must often, of course, be disappointment and despair....

So with these opinions you will not be surprised when I tell you I seriously intend studying for a profession, and I think I have chosen the medical. I am of course aware that at present women are not admitted to degrees, and that when they practise, it can be only as quacks, but I shall go though with the regular curriculum, as so many have done, in the hope that by the time I have passed all my examinations, these disabilities will have been removed....

STRUGGLES FOR HIGHER EDUCATION

Dr Maude Abbott's memoirs provide interesting evidence of the effects of the conflicting views on woman's proper sphere for one individual woman. Consumed with the desire for a higher education and for medical training on the one hand, on the other, Maude Abbott was reluctant to overturn traditional views about her family obligations, publicity, and even the appropriateness of a woman's attendance at certain operations.

Montreal, Quebec, 1885-94
Maude Elizabeth Seymour Abbott, "Autobiographical Sketch", March 31, 1928, Osler Library of the History of Medicine, McGill University Acc. 606/2. Reprinted in McGill Medical Journal, *XXVIII (1959).*

Brought up in the country by my beloved grandmother, and educated with my only sister entirely at home except for one year in Montreal at Miss Symmers and Smith School, I was fortunate in that this school was for the first time sending up a class to McGill for the June Associate in Arts examination, as the matriculation was then called. I had been very unevenly prepared in the country, well up in French and history and literature, and yet knowing nothing whatever of Latin and algebra or geometry and very little of arithmetic; but I was consumed by a great thirst for the school work, and hurled myself into it with a tremendous zest, with a result that I was so fortunate as to win the Scholarship into McGill from the school.

Had it not been for this happening, I should probably not be here today, for an Arts education for a girl was at that time considered a quite unnecessary luxury and it was exceedingly difficult for me to be spared a second year from home. But Miss Symmers wanted her first scholarship taken up for the honour of her schoool, so pressure was brought to bear at home, and I was permitted to come. Accordingly I came down (this was in the middle of September 1885), the plan being that I was to enter upon my first year in Arts and engage rooms for us all, where my grandmother and sister were to join me for the winter, in October. I had been just three weeks in Arts and all our winter's arrangements were made when I was obliged to give it up and return to St Andrews. That was the time of the great smallpox epidemic in Montreal, and my dear grandmother was anxious and decided not to come, leaving me free to do as I thought best. It was a great struggle. I had just begun Greek, and the University life seemed to me to have opened the gates of Paradise, but by all the laws of fair play it was my "turn" to stay at home and let my sister come down when the epidemic had abated, and this was what did come to pass. That quiet winter at St Andrews was not altogether fruitless however, for a kind old friend in the City sent me the modern Greek Textbooks and our own old Anglican clergyman coached me in this subject all winter long....

Owing to my domestic conditions, which were those of a very small family circle, it was impossible for me to remain away from home for two consecutive years. Accordingly, after my first year in Arts our little household moved into the city. Owing to illness at home I was obliged to drop my Classics honour course in my third year, but as I had had Greek throughout, I was able to qualify in the final year for the Lord Stanley gold medal, which I won. Of the five medals awarded that year, the nine girls in Arts '90 got three, and very proud of each other we were.

But what about medicine? The idea of studying it was not in the first place my own. My childhood "best friend," now Mrs C.H. Eastlake, who is by the way one of our leading Canadian artists to-day, said to me during my second year in Arts, as we sat one day together in the fields at home in Amonte. "What are you going to do when you leave College?" "I never thought about it," said I. "If I weren't an artist," said she, "I would be a doctor. It's a lovely life. So human and full of people." I came home and said to my grandmother, "May I be a doctor?" "Dear child," said she, "you may be anything you like." This was not a full decision, however, and I thought and spoke of the plan only in a desultory way, my great desire at that time being to remain on as a student at McGill. At the end of my second year, in May 1888, when the first class of women graduated, their valedictorian Octavia Ritchie, afterwards Dr Grace Ritchie England, who was my very dear friend, made a stirring plea for the admission of women to medicine at McGill. The authorities were however strongly opposed to coeducation and the matter rested there. Then, in my third year (1889), some kind ladies in the city, of rather advanced views, hearing that I wanted to study medicine, sent for me and offered to support any step I might take in the matter, and even undertook to go with me to call upon some of the leading doctors, to ascertain their views. The result was that I did send in, on February 12th, 1889, with the approval of some of the physicians who were more or less sympathetic or rather, not unfriendly, the following petition which I quote....

To the Dean and Faculty of Medicine of McGill University:

I, the undersigned, having decided upon adopting the medical profession, and being desirous of obtaining the necessary instruction in Montreal, do hereby petition the Dean and Faculty of Medicine that some provisions be made to this end. And I further most earnestly pray that the said provision be made for the approaching session of the college year, 1889-90.

I would solicit an early reply to this petition.

I am, yours respectfully,
MAUDE E. ABBOTT

111 Union Avenue, Feb. 12th, 1889.

Shortly thereafter some of these lay friends, who were interested, formed themselves into a Society which they called the "Association for the Professional Education of Women" (A.P.E.W.), and they also petitioned the Faculty to consider my request favourably, to inform them what requirements financial and otherwise would be needed for our admission (for there were now two of us), and they pledged themselves to raise whatever funds were considered necessary to meet these, and to this end asked for a conference. The Faculty granted this, and a deputation from it met representatives of the A.P.E.W. and us two petitioners, but the Faculty finally ruled that it was impossible for them to consider the subject favourably at the present time. This was in the autumn of 1889.

A MISSION

Born in 1839 in Parrsboro, Nova Scotia, Annie Leake lived a life that until 1887 was probably fairly typical for a spinster. She trained as a teacher at the Nova Scotia Normal School and as a young single woman took a position to teach at a Methodist academy in St John's, Newfoundland. Her religious involvement led her to seek a role in mission work that would eventually take her across the continent to work in a Victoria, British Columbia, rescue home for Chinese prostitutes. Unfortunately, the extant entries from Annie's diary do not detail much about her work in Victoria or why she gave it up after five years.

Nova Scotia and British Columbia, 1887-93
Annie Leake Tuttle Papers, Provincial Archives of British Columbia.

My heart turned to Mission Work of some kind. So I wrote letters here and there and waited and prayed, visiting here & there among old time friends in

Cumberland. It was an anxious time but I trusted and kept cool as best I could and talked Missions with friends.... I had gone to Avondale to keep house for Rev. David Hickey while his wife, daughter of Uncle Christopher Lockhart, went to visit her father. So time passed and at last I received a letter from Mrs "Dr" Huestis of Halifax an old time friend to whom I had written, seeking advice. It came in the form of an invitation to attend the Woman's Missionary Annual Meeting to be held in Yarmouth, N.S. that year, and she was the President. And so I went, in Company with our Pastor's wife Mrs Cranswick Jost.... Mrs Huestis took me under her care and I found out had plans for me of which I knew nothing at the time. Away the other side of the Continent in Victoria British Columbia there had been gathered together a few Chinese slave girls, rescued from Prostitution. The parties in Victoria who had interested themselves in those girls had not been successful in securing a suitable person to take charge of them. So they had appealed to the Woman's Missionary Society to take Charge of the work and to choose a Matron.... Mrs Huestis, who was to go to Board Meeting in Toronto, asked me if I would accept the position of Matron of this work, if I was accepted. I consented not expecting to be accepted at my age. I was 48 at that time and it was young women not over 25 who were desired for the General work. But my age and experience, and all my friend Mrs Dr Huestis felt she could say in my favour, made the Board feel that I was just the Person they needed for that work and so I was accepted.... "Our Father" had been better to me than my fears, as He had ever been through life. There was in Victoria several friends to meet me, whom I had known formerly Rev. C. Ladner, whose children I had taught in St John's Newfoundland was the first to meet me on board the Boat, as we landed. He introduced me to the friends of the Mission, Rev. J.E. Starr & the Chinese interpreter, J.E. Gardner. I was taken to a Good Hotel where I remained over Christmas and until the close of the Year. I was not introduced to my Pupils until near the Close of the year and did not take charge until New Year Eve 1887 and 1888 found me with difficult problems on my hands. But I had chosen the Position it came as I then believed from God and I now believe it more assuredly. And He alone was able to carry me through the difficulties of those Years.... I have no more doubt of their Conversion than I had of my own, and of my own I had full assurance. One year lived with them in their heathen darkness, and four after the light entered their Souls. I registered thirty names during the five years, including the child born in the Home, and the Grandmother, who sought refuge for herself and five daughters....

It was in the Maritimes that women in the British Empire first won admission to higher education. Historians Margaret Conrad and Wendy Mitchinson have shown the positive contribution of the evangelical churches in widening women's public role and in advancing women's education so that they might more effectively undertake their Christian missions. It is therefore not surprising that Mount Allison and Acadia universities, established by the Methodists and the Baptists respectively, should have been the first to admit female students. Pictured above is one of these women, Clara Belle Marshall Raymond, the first woman to graduate from Acadia University in 1884.

Credit: Graduating Class of 1884, Acadia University Archives.

COUNSEL ON SEX HYGIENE AND SOCIAL PROBLEMS

Like Annie Tuttle, whose religious involvement enabled her to take up a mission in British Columbia running a rescue home, Beatrice Brigden through the Methodist church on the Prairies found a "career" in counselling women and girls on sexual hygiene and social problems, a radical departure from the work normally expected of twenty-year-old young women. It is worthy to emphasize not only the importance of religion in securing social acceptance for this sort of work but also the role of religions in opening opportunities for leadership roles among women through missionary organizations, church auxiliaries, or support to programmes like the one in which Beatrice Brigden worked.

1890s-1915
Beatrice Brigden, "One Woman's Campaign for Social Purity and Social Reform". In Richard Allen, ed. The Social Gospel in Canada, *Ottawa: National Museums, 1975, 37-40, 44-47.*

In the summer of 1913, at the Souris and Rock Lake Summer Schools, I met a Mr Clark, boys' worker for the newly organized Methodist Department of Social Service and Evangelism. In many conversations he urged me to take on a similar task among girls, to lecture and counsel on sex hygiene and social problems. It seemed both an adventurous and a chancy undertaking for a single young woman barely into her twenties, but I allowed him to mention me to Dr T. Albert Moore, Clark's superior. Moore shortly came to Brandon to interview me, and after coming to the inevitable final and solemn question, "Are you converted?"—to which I stammered some sort of answer—persuaded me to take up the work. I was embarked on a fascinating and exhausting six-year career.

I needed preparation for embarking on such a venture, of course, and was soon on my way for LaCrosse, Wisconsin, for special studies in counselling, sex education and kindred themes. Then on to Hull House, Chicago, for two months of social studies and observation which entailed some contact with Jane Addams. Later I went to Louisville, Kentucky, for a special seminar, and in Toronto there was preliminary work in connection with city missions, the YWCA, juvenile delinquents, police women, the courts, as well as first-hand examination of industrial conditions.

Then came the travel; endless travel, including five months in Newfoundland, two winters in B.C., over all of old Ontario, little in Quebec outside Montreal, but most of all across the prairies many times, east to west, north to south. Always I was in touch with Dr Moore, reporting and seeking advice. He was utterly constant in his support. Together we worked out the format of week-long appearances in communities that requested my services. The program seldom changed, and took good advantage of my training in vocal arts.

There were regularly thirteen meetings per week, beginning with morning and evening sermons on Sunday and an address to Sunday School teenagers. On Monday morning came a recital of specially chosen stories and poems of social significance, interspersed with musical numbers. In the towns and villages especially, this combination of entertainment and thought-provoking content roused remarkably large audiences and evoked a moving response that carried through the week. Then on succeeding days came afternoon and evening meetings for mothers, girls, young women and mixed audiences. With Saturday came the parting from people one had become close to, a rush for the train, and arrival in a new strange town.

The pattern was only broken when summer came with its summer schools. There were still addresses, discussions, disputations, but the association was more sustained, intimate and relaxed. But the chattering of girls far into the night and the sagging cots did little to rest one. Only a month's holiday at home did that. Then the year began its cycle once more.

Nothing can better convey my experiences in those years of pioneer lecturing on sex education and social problems than excerpts from the letters I regularly sent to Dr Moore in Toronto.

Brandon, Manitoba, September 22, 1913
"Re—my sending you a lecture, I call them talks.... I very rarely write out anything...however while preparing the last of my talks I put it on paper [for you].... I am searching for suitable illustrations, and shall have to adapt my discussion of venereal diseases to the illustrations I am able to possess. Am not sure how you will view my introductory pages, but in teaching I have found Nature a never ending source of analogy.... Since beginning work on these talks I have resolved to use my own charts in a number of cases, drawing the desired figures or organs...."

Lumsden, Saskatchewan, May 3, 1915.
"Our first mothers' meeting was largely attended but the second was most decidedly not. When a discussion was suggested they all modestly hung their heads."

Davidson, Saskatchewan, May 18, 1915.
"We have had a splendid week here.... Our young women's meetings were most enjoyable...they begged me to go on and not stop after I had talked for an hour and a half.... I learned later there was a meeting of some fifteen disconsolate young men on the street corner, who asked one of the married ladies to take a message to me. It was this—'There must be something to you, for the girls have deserted not only us, but the Million Dollar Mystery, too.' (the serial at the moving picture theatre).

"The second mothers meeting...had one hundred and sixty women present (but) our fri. meetings were almost completely spoiled by a terrific storm...(on the way to the meeting I fell) into the ditch, full of water.... I had just stepped into the pulpit when the lights went off. We waited for awhile and then the men went out for lamps, and by the light of a miserable little coal oil lamp, and drenched to the skin I delivered an address on social ills contributing to immorality through out the land...."

―――――

A PINAFORED PRINTER

Regina, Saskatchewan, 1886-1890
Mrs May Davis, "A Pinafored Printer," Saskatchewan History, *IX (1956) 63-69.*

In glancing back over the years spent in Regina between 1886 and 1890 I cannot help feeling that some of the most important of them to me were the years which I spent in the employment of the *Regina Leader,* the city's pioneer newspaper.... It came about like this.

One evening my father surprised us all, as we sat at the tea-table, by telling mother that he had promised Mr Davin (owner and editor of the paper) to let me go to work at the "Leader Office" for a few weeks. He said that they were in need of more help in the folding and binding department, as the North-West Territories Ordinances had to be ready by a certain date, and they were short handed for the 'job'. Mother was not very enthusiastic about it, but I was quite pleased with the idea, not only because it meant escape for a time from always distasteful housework, but also at the prospect of earning a little money to 'help out'. Father said that the day's work began at 7.30 a.m. and ended at 6 p.m., with an hour off for dinner. My salary was to be $10.00 per month of 26 working days. This sounded like wealth to me and opened up vistas of new frocks and shoes all round; things which always seemed to be in short supply in the family. I was thirteen years old at this time, and as there was no young baby in the home now, could be spared more easily than usual. My mother said—so rightly—"Spared to go to school!" But I went into the "Leader Office" instead, and found it a school of sorts, and not by any means a bad one.

I was wanted 'right away', and so the morning after father had made his announcement I presented myself—with a certain amount of trepidation—the foreman took me to the south end of the long room and introduced me to Maggy Anderson, a pale-faced girl who was seated before a big table seemingly covered with sheets of printed paper. Maggy was the only binder left to cope with far too much work, and was accordingly very pleased to see me. Before he left us, Mr Burbank showed me how to fold the printed sheets of paper—which

I think had 16 pages of printing on each side—so that each one became a sort of booklet. I had to bring the numbers on the corners of the pages together, and scrape the folds down firmly with a brass rule.

Fortunately I had already learned to use my hands quickly and to work hard—when I felt so disposed (to quote Sairy Gamp)—and so it was not long before I was folding as many sheets per hour as the girl beside me, and in a few weeks—being very ambitious—more. In other words I was a success at my first job. Then followed the processes of collecting, stitching and covering the resulting books; after which the job-press man—Mr Walter Scott—who worked immediately behind our table, took piles of the ragged edged results over to a guillotine-like machine, and slicing their edges off made them much neater. When they were finished we liked their appearance very much for they were nice, compact, small books, with green or orange colored covers and entitled, *Ordinances of the North-West Territories of Canada*, 1887-88, or something of that description....

Soon after the *Ordinances* were finished Maggy Anderson left the office for her father's homestead—and I became the only book-binder.... One day Mr Burbank, the foreman, suggested that I begin to learn the cases. He followed the suggestion with a lesson, advising me particularly to "mind my P's and Q's". Before long I was given a "Stick" and "Rule" and instructed in the essential details of becoming a compositor. Next I was initiated into the process of "distributing Pi", an endless chore, after which I was never short of work.

I like better the work of "copy reading" for those employed in correcting galley proofs, and did a good deal of it, more particularly for Mr J.J. Young.

Saturday, late in the afternoon, was my favourite time, when the weekly paper came off the presses, and must be folded—by hand—as quickly as possible for distribution to the men and boys waiting about for it. All the "staff" turned to and helped with this folding, as there seemed to me to be a great deal of it to do. Speed was the important thing about it.

I always liked the damp, "printer's inky" smell, the people and the effort of trying to fold as many papers as anyone else....

I spent a good part of my time typesetting now, and enjoyed my work. The Church magazine, for which a larger type was used than for the *Gazette* and *Leader*, became almost entirely my "job"; and very proud I was of that fact. I was often very tired though at the end of the long day. Mother was less well again and therefore much of the housework fell to my lot (after suppertime) and life began to lose some of its zest....

Western women's organizations addressed a great many educational and social causes and are rightly credited with effecting wide ranging improvements in their society. They are often recognized for their contribution in developing a sense of sisterhood through the sheer joy of being together. That experience can be seen on the faces of this group of Winnipeg Jewish women as they posed for photographs at a 1920 stag party.

Credit: Foote Collection #848, Manitoba Archives.

A VON IN LABRADOR

At a time when nursing was becoming professionalized and the duties of hospital nurses specified, a quite different situation was faced by the nurses who served in remote hospitals or settlements. A Victorian Order nurse, Miss Edith Mayou, described the variety of hʳr duties at the Grenfell Mission Hospital at Harrington Harbour, Labrador, in letters of January-July 1908.

Labrador, 1908
"Extracts from letters written by Miss Edith Mayou," in John Murray Gibbon,
ed., The Victorian Order of Nurses for Canada *(Canada, 1947) 61-62.*

January 12, 1908—
As we are on an island, we cannot get any patients from the mainland until the ice is sufficiently firm and there has been enough snow for the dogs to bring them in safely on komatiks.
April 1, 1908—
Dr Hare travelled over fifteen hundred miles by dogteam last winter and saw several hundred patients. I prescribe and treat during his absence only.
Although I get up at six-thirty in the winter and at five-thirty in the summer, I never seem to have time for all I have to do. I have had night school for the men and lads and my own servants, sewing classes for the girls, and nursing talks and demonstrations for the women—I shall teach basket-making next winter. Most of the diseases we have to treat are those of semi-starvation; a continued diet of sour bread, tea and molasses does not make a very strong constitution. Our hospital treatment is principally dietetic, hygienic and eliminative, and when our patients go home, having gained ten pounds and looking pink instead of yellow and muddy, we feel that our work has not been in vain.
February 8, 1909—
The winter is fast slipping by, the cold has not been very severe, the thermometer varying from zero to 24 below, the monotony being varied by regular hurricanes and tremendous changes in the temperature, productive of coughs and colds.
March 25, 1909—
Last week I gave the mothers and wives a talk and demonstration on nursing—on an evening later gave twenty-five men and lads a practical demonstration on artificial respiration and the treatment of the drowned.
There is a terrible epidemic among the dogs. —Out of twenty-one that I treated while the doctor has been away, only seven are alive.
June 27, 1909—
An epidemic of grippe swooped down upon us.—In addition to the 160 outdoor patients, I had my own servants and hospital patients, as well as the doctor's four children and servants all on the sick list. Although I had several

severe cases with complications of ethmoiditis, bronchopneumonia, cardiac
conditions and nephritis, all are getting better.

July 1, 1909—

Could you spare the time to find out for me the cost of a black leather bag,
opening square, fitted with small screw-top bottles and space in the middle to
carry dressing, etc.—something in which to have everything ready for an
emergency—the make of bag that you recommend to your nurses who do all
outdoor and visiting work. I should like one that is not very heavy, for I am
only five five high...

CONDUCTORETTES

The enlistment of men in the armed forces during World War I opened a
number of traditionally male occupations to women. The following example
praises the work of the Kingston, Ontario, street railway conductorettes.

Kingston, Ontario, 1918
Daily British Whig. *(Kingston), 24 August 1918,9.*

"I understand that you have some vacancies on your line for conductors, Mr
Nickle. I wonder if I could fill the bill?" timidly questioned a female voice.

The manager of the Kingston, Portsmouth and Cataraqui Electric Railway
Company swung round in his easy chair at his desk and, sure enough, there
was a tall, handsome young women looking down at him appealingly. For a
moment Hugh C. Nickle was taken aback at the daring request, but a twinkle
soon came into his eye as his look of surprise wore off. The young lady was
invited to sit down and give her qualifications for a position hitherto always
held by a man.

She explained that she had seen the advertisment in the daily papers for
conductors, and that she thought she was quite capable to take over the
arduous duties. The exigencies of war, she remarked, were taking women into
new fields of endeavour, and there was a great need for men in the ranks of the
Canadian forces at the front. Women were doing all kinds of work to win the
war, and she was quite willing, therefore, to act as conductor while the boys
were away doing their bit. The women of England were running trams, and
considered it high time that the Canadians did the same.

The general manager was in a unique position and her argument could not
go unheeded. Here was a young lady anxious to do a patriotic service in a time
of need, and to release a man for the service of King and country. She was
healthy and vigorous and apparently quite able to assume the new duties. Her

earnestness did much to convince the perplexed superintendent that she would "make good" and the name of Miss Maude Chart, the first conductorette in Canada, was added to the payroll of the company on October 15th, 1917.

Since that date eleven more girls have entered the ranks of the conductorettes, and the even dozen are just one big, happy family—a unique sight as they come tripping down the main street, laughing and joking, each morning on the way to the street car barns for the day's work. There are no male conductors in the service of the company now, and the ladies have amply justified the hopes and expectations of Mr Nickle for the success of the novel experiment.

Through the bitter winter and the hot summer they have performed their duties so creditably that they have won the approbation of even the most pessimistic. From the very first, of course, there were some staid, old-fashioned gentlemen who said that Mr Nickle had been foolish to give the girls an opportunity to show their ability. Men had always been conductors on Kingston street cars, and men should always be conductors according to their views, and not even a great war should make a change. They were dubious about the long hours the girls would have to endure each day and they were not the least reluctant in expressing themselves.

When the girls first came on the cars, and they were somewhat of a novelty, the dear old gentlemen would put their heads together and if the man in the seat behind were to listen he might, too, become the victim of the contagious pessimism.

"You'll see that I'm right," he would hear the first old gentleman remark. "Some of those girls will break down some day when the temperature is about twenty below, and their hands are half frozen to the fare boxes."

And his friend would not be slow in adding, "You know that I think it's criminal to allow them to expose themselves to pneumonia and influenza these cold days. They'll come to an early end, poor dears."

What a dismal picture those pessimists did delight to paint! But they looked at the situation from the wrong angle and they are just now getting the right perspective. The girls did meet with discouraging difficulties, but even in the most trying days when their fingers were blue with cold, they carried on and collected the fares for ten hours at a stretch. Their unfailing politeness and courtesy at all times were commended by visitors as well as citizens, who did not fail to congratulate them on the splendid spirit of service they manifested. As the winter wore on the pessimists became disheartened at their inability to convince themselves and others that the conductorettes were bound to be failures.

A gleam of hope, however, came with the dawn of spring. Summer would soon be here, and the closed winter cars would have to be replaced by the open cars. Ha! Ha! Perhaps they were not so wrong after all.

"They may be pretty fair in the winter, but what about the summer?" queried the omniscient pessiminst. "They'll never be able to climb along the sides of the car to collect the fares. Mark my words. If Nickle keeps these girls in the summer, there are going to be some dead conductorettes under the sod before the snow comes round again."

And just to make it emphatic the companion in gloom remarked, "I don't see how they'll be able to walk along the sides with their skirts flying around like a couple of flags in a wind storm."

Again the pessimists were to be disappointed. During the summer months the girls have handled tremendous crowds on holidays and on other special occasions, and up to the present only one has been injured — and she was only off duty for half a day with a few bruises. Some of the "Etties" have collected as many as eleven hundred fares during one day, and registered them on an automatic recorder. It has been really wonderful to see them skip along the side steps with remarkable agility and facility. They have been especially gracious in assisting old gentlemen and ladies on and off the cars. They have easily replaced the trolleys on the wires when they slipped off. They have even turned the switches for the motomen. In a word they have performed a score of duties devolving upon them with a grace and cleverness that is exceedingly creditable and gratifying.

Clad in their natty khaki suits, they are an addition to the car service, and their courteous "Fares, please" is a delightful change from the gruff "Fares". Each girl is provided with the material for two uniforms, a peaked, brown straw cap sitting at a jaunty angle on her head under which her hair is neatly tucked, a "slicker" fisherman's hat and rubber boots for rainy days, as well as brown boots and stockings, which complete their attire on sunny days. Their suits are quite plain, consisting of a short skirt and Norfolk coat with shining brass buttons. On very warm days the girls remove their coats, and they look refreshingly cool and comfortable in pongee blouses and khaki middies. They are very business-like in appearance, and in the performance of their duties they will stand no nonsense from any of the male passengers who are of a "flirty" nature, which responds to the attractiveness of the Limestone City's conductorettes....

Their wages are also very generous and many of them make as much as eighteen and nineteen dollars a week. They are paid $2.25 for a ten-hour day, and receive double pay for overtime. At the end of the summer those who have been in the service during the whole of the season are to be granted a substantial bonus by the company as a mark of appreciation for their steady work. Altogether the majority will have averaged about $18.50 a week when their bonus is given.

Some of the girls start as early as six o'clock in the morning on their trips, and Mr Nickle stated that as a rule they were more regular than the men in arriving for the "dawning" cars. During the day they have few idle moments until the last car enters the barns shortly before eleven o'clock at night.

---

2. THE VOTE

CAMPAIGN ECHOES

Letitia Creighton Youmans was educated in the public common school and at ladies' academies and eventually pursued a teaching career at the latter. When she married a widower with eight children, she gave up her teaching to attend to his household and her stepchildren. Her concern with the effects of intemperance and her voluntary activities in the Sunday School movement directed her eventually, when her responsibility to her stepchildren was over, to active involvement in the temperance movement, through the Woman's Christian Temperance Union. As an active organizer, speaker, and leader of this cause, she was drawn to support the granting of woman's suffrage as a means of securing prohibition legislation. In 1885 as a propertied widow, she cast her first two municipal ballots in Picton, Ontario. In the excerpts from her autobiography below, she recalls her philosophy and her emotions at that time.

Picton, Ontario, 1885
Letitia Youmans, Campaign Echoes *(Toronto, 1893) 206-209.*

In the year 1885, the Ontario Legislature gave unmarried women the power to vote at the municipal elections. I had always believed that when I had the privilege to vote it would be my duty to do so; for I was firm in the belief that it is a duty to "Do all the good you can, to all the people you can, in all the ways you can, and as long as you can." So strong was the opposition in Canada to what was commonly termed "woman's rights," that I had good reason to believe that, should I advocate the ballot for women in connection with my temperance work, it would most effectively block the way, and it was already uphill work for a woman to appear on a public platform.

It used to seem to me that I was just the snowplow preceding the train to clear the track.

I saw, in this respect, the necessity of being as wise as a serpent and as harmless as a dove. I was firm in the conviction that it was my duty to appeal to the men, the natural protectors of the homes, to use the power that was in their hands to protect those homes; and that this could only be done at the ballot box.

Even the term prohibition, when applied to the liquor traffic, was obnoxious, so much so that I would announce my subject as "home protection," assuring my audience that I had not come to advocate woman's rights, but to remonstrate against women's wrongs; to claim for every wife the right to have a sober husband, and every mother to have a sober son, and a comfortable home for herself and children. This assertion of rights would invariably insure a hearty response.

When in 1885 the Ontario Government gave unmarried women the municipal vote, my duty was quite plain, to vote myself and urge my sisters to do the same.

It did seem a dear price to pay for a vote when my husband was taken away; however, I was thankful for even this innovation on the laws of the past.

It is a problem I have not yet been able to solve, why a woman having a husband should be disqualified from voting any more than a man who had a wife. An old-fashioned maxim declares, "It is a poor rule that won't work both ways."

If only widows and spinsters are allowed to vote, then surely bachelors and widowers should be the only men eligible to the same privilege.

If this amendment to the municipal vote could be secured, it would no doubt adjust matters.

The first Monday in January, 1885, found the W.C.T.U. of Picton assembled in the house of their President to discuss the momentous question of going to the polls. As Samantha Allen says, some of the number "had been to the well pole, the hop pole, and the bean pole, but none of these seemed anything like as hefty as the one where a little slip of white paper had to be lifted into the ballot box."

The question now to be decided was, "Shall we go in a solid body, or go one at a time, in a sort of Indian file?" The latter mode was adopted, and I was selected as the first offering on the altar of female suffrage. A sense of responsibility aroused all my energies as I started across the street (for we were just on the opposite side of the way from the polling place). On opening the door, I found the room occupied by a number of men, and dark with tobacco smoke. The sickening fumes struck me full in the face. Just as it had often been said, "The polling place was not a fit place for women." Nevertheless, I ventured inside. The men gazed at me in astonishment, and then at each other, as much as to say, "What does the woman mean?"

Fortunately I espied a little group standing apart, composed of good temperance men. Bowing to them, I said, "You will remember, gentlemen, that I am a citizen this morning." A smile of complacency passed over every face, and pipes and cigars suddenly disappeared, and I was politely escorted into the inner room, the mysteries of the ballot paper explained, and a still more secluded spot pointed out where I could designate the men I chose to represent me in the town council.

While alone marking that paper, a deep sense of personal responsibility rested down upon me. None but the eye of God was cognizant of the act, and I would not have dared to be influenced by mere party principles, or any other unworthy motive.

This wondrous feat being accomplished, I returned to the outer room, and found the windows open and the smoke all cleared away. My mental inference was, such will be the effect of women taking part in public affairs, it will clear up the moral atmosphere most amazingly. My report to my sisters induced them to go without hesitancy and deposit their votes.

Having a vote in another ward of the town, a carriage was sent to convey me; and aspiring candidates, waiting at the door, eagerly helped me to alight, notwithstanding my inconvenient avoirdupois. I had always been treated with kindness and respect in the town of Picton, but that morning I was evidently of more consequence than ever I had been before. That little slip of paper had a wonderfully elevating influence. The superintendent of the railway offered to hold the train fifteen minutes, to enable me to vote before starting to meet an engagement in the West.

OPINIONS ON WOMAN SUFFRAGE (1)

In 1893 the Quebec women's journal, *Le Coin du Feu,* surveyed prominent men and women of that province on the question of woman's suffrage. These solicited correspondents were invited to address the issue as follows:

>It is certain that the mixing of women in politics
>will completely change the conditions of social
>life as they have been established for centuries.
>Will it be for the best?

Two of the responses received from women are reproduced below.

Quebec, 1893
"Le Suffrage Feminin," Le Coin du Feu, *I (1893) 359-62.*

No one more than myself wants women to be accorded the full range of her rights. However, her emanicipation—in my humble opinion, at least—should not extend to political suffrage. If one gives her the right to vote, it would be necessary, as a logical consequence, to accord her the right to aspire to representation. But, a woman must keep herself far removed from these noisy places where, in the excitement of the battles, the heat of emotions, the dignity and respect due to her would be in danger of compromise. And because politics are often the reef where fine intellects and honest intentions founder, let us keep away from this new danger, which would only add to the difficulties with which our route is already strewn.

Françoise

Female suffrage is no more than the strict consequence of a real democracy; that is why I think that as one penetrates the inner meanings of this form of government, one will accord the right to vote to women.

But, it would be dangerous to augment the responsibilities of the latter [women], without previously supporting a number of changes in their education.

Yvonne

OPINIONS ON FEMALE SUFFRAGE (2)

Fifteen years later, in 1908-1909, the *Journal de Françoise* conducted a similar plebiscite among prominent women. Of the published replies, nineteen favoured woman suffrage while a majority of thirty-five opposed the proposition. A remaining four were undecided. A sampling of their letters is presented below.

Quebec, 1908-1909
"Notre plebiscite," Le Journal de Françoise, *VII, December 5, 1908, 262-65 and January 2, 1909, 295-99.*

Mme A. -R. Angers,
Wife of the Honourable A. -R. Angers, former Lieutenant-Governor
of the Province of Quebec.

In reply to the question posed by your journal: "Should women have the right to vote?" I consider that the role of women is to govern her home and to direct the education of her family. In my opinion she would gain nothing by descending into the political arena in becoming an elector.

Mme A. -R. Angers

Mme Marcil,
Wife of Charles Marcil, Deputy of Bonaventure and the next
President of the Chambre des Communes.

I have not had the time to examine thoroughly the question of woman suffrage, but I must confess that my first impulse is in favour of the right to vote for women. There are a multitude of reforms which women could effect—questions of detail which escape men and which are in woman's sphere. Naturally, this right to vote which I claim in favour of my sex would have to be exercised with prudence and judgement.

Louise Marcil

Miss Hurlbatt
Principal of Royal Victoria College
I am in favour of the extension of the parliamentary franchise to women in the same terms as it is or may be extended to men. If women are different from men, representative government without them is incomplete representation of the State. If women are the same as men they presumably have the same need to vote as men. In the past fifty years three great changes have come on western civilization each of which, and all of which in conjunction, have given a very strong colour to the women suffrage cause, first: the achieved economic independence of women; second: the great development of town centres and the consequent extension of state activities which demand the services of public servants of new aptitudes and qualifications, third: the spread of education among women. Then great changes have led us unto claim the suffrage. As members of the modern industrial state seeking to represent their own interests, to remove their own disabilities and to perform with the fullest opportunity their work of social service. Parliaments and departments of State legislate or deal with vital questions affecting the welfare of women and children and in these matters women should have the fullest opportunity given them to do what they can to raise the standard of public opinion and to him improved conditions to beat upon the homes and work places of the Empire....

Ethel Hurlbatt

Madame Lepage
Bagotville, (Chicoutimi)
On the question which you gave me the honour of addressing, I reply:
For single women: Yes.
For the woman under the power of her husband: No

S. -G. Lepage

REPRESENTATION IN EDUCATION

As the nineteenth century progressed, children spent more and more of their time in schools and these institutions replaced in many families the mother's role as formal educator, although her educating function as model remained. As the educational system appeared to have taken over a vital role, some women sought to continue their influence on their children's formal education by demanding the right of women to vote at school meetings and their right to be elected as school trustees.

Nova Scotia, 1895
Nova Scotia Provincial Education Association, Report *(1895) 55-57.*

A few years ago I taught in a section only a few miles from Truro where lived a family who, owing to the illness of the father, were very poor. With the aid of one or two kind-hearted mothers I succeeded in getting two of the children, a girl of 13 years and a boy of 11, to attend school a short time. Thinking that the rising generation of Nova Scotia were being properly educated, I spent some time teaching Hindoos to read and write English. Last week I returned to this section and found that in this same family there are four boys, between the ages of 6 and 18, who can neither read nor write. The girl already referred to never attended school after I left and is now—poor child—an ignorant wife, nineteen years of age. Yet these four boys can, by their united votes, help to send a man to Ottawa or Halifax to represent the people of Colchester, while the intelligent mothers of our land who *can* read a newspaper—tho' they may find it necessary to ask their husbands to explain the profound (?) editorials in our Canadian papers—have not the right to vote at school meetings!...

But 'tis not for the sake of the poor classes that I would like to see women represented on our school boards, but 'twould be for the benefit of every boy and girl attending our public schools.

That it would be for the better were our schools more homelike no one will dispute, how then shall we give mothers a deeper interest in the school? True, individuals here and there may do much to improve school rooms, surroundings, etc., but institutional wrongs can never be righted by individual reform— though moral reforms can—and to my mind it *is* an institutional wrong that women should not vote on all that pertains to the educational welfare of their children, and it can be righted by amending section 44 of the Revised Statutes, "Of Public Instruction", so as to include women....

The following resolution was moved by Insp. Craig and Principal Miller: Believing that a closer relationship between home and school is desirable, and that much good will result from having the mothers of our public school children take a more active interest in the school, this association endorse every effort made to amend section 44 of the statutes of public instruction, by adding the words "and female". Discussion.—Principal McLeod, Kentville Academy:—Women are all right where they are. Their sphere is the home, and if they do faithful work there, it will not be necessary for them to take an active part in affairs outside the home. We have it on record where woman's influence over man, when on an equality with him, resulted far from satisfactorily. Do not want to see the like repeated. Mr Andrews said he thought women took a deep interest in teachers now, as was often evinced when a child was punished.

Principal Kennedy said that women had the power now, and if they desired to pay a poll tax he was thoroughly in favour of it. They were going to run the civic machine anyway, and it was just as well to stand out of the road.

On the vote for the resolution 23 voted for and 28 against, and it was declared lost.

•

British Columbia, 1895
Petition of the Local Council of Women of Victoria and Vancouver Island, Journals of the Legislative Assembly of the Province of British Columbia *Volume XXIV (1895).*

PETITION

To the Honourable the Speaker and Honourable Members of the Legislative Assembly of the Province of British Columbia, in Parliament assembled:

The petition of the Victoria and Vancouver Island Women's Council humbly sheweth: —

That your petitioners have learned that women are not eligible in this Province to become members of the Boards of School Trustees.

That your petitioners have learned that in many parts of the Dominion of Canada, of England and of the United States, efficient women have materially helped the Public Schools by occupying seats in the School Board of Trustees.

That your petitioners have learned that the sex most largely represented at our Public and High Schools is the female sex.

That your petitioners humbly think that the time has arrived when woman should be granted the privilege of her influence and voice in the education of her children.

Your petitioners therefore humbly pray that Your Honourable Body will so amend the "School Act" as to allow women to become members of the School Board of Trustees.

And your petitioners, as in duty bond, will ever pray.

Signed on behalf of twenty ladies' societies.

Louise Baker
President of Local Council of Women of Victoria and Vancouver Island.

———————

MUNICIPAL POLITICS

In 1892, *An Act to Extend the Franchise to Spinsters and Widows in Municipal and School Matters* (55-56 Vict., C. 35) gave widowed and unmarried women in Quebec the right to vote in municipal and school elections. Although married women in that province did not acquire these rights until 1941, the major Quebec women's organizations involved themselves in petitioning for suffrage, in politicizing women through the media, and, as the following report shows, in actively organizing the female vote.

Montreal, 1914
"Women in Municipal Elections," Reports of Women Correspondents, Montreal, Labour Gazette, *April 1914, 1159.*

The approaching municipal elections are the occasion of much activity in the leading women's organizations of Montreal.

It is estimated that nearly one-twelfth of the total vote can be polled by women, there being the names of 11,000 female voters on the election rolls out of a total of 135,000.

That the feminine vote be used and be properly directed is the aim of both the Local Council of Women and "la Fédération Nationale St-Jean-Baptiste." The first named organization has made detailed arrangements in the different wards of the city; conveners have been appointed and committees formed. These volunteer workers will, when necessary, accompany the women voters to the polls. These will have been reminded of their duty in personal visits from members of the council. This body had adopted the Citizen's Association slate as the list of candidates believed by them to be best qualified to make good civic administrators.

"La Fédération Nationale St-Jean-Baptiste, at its February meeting, discussed what line of action would be advisable in relation to the coming municipal election.

The practical result of the society's deliberations was made evident at a meeting held on the afternoon of March 28. A permanent league was formed, having for its object the civic education of the women voters of Montreal. Lectures will be given at intervals by competent men. As regards the present elections, French-Canadian women voters are being reminded of their duty in articles inserted by "la Fédération" in the daily papers.

A WOMAN REFLECTS ON THE VOTE

On 17 December 1917, women with close relatives in the Canadian or British armed forces voted for the first time in a federal election. The next day, a Toronto woman, Janie Smythe, penned the following letter to suffragist Flora Denison and expressed her optimistic sentiments as a woman in a "new state of equality."

Toronto, 1917
Janie Smythe to Flora M. Denison, Dec. 18, 1917; Mrs. Flora M. Denison
Papers, Thomas Fisher Rare Books, University of Toronto. Library, Mss Coll.
51.

22 Glengrove Ave. W.
Toronto Dec. 18, 1917

My Dear Mrs Denison.
It is befitting that you should be the first one I should write to since I recorded my *first* vote. It was a proud day yesterday for me and an hour which you and others have by unceasing devotion to the cause, made possible. I may now be recognized by humanity at large, as having a complete number of organs and faculties with more or less average mental ability to use them! In a word, am equal of my husband, at least technically speaking. I have my vote owing to my sister nursing soldiers. Stepmothers are not fully qualified for such a high honour as voting. I trust that when next we shall meet that I shall bear myself with true and becoming dignity in my new state of equality....

Janie Smythe

---

3. NEW WOMEN, NEW ISSUES AND NEW ACTIVITIES

THE FIRST LADIES' BIKES

The introduction of the bicycle for women in the late 1880s produced a visible social change. Cycling was a relatively inexpensive form of fun and exercise for women and it enabled them to travel, at least short distances, independently. Moreover, it has been credited with increasing the movement to dress reform as female cyclists sought clothing that allowed greater freedom of movement than current fashion and modesty dictated. As the following comment on the first bicycles brought to West Jeddore, Nova Scotia shows, "that contraption" drew out local ambivalence about social change in the role and image of Canadian women.

Nova Scotia, circa 1890
Grace Forsythe, ed., Tales of the Yesteryears: The Writing of Mrs. E.S. Williams, West Jeddore, 1888-1977, *Book I, 29.*

Two of my cousins brought the first ladies' bicycles to the Cove. In their late teens they had set forth to USA, and were employed at the Dennison factory in Framingham. It was quite the fad then for groups of girls to go bicycling out on the country roads.

After a year away from home, they returned for their holidays. Arriving in Halifax, they contacted Capt. John Weston of East Jeddore and started for Jeddore on his vessel. A blast from a horn echoed over the air. Uncle Jeremiah launched his rowboat and went out to meet the vessel that was coming round the Heads into the Cove. The Captain was by no means happy to transfer the girls, their luggage, and their bicycles into a small rowboat. However, the transfer was made safely, and the vessel went on its way up the harbour.

Consternation and dire predictions reigned among some of the older folks who saw tragedy ahead. "Those girls will land with broken limbs." Etc. We younger ones were audacious enough to admire them, and some of the boys who had never seen a bicycle except in Eaton's catalogue, looked upon them with the "green-eyed monster" showing in their eyes.

One fine evening the girls set forth on those bicycles to ride from the Cove to farther up the road, which was "Up-Along", while we lived "Down-Along". Although the girls wore heavy tweed circular skirts that politely hid their ankles, it was impossible when pedalling not to display those ankles. The predictions of what might happen seated high on "that contraption", as well as the display of ankles brought sighs and groans. They were the first bicycles seen in the Cove and "them girls" coming from Boston were more than some dear saintly souls could tolerate.

However, the rough country roads were unkind to the machines, and they were laid aside. The girls returned to Boston, where they could ride in ease, removed from the seat of condemnation, and could display their ankles.

———————

THE ISSUE OF DRESS

With issues such as woman's suffrage, the reform of female clothing received attention in the late nineteenth and early twentieth centuries. As Canadian women assumed larger roles in the public sphere of society, some began to seek more comfortable and mobile attire. In the brief article which follows the editor of "Woman's Sphere" considers specifically the possibility of the revival of the crinoline and more generally the problem of defying trends in female fashion.

Toronto, 1905
"The Dreaded Crinoline", The Canadian Magazine, *XXV (1905) 367.*

Crinoline is in the air and every woman shudders as she says—"Oh, I hope it won't come." Occasionally a woman is brave enough to declare—"I won't wear it if every other woman in Canada goes with the fashion." We are all afraid of it but most of us have the sneaking dread that we also shall appear in the hideous garb of "hoops" dimensions.

The *Rational Dress Gazette* indulges in the following mournful reflections: "Once more we are threatened by the crinoline. The newspapers are full of disquieting rumours; an Anti-Crinoline League has been formed. We would fain have faith in popular intelligence; we would fain believe that the crinoline is an extinct thing. It is so preposterous, so unjustifiable, so unaccountable. We know that hoops did once encumber the earth, but we find it hard to believe that these things could happen again. Possibly, possibly, they will not happen again. But the portents are about."

FREYJA

The Icelandic women of Manitoba played a role in their community that was not as circumscribed as that of their non-Icelandic contemporaries. By the turn of the century, local custom had established women's cultural, economic, and community participation and before Anglo-Saxon initiatives, Icelandic women in the province had formed suffrage associations and had petitioned the provincial legislature. A part of this tradition was *Freyja*.

Freyja, which is the Icelandic word for woman, was the title of an Icelandic women's magazine published in Manitoba from 1898 until 1910. Its founder and editor, Margret Benedictsson, outlined *Freyja*'s aims in its first issue. These are reprinted below. Dr Mary Kinnear, who provided this translation from the magazine, describes *Freyja* in an unpublished research paper as "an expression firstly of the culture shared by all Icelanders in North America, and especially Manitoba; secondly of the attitudes of, and towards, the Icelandic women; and thirdly it was the voice of one particular Icelandic woman, Margret Benedictsson."

Manitoba, 1898-99
"The Aims of Freyja," Freyja, *Selkirk, Manitoba, I (1898-99) 4.*

Freyja shall be quite independent in all matters, her purpose is to bring knowledge and enjoyment to her readers. *Freyja* will not, without cause, get involved in matters that cause dissension such as religion and politics. There is however, no subject matter pertaining to human or moral issues that does not concern *Freyja* and she will not pledge herself to keep silent about such matters.

Freyja will bring informative and amusing articles, original and translated, whenever possible. There will also be fiction, poetry, jokes, housekeeping hints and husbandry.

Matters pertaining to the progress and rights of women will always be her first and foremost concern. *Freyja* will support prohibition and anything that leads to the betterment of social conditions.

Freyja will accept with thanks, original stories and poetry and in fact anything pertaining to the good of all.

Articles not accepted will only be sent back to sender if a stamped, self addressed envelope is enclosed.

Write distinctly and have it short. Be careful how you write because nothing personal or libelous will be printed in *Freyja*. Our motto is: Humanity and equality. Discuss the subject, but not the person.

"THE SAME SOURCE OF STRENGTH AND PLEASURE"

In the introduction to her report to the Royal Commission on Industrial Training and Technical Education (1913), Miss C. Derick, Assistant Professor of Botany at McGill University and President of the Montreal Local Council of Women, addresses the issue of economic change as it transformed women's public and domestic roles. Her perspective and arguments concerning the value of women's public work and her changed private role are radical when compared with most of the other contemporary writers on these topics.

Montreal, 1913
Miss C. Derick, "General Report on Women's Work," Royal Commission on Industrial Training and Technical Education, Report (Ottawa, 1913) 1974.

Many people are uneasy at the employment of a large number of women and girls in wage-earning positions (probably about 33% of those between 15 and 24.) Economic changes have taken women's work from the home to the shop; the home is still the centre, but has become the centre of consumption instead of production, thus losing many of its educational functions. It has therefore become necessary for girls to take up definite work outside the home, to gain the mental and moral discipline resulting from the performance of regular duties and save them from seeking idle tasks to fill idle days.

A woman's work is to her the same source of strength and pleasure as to a man; self-respect is deepened by economic independence and her true womanliness is only fully revealed when every power is given opportunity to exercise. But this ideal has yet to be realized. In partial adjustment to new conditions, abuses have arisen; the remedy is not in restriction, but in liberty, provided that protection is given to children, that a good primary training followed by vocational training is open to all, and that reasonable hours, sanitary surroundings and fair remuneration are secured for all alike through legislation. This would deplete the ranks of the unskilled and thus improve the conditions of the labour market. The power derived from training and the stimulus given by the opening of all the highest positions to women would combine to produce desirable changes in their economic and social condition which restriction could never secure....

REFLECTIONS ON WOMAN'S LIFE

Jessie Sime's book, *In a Canadian Shack,* from which the following excerpt comes, is both a descriptive and an introspective volume. An educated, urban woman, Sime left the city on three separate occasions to work as a housekeeper for a female poultry farmer in St Aniel, Quebec. These changes from her normal life gave her time to reflect on herself, on the changing roles of Canadian women and on the need to redefine their image.

St Aniel, Quebec, circa 1915
Jessie Sime, In a Canadian Shack *(Toronto, 1937) 123-24.*

What a queer thing a modern business woman's life is! She is, more often than not, divided from nearly everything that was originally thought to constitute a woman's lot. If she is married and works, she is divorced from her house (which at one time fitted her as his shell fits a snail): if, as is too frequently the case today, she is obliged to be the bread-winner for her family—for in these abnormal times women can often enough find work more easily than men— she is divided from more than her house: she is separated from what was once regarded as almost identical with herself, her children. If she has a lover, she cannot live with him (except in the special sense in which that phrase is used), and if she is a spinster and a virgin and has no connection with man or child, she runs the risk of desiccation. It is very difficult for a woman divorced from "rights" to—what shall I call it?—remain unspoilt.

"SOME KIND OF DOMESTIC REVOLUTION IS NECESSARY"

Concern for the demands that housekeeping made on Canadian women and for their wasted talents sparked Margaret Fairley to pen the following proposal for a reorganization of household and child care responsibilities. A founder of the *Canadian Forum,* Margaret Fairley was an outspoken advocate of women and the working class among left-wing thinkers in Toronto and, through her writings, across the nation.

1920
Margaret Fairley, "Domestic Discontent," The Canadian Forum, *December 1920. Reprinted in* The Canadian Forum, *September 1975, 31-32.*

There is in Canada a fast increasing number of well-educated women. And far too many of them are unable to follow up the interests which have been awakened and developed in them. What hope is there of free intellectual life for them? Thoreau was convinced that the machinery of life, the acquiring of food and shelter and clothing, should occupy but a small portion of a man's time and it is probable that, if educated housewives are to do more than like on their intellectual capital, some kind of domestic revolution is necessary. Courageous experiment is required to break down conventions and traditions based on two outworn practices—that of living as a clan, many branches of a family in a house, and that of educating the girls far less than the boys. Perhaps our habits of eating and drinking are based on these practices and the dimensions of dish-washing are, in consequence, quite disproportionate to the spiritual demands of women. Let us then break through some of these dishes and do something drastic to win back our self-respect....

Only those housewives who value their time more than their jam can contribute much towards that new order where the life can be more than meat and the body than raiment.

But not much can be done by individuals. Thinking women as a whole must change their standards, their domestic customs, and their methods of enticing help. There might, for example, be far more entertaining without the inevitable meal. Invitation cards might be printed with "Please eat at home" in the corner. Even so the margin of time left for pursuing vital interests will be small, and some paid help was still be desirable. What is the most likely form that this help will take in the future? Everything indicates that the number of girls willing to live and work in other people's houses is on the decrease. The reasons are obvious. It is pleasant to have a work place and a living place. It is pleasant to live with people with whom you share a common point of view and a common idea of amusement. It is pleasant to be your own mistress over the ordinary little details of your off-time, your bed time, and your rising time; your bath, your exercise, and fresh air, and recreation.

Any organization dealing with domestic work could, if it had the confidence of employers and employed, do much more than handle casual appeals for help or for work. The women of an energetic community who feel the need of organized domestic work could get together and work out some scheme whereby this eternally recurring worry could be compelled to take a back seat. Their aim should be to make the good life possible for housewives and for paid assistants alike.

A comparatively small district could set the example, say the streets lying within a given square mile. Every house in the district might receive a letter asking for answers to some such questions as these:

1. Do you desire help in your house or with your children?
2. If so, for what work? at what hours? for what pay?

3. Is there any woman or girl in your house ready to give help to another house?
4. If so what work? at what hours? for what pay?
5. Are there children in your house?
6. Is there anyone in your house willing to take her turn (say two or three evenings a month) at staying with neighbours' children in the evenings when their parents are out?

The enterprising two or three who have made themselves responsible for canvassing the district will, if they get much encouragement from the returns, probably appoint a secretary whose duty it will be to try and turn the good will of the district to practical account. The answers to 6 will have to be classified under very small areas. It is conceivable that the answers to questions 3 and 4 might bring to light a girl with a gift for cleaning silver who could work for half a street, another who was a skilled bedmaker, a third who liked nothing better than dishwashing. So a procession of experts might be at our service and we should have merely to be at hand to let them in and out of the house. We should in our turn become expert door-openers.

It is surely true that if a determined effort were made, as far as income allows, to reduce work, to make use of outside help such as that of laundry, bakery, nursery school; to organize paid help in the house for certain parts of the work, and to organize the neighbourly interchange of responsibility for the children in the evenings, this wearisomely monotonous discontent over the domestic problem would in great measure disappear. There would surely be more happiness, though of course there would have to be some hard thinking for topics of conversation.

STOPPING THE RAILWAY

Although the image of the Victorian woman is one of passivity, Canadian women of the era proved themselves to be active and effective when their interests or those of their families were involved. When the women of Foxtrap, Newfoundland, believed their dairies to be threatened by the arrival of the railway, they quickly took matters and weapons into their own hands to prevent the intrusion.

Foxtrap, Newfoundland, 1882
Michael McCarthy, "The Role of Women in Newfoundland History," The Newfoundland Teachers' Association Journal, *Summer 1974, 44.*

The year was 1882 and railway talk was strong in the air. On April 12th, surveyors had reached as far as Foxtrap, however, some evil disposed person who did not favour the railway, had been busy in the settlement. The women were told that the train's whistle would frighten their cows and cause their milk to turn sour, their turnips and potatoes would be shaken by the passage of the train that they would not grow, and if they did the soot cast by the locomotive would cover the entire area. The men were absent, the ladies had to make a decision, they approached the surveyors and asked them to go away, the surveyors paid no attention, then the Foxtrap ladies gathered themselves together collected blubber from the stage head and pickle from the winter beef barrels, and armed with these offensive weapons of war descended *en masse* upon the intruders, the surveyors retreated blubbered and pickled and the doughty old Judge Prowse was sent out to restore order, he too was treated to a similar fate, but gradually the railway was explained and the ladies then very courteously agreed to let the survey continue, this incident of amazon warfare has gone into our history books as the Battle of Foxtrap.

UNION WIVES PROTEST BLACKLEGS

Labour relations in British Columbian coal mines in the late nineteenth and early twentieth centuries were dominated by conflict and violence. Union men striking for wages and improved working conditions faced the force of large companies backed by the provincial government and its police. In the Northfield/Wellington area in 1891, a number of striking workers had been arrested and protest action by other union men would have brought stiff and immediate reprisals. It fell to the wives and children of striking miners to demonstrate against strike breaking workers or blacklegs, as they were known.

Northfield, British Columbia, 1891
Report of Select Committee on the Attack on Funeral Procession of Ellis Roberts. British Columbia Legislative Assembly Journals, Vol. 20, 1891, lxv, lxxiii, lxxxvi, xciv-xcv.

Mr Speaker,—Your Select Committee appointed to enquire into the attack made on the funeral procession of the late Ellis Roberts, of Wellington, on the 4th inst., beg respectfully to report as follows:—

That we proceeded to Wellington on the 14th instant, and held an enquiry at the Court House at Wellington on the same day, and examined witnesses, and we consider that the question of the conduct of the people at Northfield towards the funeral procession which carried to the grave the body of Ellis Roberts, may be divided into three parts: —

    1st.   The procession to the grave.

    2nd.   The service at the grave.

    3rd.   The return of the funeral procession.

The Union men had assembled for a procession at the starting point of the funeral procession of non-union men, and waited for them. They parted to let the funeral procession through, and lowered their flags to the corpse.

With regard to procession to the grave there is little or no evidence to show that any very hostile expression of opinion was exhibited. During the service at the grave there was nothing to call for comment, and the minister who conducted the service testifies that he heard no unseemly interruption. The return of the procession from the grave was evidently seized upon by the inhabitants of Northfield at the Half-way House (who were Union men) as an opportunity for an exhibition of their hostile feelings towards the non-union men who formed the funeral procession, but care was evidently taken that there should be no violence. That the demonstration was premeditated is shown by one or two effigies which had been previously constructed, and were placed on the side of the road, and these effigies from their character were intended to indicate blacklegs. As the procession passed the Half-way House it was assailed by insulting cries and jeers from several men there. As it approached and passed through Northfield large bodies of women and children lined the road and flung snowballs at the procession, and by their jeers and insulting expressions showed plainly that the intention was to indicate their hostility to the non-union men, but the men of Northfield took no part in the snowballing, and confined themselves to encouraging the women and children. In fact it appeared as though care had been taken that no act of violence should accompany the hostile expression of feeling.

Having considered all the evidence available, your Select Committee is of opinion that the conduct of the people of Northfield to the non-union men returning in procession from the funeral was unseemly and insulting.

All of which together with further evidence is

Respectfully submitted.

Geo. W. Anderson

Chairman.

18th March, 1891

Thomas Richards (Miner)

Q. Chairman: Did you see any woman put herself into an unseemly position?

A. Yes, sir; I did.

Q. In what way?

A. Lifting her clothes up and jumping; whether she was going to show her black legs, or show her white ones, I don't know, but it was very ridiculous, the one, sir, I saw. There was three ladies together.

Q. Mr McKenzie: I don't quite understand. What unseemly thing did she do?

A. Lifted her petticoats as high as that (illustrating), and shouted "blacklegs! blacklegs!"

Q. As high as the knee?

A. Yes.

Q. Do you know her name?

A. I don't know her name, sir.

Q. Mr Bodwell: When was that?

A. When we were returning; I don't know her name, sir...

D.J. Thomas (Fireman)

A. When we came back through Northfield there were women coming out in crowds, shouting after us, and one, especially, called out to us that was in the sleigh to throw us over, throw us out; "throw them Aberdare men out!" and that is the very place I come from—South Wales. And there were women there. I don't like to say anything, as I am ashamed of it.

Q. Well, you had better tell the Committee?

A. There was two women there came out from the house—I think it was about the third house from the corner, that is the right-hand side coming out to Wellington; they came out there and shouted; I don't know what they were shouting, because the two were shouting together, and I could not understand what they were saying, but they showed their legs to us, and they went rather too far, I should think. They raised their clothes rather too high.

Q. Mr McKenzie: How high?

Q. Col. Baker: Did they lift their clothes above their knees?

A. Yes, sir; above their knees. I had no snowballing at all; I was in front of the others...

Alexander Sharp (Manager of Mines)

Q. Then you left the Cemetary after the service, and started on your way back?

A. Yes.

Q. You were with the body of the people returning?

A. There was one sleigh immediately in front of us, and all the others was to my rear. While we were just entering the village of Northfield, I could see that there had been quite a lot of preparation made for our return. The women were running from one door to another, somewhat excitedly, and I could see several effigies standing by the roadside.

Mr McKenzie: Several?

A. There was one distinct effigy of a woman—at least, I took it to be—on a pole about this high, and it had a woman's dress on, and there was nothing shewing the head, but just on top of the dress there was a deep mourning veil. That was standing on the right-hand side of the road, I think opposite about the second house in Northfield, coming to Wellington.

Q. Do you think that had any significance with reference to the funeral procession?

A. Well, I took the thing just to be a complete insult, and felt very much aggrieved to think that people was so ignorant and stupid to do that while we were returning home from such a solemn ceremony. I want to explain what I mentioned about several effigies. There was two. My attention this time was somewhat taken up with the snowballing, which was being commenced; but there was a second one there. I think it was just the trousers of a man that was put on a pole, and a pit cap on the top of it; and in the rear was another sort of a thing, indicating a rig of a miner, and some sort of mourning cloth hanging on it. Then the women began snowballing on each side of the road at a lot of men that was immediately in front of me in the sleigh, containing, I would say, a dozen of men. They would pelt at that sleigh, I would say, not less than 30 or 40 snowballs.

Mr McKenzie: Who would do this?

A. There were three women particularly engaged, standing each side of the other, and then there would be about a dozen boys and girls, of ages ranging from 9 to 11 years. The boys and girls that was snowballing at this end of the town they did look to me a year or so older than the ones that we met coming in, but there was quite a number, because they were throwing these snowballs; they were shouting every conceivable insult: "blacklegs," and "sons-of-bitches," and so on, and hooting and bowing; and two or three girls and boys on this side had oil-cans, rattling them with pieces of sticks. Every man in this part of Northfield was standing in the doorways, shouting to the women as if encouraging them, and every woman stood in the doorways waving something in their hands, and bowing in this sort of way (illustrating).

Chairman: What was that something they were waving?

A. Well, at least one woman, I would know her if I saw her. She was standing in the door, and she had a piece of cloth or something just in her hand. I think there would be, perhaps, 4 or 5 women standing in the door as we passed at Northfield. Then, the snowballing was evidently going to be directed towards me, and it was at this particular time that this remark was made we formerly spoke about. I think I would be about 5 or 6 feet, then, from these women. I had turned the buggy a little, so that I could call, in order so as to speak to the women that I thought I should hear from, and I could see their hands—we were not 5 or 6 feet away—and I laid the reins down, and spoke to the woman and said "If you throw that snowball here, I will come out of it," just through the bars in the covered buggy. They dropped their hands, and just as I was moving a little further, a snowball came and struck the arm of the buggy, just where my cheek was.

Q. Was any remark made?

A. Oh, yes; all these women made several nasty remarks.

Mr Croft: What remark did they make?

A. Oh, the old story over again: "Give it to the blacklegs," "let the blacklegs have it." In coming further up towards Blakeley & Rogers' boarding-house, several men were standing there shouting "blackleg," and coming to Young & Bickle's store, I would say there was no less than 20 men standing on the verandah, with 8 or 9 boys standing in front of them, all having snowballs prepared.

Mr McKenzie: The men, too?

A. No, sir; no, they hadn't the courage to do that...

RURAL WOMEN'S ORGANIZATIONS

By the first decades of the twentieth century, a variety of associations and clubs had been established for rural women. Some of these were national and international in scope, while others were community based. All provided an opportunity for leadership and fellowship among rural women by aiding them in forming networks and helping them to develop the skills required to operate effectively in the public sphere. Through the initiative of Adelaide Hoodless the first Women's Institute was organized among the women of Saltfleet, Ontario, in 1897. The following letter provides evidence about one Institute's debating programme. Such programmes would accustom rural women to public speaking, teach them to develop an argument effectively, and expose them to new information and a variety of opinions. Similar benefits would accrue from monthly clubs like the Women's Maple Leaf Club of Sundre, Alberta, whose brief minutes are also reprinted here. The minutes are evidence of the range of concerns addressed by these western women. The Sundre women's ingenuity for entertainment is also shown by their approach to the calling of the membership role which required each member to respond by name and with a comment on a monthly topic, for January, on kitchen appliances and conveniences, in February, with a comic saying, and so on.

Ontario, 1909
Department of Agriculture and Food, Women's Institute Branch, Correspon-
dence Files, 1909-1910, Public Archives of Ontario.

Old Castle   Dec. 15, 1909
Miss Watson
as a friend of institutes I am taking the liberty of asking you a few questions at
our next meeting at Old Castle we are having a debate the subject to be
discussed "Resolved that a farmer's wife is more of a benefactor to the country
than a merchant's."

and I have been appointed to take part and fight for the merchant wife
(although it goes against the grain to do so) and not being very well posted on
debating thought perhaps I could get a few points from you to help me out a
little for of course we shall work to win [even] if it is against our will.

Truely Yours,
Mrs C.A. Allen

P.S. Next meeting the first Wednesday in Jan.

•

Sundre, Alberta, circa 1914
Robert Dean Papers, M310, Glenbow-Alberta Institute Archives.

Jan. 28 Creed. Roll Call—Kit. appliances and conveniences Minutes of last
meeting. Business. Paper on "Household Economics" by Mrs Jackson. Discuss
Banquet for U.F.A. by D.E.L.W.I.* Household hints by Mrs A. King.
Recitation by Miss Watt. At Mrs Jackson. Snow on the ground.

Feb. 25th. Maple Leaf Club Roll Call, by, a comic saying. Minutes of last
meeting. Business. Paper on child welfare by Mrs Miller. Discussion by three
members on these subjects (no. 1) Squabbling and how to deal with it (no. 2)
Unselfishness (no. 3) Equal rights for boys and girls. Valentine box. Valentine
tea. Community Singing. Speakers on Discussion are Mrs Nelson, Burke,
Overguard at Mrs Burns.

March 31st. O Canada. Roll Call—by—Irish Jokes. Min. of last meeting.
Business paper on "Canadianization" by Mrs Burke. Discussion on local
civics. Grab bag. Lantern Slide Lecture. At Mrs Nelson—muddy roads.

April 28th Creed, Roll Call—a verse from Shakespeare. Min. of last
meeting. Business. Paper on "Emigration" by Mrs A. King. Debate—

*[United Farmers of Alberta by a particular Women's Institute]

Competition on—Some article you have brought from your Native land. At Mrs Miller's snow everywhere.

May 24. Maple Leaf Roll Call by—helpful hints on vegetables & Soups. Min. of last meeting. Business. Paper on "Agriculture" by Mrs Peksie talk by Mr Kemp on "Gardening". Discuss—Trip to A.S.A. at Mrs Farris off muddy roads.

June 30th (O Canada) Roll Call by personal reminiscences of childhood days. Min. of last meeting. Business. Paper on "Education and Better Schools" by Mrs Overguard. Reading "The Children's Hour" by Mrs Lobley. (At Mrs Burkes Lovey Day) Musical programme. Discuss picnic and Sale of work.

July 28th Creed. Roll Call—name a Canadian industry. Min. of last meeting. Business. Paper on "Canadian Industries" by Mrs Nelson. Round table talk "How to improve home marketing" led by Mrs Jackson. Picnic and Sale of Work. At Mrs A. Dean.

August 25th. Maple Leaf Roll Call by current Events. Min. of last meeting. Business paper on Legislation by Mrs G.R. Batham. A Reading by Mrs A. Dean. Recitation by Mrs L. Ferguson. At Mrs Lobly.

Sept. 29th. O Canada Roll Call—quotations from B. Burns, Min. of last meeting. Business. Sketch of Burns life—by Mr Jackson. Scotch Songs. Competition of Scotch cakes. At Mrs Blackhurst.

Oct. 27th. O Canada. Roll Call—A Thanks - giving verse. Min. of last meeting. Business. Reading by—Mrs Leacock—Debate WI versus U.F.A.* Halloween Banquet. Invite Girls Club. At Mrs Bothens.

November 24th. Maple Leaf. Roll call by—Supper Ideas. Min. of last meeting. Business. Entertain children, party games, etc....

*[Women's Institutes versus the United Farmers of Alberta]

---

4. DEVIATING FROM EXPECTED ROLES

A LOCAL CELEBRITY

Unlike the reforming women who challenged their prescribed roles through organized groups or education, some post-Confederation women confronted the prevailing female images individually. Such was the case for Thérèse Dionne whose attire, habits and lifestyle challenged the social norm for single women and sparked the following speculation from a male observer.

Saint-Thomas, Quebec, 1872
J.M. Le Moine, L'Album du Tourisme, (Québec, 1872) 288-89. Translated by the editors.

Saint-Thomas includes another local celebrity, going by the name, Thérèse Dionne. Thérèse wears men's boots, a man's hat of rather the same volume; short skirt and long hunting knife in a sheath hung on her right side.

At the end of April, Thérèse preceded all the other regulars of the fishing hole and spent the day, in ice water to her knees and sometimes to her waist, fishing for *éperlans* or carp with a hand net. Alert, jesting despite her sixty years, gay as a finch, in her normal state: only, beware to the youngster who plays pranks on her! The sybille of Cumes is nothing compared to her; her eyes flashing with lightning; heinous swearing leaving her mouth: the knife drawn from its sheath. She would follow her enemy to the foot of the altar. In the eyes of my colleagues at school she was much more than an ordinary sorcerer. In short, her demeanour was so masculine as to put in doubt her sex. Was she man or woman or hermaphrodite?...

THE CASE OF MADA PINAULT

Although school teaching in the nineteenth century seemed a new opportunity for women for independent employment, the female school teacher's life, especially in rural areas, was not necessarily her own. Her movements, language, and behaviour, both inside and outside the classroom, were subject to microscopic examination by the parish and its authorities. In the case against Mada Pinault, we are presented with perhaps an extreme example of this examination and we have only the authority's side of the case. The case, however, does demonstrate the community consensus that in accepting public employment as a teacher, the woman gave up the right to a private life outside the school house and school hours, a view that Mada Pinault challenged.

Mont-Joli, Quebec, 1887
Testimony in the case of Mme Pinault.
Corréspondence Générale, 1887 No. 706, Education, Archives nationales du Québec, reprinted in Jacques Dorion, "Mathilde Milette, Eugène Morin, Lenaide Lemay, Dame Pinault: Coupables ou non-coupables?" Culture & Tradition, *II (1977) 61-63.*

Testimony of J.B. Beaulieu
    Twelfth day of October in the year one thousand eight hundred and eighty-seven before the Honourable Gédéon Ouimet, of the City of Quebec, Superintendent of Public Education, and Justice of the Peace of the Province of Quebec,...appeared Jean Bte Beaulieu of Mont-Joli, Rimouski, in the said district, aged seventy-four years who solemnly swore as follows:
I am the President of the school commissioners of Mont-Joli. The teacher of Mont-Joli is Mada Pinault. The husband of the teacher does not live at all with

his spouse; he lives in Ste-Flavie on the edge of the water three miles from Montreal. I have had occasion to receive complaints from the ratepayers of Mont-Joli about the conduct of the teacher. I have received these complaints ever since I became president, that is to say since the month of July and before that I received them when I was steward and school commissioner. They complain that the teacher lives in a *maison publique** which takes in travellers and they say that this is not proper for the schoolmistress. I cannot say whether it is a boarding house. I can say that this house has a license and possibly one can board there I do not know. They complain that it is not moral for a female teacher to sleep in a house like that. They complain that there are a lot of people in and out of the school house at night; they say that they are men and they complain that there is not an ounce of morality in the teacher, that she travels here and there.... Last July, I had occasion to meet the teacher on the public road and when she recognized me the teacher lay down on the ground, threw open her clothes and, laughing, said, "I greet you." At that time I was a school commissioner and I did not find her behaviour suitable. (Here the witness made the gesture the teacher made during this encounter). Two years ago this summer or thereabout, I was steward, in July or August. I was working in the teacher's room, she was sleeping in the bedroom of the school house, about ten o'clock in the morning, a man came in and sat down on the edge of her bed, then I was a bit embarassed and I left, this man stayed in the teacher's room about one half or three quarters of an hour. When he left she conducted him out through the private door and when he had gone, I resumed my work as steward in the teacher's room. One time, we were waiting here for the teacher to give the evening prayer in the chapel below the school and she arrived, between six and seven o'clock, from a walk with a man who was not her husband. We have on the floor below the school a chapel where until last spring we conducted religious services in that chapel but since that time, the parish priest has stopped coming to conduct these services in light of the gossip about the behaviour of the teacher....

J.B. Beaulieu

*[In the twentieth century, the term *maison publique* has come to mean brothel. At the time when this document was written, however, it might also mean boarding house or hotel. Eds.]

Testimony of Marie St-Pierre

The twelfth day of the month of October... Marie St-Pierre, daughter of Mathias St-Pierre, aged 19 years, appeared, was sworn in by the undersigned, gave evidence and said: I live with my father near the school in Mont-Joli. I know Miss Pinault. Her husband does not live with her. I went to the school about ten or eleven o'clock at night to have her read the directions on a seed package, it was a year ago this summer, about the month of May. I knocked on the door, the schoolmistress opened it and I found her there with Joseph St-Amant. I had the directions on the seeds read and I left.

The summer before in the month of June or July the following happened. I went to sleep at the school, my aunt was sleeping with the schoolmistress, she asked me to go to sleep with the teacher, I went there with her. After my arrival Joseph St-Amant, came in and went to sleep with the schoolmistress in her bed. It was ten or eleven o'clock at night, my aunt was 23 years old she was a girl: we were all four of us in the same bed. Another time in the same summer we the four of us went for a ride. Joseph St-Amant had some liquor, he rested his head on the teacher's shoulder. We left in the day and came home in the evening. I told my mother that I slept in the same bed with the schoolmistress, my aunt and Joseph St-Amant. Afterwards, after that experience, I did not go back to the school, my mother forbade me and I would not have gone back myself, if I had known what would happen, I would never have asked to sleep at the school....

Marie St-Pierre

THE UMBRELLA LADY

Single women outside the supervision of a family or their employers were a rarity on the prairies. Miss Gardiner, the umbrella lady described by Harriet Neville, was ridiculed for her dress and her eccentricities but for countless isolated prairie women her company and nursing made her an angel in disguise.

North-West Territories, 1887
Harriet Purdy and David Gagan, eds., "Pioneering in the North-West Territories," Canada: An Historical Magazine, II (1975) 42-43.

Many times men and a few times with women along have found shelter with us. There was one precept which my father inculcated in our education. "Be careful to entertain strangers, for thereby ye may entertain angels unawares." No stranger was ever refused meals or shelter night or day at our home. Many times peddlers with their team or only carrying their two heavy grips came near night saying they could not find any place to stay but always were told to go "there" pointing to our house with trees around it, as the place where they might stay all night. Once it was truly an angelic messenger. My husband home but about deluged with fall work. Two eldest daughters (May and Elsie) away teaching school. Our youngest (Brenda) having to milk cows and do all the housework as I had been sick in bed about two weeks. The first day I could sit up awhile, my daughter came and told me that some person wanted to come in and said Papa had just gone away. I said "Why bring him in, perhaps he is hungry." "But Mamma it is a woman." That was stranger still.

What woman could come unless driving, without a man with her? "Bring her right here," I said. I did not wonder at my small girlie's puzzle when the traveller entered. Small, not very young, but still not old, dressed in wide skirts with the long ago crinoline under them, hair in curl papers with a man's straw hat over them, man's number nine heavy boots on and carrying an immense green umbrella and a heavy bundle. The first thing she said "Is there a man here." Thinking she perhaps wanted my husband as magistrate to do something for her I answered, "No, he is away now." "Well when I hide my bundle I will come in then." I told her to leave her bundle in the porch or bring it in the house, it would be safe here. She would not but went out and came back without it. I told her to take off her things for she could not go any farther that night. She looked at me and said "You are very sick." I told her I was better but not able to help with the work yet. She said "That is just what I came for," and forthwith followed [Brenda] into the kitchen. It was milking time and she took a pail. Then my scared girl came to me and said not to let her go where the cows were in the nearby field for she was sure they would be frightened. I could not stop her but she never got near enough a cow to milk. She carried the milk in, strained it into the pans and washed the pails, when she heard my husband drive to the door with some things to bring into the house. Whether afraid of a man or not she insisted on helping him water and feed his horses and taking them to the stable. Of course my husband was amused and tried not to show it but used her as he would any other lady so kind as to be helpful, then brought her in to tea. She would not sit at the table but by the stove, and took some lunch out of a parcel. I handed her a cup of tea but at first she did not want to take it as she said she had some tea if I would allow her to make it. However I coaxed her a little and she soon began to talk.

Her name was Miss Gardiner. She was looking for a nephew who was poor and had no one to take care of him. She had a fortune and was going to help him and leave him her money. But as she always helped sick people she would stay here till I got well. We made her a bed so she could sleep comfortably but I was careful to fasten the hook on inside of the kitchen door when we said good-night to her. First thing in the morning we heard her start the fire, and I called Brenda to hurry down and see after the breakfast. She was very attentive to prayers, ate a good breakfast, and asked if the week's washing had been done. Then started preparations for washing. I thought that was better than some other work she might attempt, but she went all over the house trying to find more things to wash. She took all day to it but did it well. Next morning she went at the kitchen, cleaned the stove all the woodwork and floor, every crack and corner and folded the clothes to iron, which she did in the afternoon.

Next day she insisted on churning and certainly worked the butter as it never had been before. She was thorough and also very attentive to me, [although] I was glad she did not try to dose me with some imaginative remedies.

Of course I got well as soon as possible and as I thought I would like a short drive my husband got ready the buck-board and pony for me, and my friend said I was not able to go alone, so she came along. I did not dress up in Sunday clothes but just went in my ordinary work dress and sun hat. A few rods from the house she burst out laughing and When I asked what was the matter she said "I was just thinking there was a pair of us." Well there just was. I had to laugh too and it did me good. I asked her why she carried that large umbrella. She said for two reasons. When boys came out of schools and made fun of her she just shut it up and charged at them and I should see them run. Another reason was so that when a storm came up, all she had to do was to open it and sit down close to the ground and she was always safe. She stayed a month and worked all the time at something. Helped pick potatoes and other things from the garden to the cellar, then said she must go, as I was quite well. I coaxed her to stay all winter and we would pay her but she would not. Then I fixed her a good lunch and gave our daughter [Brenda] money to buy a ticket, sent her to take her to the station. Ticket bought and having to wait awhile in the station she went out, and when she did not return soon my daughter went out to look for her and saw her a long ways down the track. She had taken the ticket farther west but whether she got on the train or not we never knew. This was my "angel unaware." We heard of her afterwards under several names, always stopping where there might be sickness and trying to help others. Who knows but what she had come for just such times as those. Perhaps helping some poor lonely woman on the prairie who needed the help much more than I did. She might find plenty of those I know....

WITCHES AND WITCHCRAFT

Societies commonly regulate the behaviour of their members through rules, whether enacted by legislation or by the force of community pressure. Branding those women who deviated from community norms as witches was one way of controlling behaviour through the exclusion of these women from normal social interaction. The following excerpt documents practices found as late as the turn of the century in some German-Canadian communities.

Ontario, 1901
W.J. Wintemberg, "German-Canadian Folk-lore," Ontario History, *III (1901)* 95.

About twenty years ago there lived an old woman not far from the village of New Dundee, who was popularly regarded as a witch. She is said to have possessed the sixth and seventh books of Moses, and it was believed that she could transform herself into any animal she chose. She sometimes transformed herself into a cat and prowled around her neighbour's premises. She once said that if she had a grudge against some person and could possibly get possession of some of his belongings, she would make him suffer.

Some time ago I was told of a bewitched sow and her litter of ten pigs. One day the sow started to run in a circle around the barnyard, the pigs following close at her heels. Every few minutes one of the pigs dropped and died. This continued until only a few pigs were left. The farmer went to consult a witch-doctor, who lived about three miles from his home, near the village of Petersburg. The doctor broke the spell which the witch had over the pigs, and told the farmer that the witch would call to get the loan of something, but he was not to let her have it under any circumstances for thus she would regain her power over the pigs. The witch-doctor's word proved to be true, for before long a woman came to borrow some article and he refused to let her have it. She called several times, but was always refused and her plans were thwarted.(!)

An old woman told me that one day a woman came to the place where she was working and asked for some food which was refused her. She left, much incensed at this refusal, and as she passed down the lane she began calling the cows, meanwhile holding up three fingers. The farmer did not think much about the matter at the time, but when the women began to milk, they found that on every cow only one teat produced milk, the other three, blood. The following morning the same thing happened again, and the farmer becoming alarmed, consulted an Amish witch-doctor, who cured the cows by a process of charming....

"LIKE A LIONESS WITH HER CUBS"

Although turn-of-the-century white women faced a social ideology that demanded obedience and dependence, these strictures were doubly strong for black women. However, as Carrie Best recalls, her mother demonstrated throughout her life a tenacity and will power that challenged the stereotype of black womanhood.

New Glasgow, Nova Scotia, circa 1917
Carrie Best, The Lonesome Road: The Autobiography of Carrie M. Best, *(New Glasgow, N.S., 1977) 43-44.*

Compared to our present life style, we would I suppose be classified as 'respectable'. If we were poor, we as children were never conscious of it, for we were never lacking in food, clothing or home comforts.

My mother was a meticulous home maker and cook often catering for social gatherings in the town. Although kind, loving and generous she was none the less a disciplinarian guarding the sanctity of the home and the family's safety like a lioness with her cubs. Black womanhood was held in low esteem during the early part of the twentieth century and only the home afforded the protection needed to ensure security from outside influences.

An incident that occurred at the close of the First World War tells its own story. A race riot erupted in the town of New Glasgow as the result of an altercation between a black and a white youth. Bands of roving white men armed with clubs had stationed themselves at different intersections allowing no Blacks to go beyond that point. We had learned of the riot from our father when he came home from work. My oldest brother was at work at the Norfolk House and my mother who had been driven home by the chauffeur of the family for whom she had been working knew nothing of the situation.

Finding my younger brother my father and myself at home and my older brother missing my mother inquired as to why he was not home. It was dusk.

In all the years she lived and until she passed away at the age of eighty-one my mother was never known to utter an unkind blasphemous or obscene word, nor did I ever see her angry. This evening was no exception. She told us to get our meal, stating that she was going into town to get my brother. It was a fifteen minute walk.

At the corner of East River Road and Marsh Street the crowd was waiting and as my mother drew near they hurled insults at her and threateningly ordered her to turn back. She continued to walk toward the hotel about a block away when one of the young men recognized her and asked her where she was going. "I am going to the Norfolk House for my son," she answered calmly. (My mother was six feet tall and as straight as a ramrod.) The young man ordered the crowd back and my mother continued on her way to the hotel. At that time there was a livery stable at the rear entrance to the hotel and it was there my mother found my frightened older brother and brought him safely home.

––––––––––

"SHE HAS CHOSEN HER LIFE"

Many of the young women who became prostitutes in the decades after Confederation undoubtedly faced situations similar to that confronted by

Cora Lee in the account below. Alone in a city without money, family, or friends, she would have had little other chance for survival than to accept the prostitute's work that was pressed on her. Her case caught the sympathy of many reformers, a sympathy that was quickly revoked when she returned to the brothel. While they judged that she had "chosen" an immoral life, one must wonder what alternatives she had in a society that would continue to brand her a fallen woman.

New York and Saint John, New Brunswick, 1888
Progress [*Saint John*] I(30) November 24, 1888, 1 and I (31) December 1, 1888, 1.

New York, Nov. 21—New York has heard no story in many a month that has stirred it to its depths like that of poor, unfortunate, hapless Cora Lee of your city. The tale is a brief one, but it is graphic with nameless deeds practised upon a homeless girl who left an orphanage only to be forced to live a prostitute.... She is of slight, willowy, sensuous build, is scarcely five feet tall and has eyes which at a distance seem black but melt into blue on a nearer approach. She is only seventeen years of age, hardly that in fact, and yet she has passed through an ordeal such as would wring pity from anyone but a demon. She has fallen, but it was a fall such as might happen any girl who landed in this city and had no help extended her to wrestle with the evils that abound. The whole gauntlet of crime she has been forced to run. She is ruined in body. In soul, let us trust that her present grief may wash the hideous immorality which perhaps over-confidence at first and force subsequently compelled her to practice....

"I was brought up in Saint Vincent's orphanage," she said, "away down in Saint John. I was only a child when I went there and the sisters took care of me. I had an uncle who was wealthy and after my father's death, my mother thought that he would leave us enough to keep us. He gave it all to our cousins and the orphanage was the only place for us. My mother died, long, long ago, and that today is the only thought that comforts me. I can remember Saint John as well, too! I often went with one of the sisters shopping and they were so good to me. They little know who it is that is now poor Cora Lee!" she said as she burst out sobbing.

"Oh, for God's sake don't give my name away!" she cried, as she looked at your correspondent and her face blanched. "I have two sisters married down home. It would kill them to know that I was so fallen. I was not to blame. I thought when I came to New York that I was coming to a home. So did poor Mother Augustine or she would not have let me come. I know she would grieve to death if she learned that the little girl who went out so often with her was the—oh, no! my God! Oh no! I cannot say what I was going to. I did not fall through my own fault. I was nearly fifteen years of age when one day, about two years ago, a lady from New York called at the orphanage, on Cliff street, and offered me a home here. I was glad of it in one way, though I remember how the poor mother pressed me to her and said she did not like to part with me. Sister Joseph, I think was her name, as well took me to her room the night before I left, and together we knelt down and prayed, and the sister warned me always to be good. She gave me some articles of devotion, and I left. I do not want to say who the lady was who took me away, except that she did not use me well. She imposed both on me and on Mother Augustine. She told the sister great stories about her being a relative of Judge Hayes, of California, and of the nice home I would have.".…

The next we learn of "Cora Lee" was that she was an inmate of the notorious House of All Nations in West Thirty-Second street, the most gorgeously fitted up palace of sin on the continent. It is the place where the gilded youth go to wear out the hours of the night in ribaldry and crime. Their means protect them from the police, and induce the procuress to do her devilish work. More young girls have been sent to shame and suicide out of that place than ever were victims from Monte Carlo.…

New York, Nov. 28. The sensation created by Cora Lee has collapsed. All our sympathy for the unfortunate girl has vanished. She is no longer held in the House of Detention as a witness against the notorious Carrie Baker. She is back again in the very hell from which she professed less than a week ago such a delight at being freed.

How was it done? There was too much money behind the House of All Nations; there were too many men in high places who had to be shielded. She succumbed to entreaties. She accepted bail for her appearance, and here the case ends. All her professions of reformation have been cast to the winds, and she is back at her old life of sin and shame. Her harrowing tale, I have now good reason to believe, was a sham—not the part of it concerning the orgies in which she was obliged to take part—but that portion which related to her being entrapped in the place. I have taken some pains to find out her history, and have discovered that before she went to the notorious Thirty-second street house she was the principal attraction in a low concert dive at Harlem.

Cora Lee played her part well, but Cora Lee has spurned what may be her last opportunity for reformation. It is sad, but she has chosen her life. It is sadder to think that she is a Saint John girl. The only bright spot in the whole affair is that she is unknown to anyone here. Her friends, if any still live, will be in ignorance of her fate. Even if they did know, they may not grieve. Her history deserves no other ending than the one it will surely have. Her life will necessarily lead her to one of two places, the prison or the insane asylum, for the deeds carried on where she now is are nameless ones. It may be, the sooner the better.

———

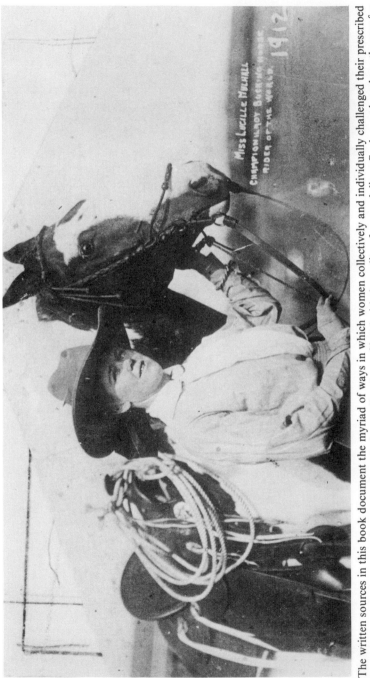

The written sources in this book document the myriad of ways in which women collectively and individually challenged their prescribed image. They also show many instances where the image directly conflicted with the reality of women's lives. Such must have been the case for Miss Lucille Mulhall, the 1912 champion lady bucking horse rider of the world.

Credit: Lucille Mulhall Collection, Manitoba Archives.

CHARGED WITH MANSLAUGHTER

As a spinster farmer, Helen Findlay needed assistance working her land. She hired George Everitt Green, a British child immigrant from Dr Barnardo's Homes. The boy was blind in one eye and, possibly, mentally slow but Findlay was desperate for help. As a spinster farmer out of grace with her family and exposed to hostility from her neighbours she was under extreme pressure. She used scolding, shoving, and beating to make George work harder. When he died as a result of external injuries, Findlay was charged with manslaughter but was not convicted.

Ontario, 1896
Alfred B. Owen to The Secretary, Department of the Interior, Jan. 18, 1896. Immigration Branch, RG 76, Vol. 124, File 25399. Public Archives of Canada.

Dr Barnardo's Homes.

Toronto, Jan. 18th, 1896

The Secretary, Department of the Interior,
Ottawa.
Sir,
It remains for me, therefore to deal only with the case of the unfortunate boy George E. Green, who died some time ago, in the Township of Keppel, in the County of Grey, and whose death led to his employer being tried on a charge of manslaughter. The boy Green arrived from England in April last having been for several months prior to his leaving an inmate of our London Institutions. Before his departure for Canada he was submitted, as is the case with all the boys who are sent out from our homes, to a close, thorough, and searching examination on the part of the Medical Officer of the Institutions.... At Liverpool he passed inspection at the hands of the medical officers of the Allan Steamship line and of the Board of Trade.... At Portland, where our party landed, we were subject to an unusually rigid examination at the hands of the United States medical officers.... The boy Green passed this without any question arising as to his physical or mental condition, or desirability as an immigrant. On our arrival at the Home here our medical officer, in accordance with our invariable custom, examined each boy in the party. He remarked that Green had lost the sight of one eye, and that he was not a boy of robust appearance, but there was absolutely no appearance or indication of deformity or disease. On the 6th of April he left us to enter the service of a farmer named Cranston, in the Township of Windham, in the county of Norfolk. His engagement with that gentleman, beginning, in accordance with our custom, with a month trial. At the end of the month Mr Cranston wrote us that he was returning the boy, as he found that owing to his defective vision he was not capable of performing the work required of him. In his evidence at the trial of the woman Findlay Mr Cranston swore that, apart from his defective vision,

the boy had no physical or mental defect, that he was clean in his habits and capable of performing a reasonable amount of work, and he swore that he was not humpbacked or in any way deformed, other than being left handed which, I presume can hardly be described as a deformity. He returned to the Home on the 4th of May, and three days after was placed with Miss Helen Findlay. I may say of Miss Findlay, that she was a member of a family with whom we have for several years placed boys. She herself kept house for her brother, George Findlay, and the latter employed one of our boys for four years, the boy during that time, doing exceedingly well and being contented and happy. He was visited several times by our Inspectors, and we had numerous letters from him, so that during the time he was there we had no reason whatever to question the suitability of the home. In 1894 George Findlay died, and, after the division of the property, which was attended we understand by a good deal of dispute and ill feeling among the members of the family, Miss Findlay was left in possession of the farm, with the stock and implements, but with little or no ready money in hand. The other members of the family, as we are informed, were much opposed to her carrying on the farm but she insisted on doing so and as the boy, who had been with her brother, did not remain with her, she made an application to us for another boy. Considering that we knew the place from our experiences in the past, we had no hestitation in entertaining the application, and the boy Green was sent to her as already stated....

After he had been in his place a short time we entered into correspondence with Miss Findlay in regard to the terms upon which she should engage the boy, and the usual agreement was signed, under which Miss Findlay undertook to engage the boy for a term ending on the 7th May 1898, furnishing him with his board, lodging, washing, clothing and all necessaries and paying him the sum of seventy-five dollars ($75.00) in cash. The agreement was finally received duly executed on the 1st of August, and from that time we heard nothing from either Miss Findlay or the boy, until we saw the paragraph in the papers that his death had taken place, that an inquest had been ordered and a verdict found implicating her with having caused his death by neglect and cruelty. The preliminary hearing took place before the Magistrates on the 19th, 20th and 21st days of November, ending in a disagreement of the Jury. The medical evidence adduced at the trial was extremely conflicting, and it is not remarkable that with this conflicting evidence before them the Jury was unable to agree upon a verdict....

Women's motives for participating in the Klondike gold rush were as varied as those of men. Some followed husbands, while others sought riches or adventure. In the Klondike they ran businesses, kept hotels, prospected, nursed, or maintained households. Hundreds of others ignored the strictures of Victorian morality to work as dance hall girls and prostitutes, as did the "group of hard workers" in Dawson pictured above. The North West Mounted Police estimated that over six hundred women passed the Lake Tagish Post in 1897-1898 alone.

Credit: Public Archives of Canada, C-14478.

FEMALE SUICIDE

It is difficult to determine the extent of female suicides in 1909 Canada because aggregate statistics are not available. However, to at least one writer, Jean Graham, the number of women taking their own lives was sufficient to prompt the following comments by way of explanation.

1909
Jean Graham, "The Tired Woman," The Canadian Magazine, *XXXIII (1909) 277-78.*

Suicide is not a particularly pleasant subject; but surely we read of an unusual number this spring among respectable women who were simply tired out or "suffered from poor health." The woman who has never been so weary of the daily grind that a grave seemed a nice, comfortable resting-place is to be envied. It is all very well to hang up hateful little mottoes, such as "Don't Worry," "Be Sunny" and "Do It Now." If I had my way they would be banished and soothing selections from "The Lotus Eaters" substituted. The truth is, that too many of our Canadian women have all work and no play and the result is physical disaster. The parsons and editors who are warning us against bridge and cocktails are wasting their paper and pulpit energy. The Canadian women who are alcohol fiends or given to excessive bridge are so few in number that they are hardly worth bothering about and regard these exhortations, if they ever hear or read them, with an amused scorn for the writer or speaker. What the clergy and the editors do need to talk about is the duty of giving the tired woman a rest and a change. Constant toil and drab monotony are enough to drive any woman to the nearest river or the most convenient carbolic acid. Then everyone wonders over the tragedy, an attempt is made to prove that the woman was insane, and some kind friend remarks: "She complained a good deal of feeling tired."...

Every sane and healthy woman likes work and takes praiseworthy pride in it. But drudgery is quite another story, and it is that sort of thing which depresses even unto death the woman who has no play, no variety. If advice is to be given, let some of the selfish men, who never dream that looking after the meals and material comfort of a large household is not enough to keep a woman bright and happy, be told of their shortcomings and shown the way of decent appreciation. There may not be a great deal of such selfishness in the community, but no one who has seen the drawn, gray faces of these over-worked, oppressed women can wonder that the burden finally becomes too heavy for human nerves and strength and is flung off by wearied hands that open the gateway to—let us hope, a long rest.

———

CHAPTER SIX

WIDOWHOOD, OLD AGE AND DEATH

In the half century after Confederation a woman who survived her most active childbearing years and reached age forty could expect to live for thirty years more.[1] Within those years the boundary between middle life and old age was indistinct so long as families remained large. At sixty as at forty a married woman had dependent children around her.[2] A rural woman whose oldest son stayed nearby to inherit the family farm probably saw her last children and first grandchildren growing up together and continued to participate in child care until close to her dying days. In smaller urban and rural households at the turn of the century all of the children of the marriage might be gone from home by the time the wife reached fifty, yet family concerns continued to figure prominently in the lives of older women. In the best of circumstances, the succession of generations represented a comforting continuity and children offered their mothers a sheltered and honoured dignity in their later years. For example, Ellen Osler lived until she was a hundred, dwelling in a comfortable Toronto home, dispensing advice and small gifts to her spreading family, placidly accepting a certain distance from crises in the lives of her offspring.[3] Other mothers measured their own worth by the respectable positions in which they were able to establish their children.

For couples whose marriages were happy and whose material circumstances were ample, the rewards of these last decades of life were many. It was possible for wife and husband to have some leisure together, to spend time helping family by choice rather than obligation, to cultivate the dahlias, and watch the sunsets.[4] Regrettably many marriages were not companionable, most couples were not prosperous, and widowhood was, statistically, a woman's most likely condition in the final years of life. By 1881 women's life expectancy exceeded men's in Canada, the excess in female survival rates being most marked in the years after fifty.[5] A woman who had buried several young children might count upon burying her husband as well before she herself died, and be reasonably assured that demography would make a second marriage improbable; social convention, we suspect, was increasingly set against the unions of older women and younger men.

Of course many women were widowed at a relatively young age, male probabilities of death already exceeding female among those who survived to age forty.[6] Vigorous and strong-willed women in this predicament achieved prominence in some European and American settings, using their widows' weeds to deflect discussion from the presumed disabilities of their sex and the skills learned in private life to command the commercial or agricultural enterprises bequeathed them by their spouses.[7] In the period immediately following Confederation, women in agricultural Canada did not often have this option. They were more frequently left dependent on their sons, sons-in-law or on their husbands' executors. Not even one in four of the Peel County, Ontario, widows studied by David Gagan was recognized in her husband's will as "mistress of her own future."[8]

The barriers to a widow's independence were social as well as material. Letitia Youmans, the Ontario school teacher and suffragist, was admonished against travelling alone in the continuation of her political work as a widow. The taboos against unaccompanied travel made women fearful, and amplified the unpredicatability and vulnerability of their situation. Note for example the trepidation of Madge Strong attempting to find her way home accompanied only by her mother and a young child.[9] In late nineteenth-century Canada widowhood was not an honourable station but a position popularly recognized as a kind of half life whose limits were defined by the absence of a male protector, breadwinner, and progenitor of social standing. Yet Youmans went on with her campaigning. The proportion of widows able to remain mistresses of their own households increased through the decades. Widows of some means could insist on more autonomy by the First World War.[10] Still, at the close of the period considered here, beyond the grief, the loneliness, the stunned adjustment to an abrupt and radical transition in their lives, the most common shared condition among widows, old and young, was poverty.

In 1885 a Quebec woman summarized her condition thus: "Little money, little means, and alone afflicted." Maria was 78, "rather old to work," ailing, and possessed only a cow, which she did not have money to feed. Her predicament sounds dire, even discounting the fact that we learn of her through a begging letter, a medium not characterized by great moderation. Widows were the prime recipients of late nineteenth- and early twentieth-century philanthropic aid not only because they were socially acceptable beneficiaries, but also because they were in unquestionable need. Their position was so bad that they were the first candidates for twentieth-century income assistance programmes.[11]

In the final patterns of life, those of death, Canadian women differed from Canadian men.[12] In 1881 although infant girls were more hardy than infant boys, young girls aged one to seven were more likely to die than young boys, and less likely to survive until their next birthdays in each succeeding year up to age forty-two. It was probably the poor diet and physical confinement of girlhood and the high risks of motherhood that caused this excess of dying in women's early years. Those who survived to age forty-two became the relatively long lived. Their male peers whose early years had been more healthful began to show their waning strength in increased vulnerability to accidents and disease.

By 1921 overall female odds against premature mortality had lengthened. Women's life expectancies generally had become greater than men's. Their largest gains occurred in childhood and adolescence, periods during which all mortality rates dropped radically, but the decline in girls' incidence of death was especially marked. The last age group during which relatively high female mortality lingered in Canada was thus the child-bearing years. In this, the Canadian pattern differed from those in some western European countries. While in Britain, the struggle against maternal mortality was beginning to show some success by the early twentieth century, in Canada progress was considerably more slow. In Canada, too, female death rates from respiratory diseases, particularly tuberculosis, remained high, markedly higher than male rates, a reproach in an era during which women in other countries had been the prime beneficiaries in the struggle against the white plague.[13]

The rituals of death sustained life. The funerals of those who had managed to stay in one place and build an honourable connection of neighbours and kin were not only well attended celebrations of a life well lived but also affirmations of loyalty to lineage and community.[14] The final reckoning was edited of all but virtuous accomplishment and notable contribution (note the eulogy for the forger Cassie Chadwick)[15] as a gesture of atonement and to assuage the fear of death. Thus the masked testimonies of death camouflaged life's contradictions and wives, mothers, and widows denied a fair portion of honoured dignity in life were offered sentimental sanctification in death.

NOTES

1 M. C. Urquhart and K. A. Buckley, *Historical Statistics of Canada* (Toronto, 1965) 41. This probability remained relatively constant through the period under consideration here.

2 David Gagan, *Hopeful Travellers: Families, Land and Social Change in Mid-Victorian Peel County, Canada West* (Toronto, 1981) 87-89.

3 "A Grandmother's Letters" in this chapter.

4 "A Succession of Fine and Lowery Days" in this chapter.

5 Dominion Bureau of Statistics, *Canadian Abridged Life Tables, 1871, 1881, 1921, 1931* (Ottawa, 1939) 13.

6 Male life expectancies decline below female in 1871 and 1881 at age 37; by 1921 female life expectancies are greater than male continuously from age seven.

7 Iris Origo, *The Merchant of Prato* (London, 1957); Diane Hughes, "Domestic Ideals and Social Behaviour: Evidence from Medieval Genoa," in Charles Rosenberg, ed., *The Family in History* (Philadelphia, 1975) 115-43; David Herlihy, "Land, Family and Women in Continental Europe, 701-1200," *Traditio*, XVIII (1962); Julia O'Faolain and Lauro Martines, *Not in God's Image* (London, 1973) 149, 229-35; Lawrence Stone, *The Family, Sex and Marriage in England, 1500-1800* (London, 1977) 196, 244; Sheila Rowbotham, *Women, Resistance and Revolution* (New York, 1974) 19-20; Isabel Foulché-Delbosc, "Women of Three Rivers: 1651-

63," in Trofimenkoff and Prentice, *The Neglected Majority;* Ann Douglas, *The Feminization of American Culture* (New York, 1977) 59.

8   Gagan, *Hopeful Travellers,* 55-56; "Widows" in this chapter.

9   "Benediction," and "Worrying and Wondering" in this chapter.

10 "Plans in the Morning" in this chapter.

11 "Seventy-Eight is Rather Old to Work" in this chapter. See earlier discussion of this point in chapter four.

12 This discussion is based upon the life tables 1871, 1881, 1921, and 1931 found in Urquhart and Buckley, *Historical Statistics,* 41, *Canadian Abridged Life Tables,* 5-20, and S. H. Preston, Nathan Keyfitz and R. Schoen, *Life Tables for National Populations* (New York and London, 1972) 120-23. Under-registration of deaths limits the reliability of these figures for 1871 and 1881 and it is likely that under-reporting distorts data most seriously for the elderly in all years. We are grateful to R.M. McInnis for alerting us to difficulties in the data and pointing out parts of the literature we had not explored. See also Warren E. Kalbach and Wayne W. McVey, *The Demoraphic Bases of Canadian Society* (Toronto, 1971) 44-45.

13 Sheila Ryan Johansson, "Sex and Death in Victorian England: An Examination of Age- and Sex-Specific Death Rates, 1840-1910," in Martha Vicinus, *A Widening Sphere* (Bloomington, Indiana, 1977) 163-81; Preston, Keyfitz and Schoen, *Life Tables,* 120-123; George Wherrett, *The Miracle of the Empty Beds* (Toronto, 1977); R.J. Dubos and J. Dubos, *The White Plague* (London, 1953). On the tuberculosis campaign in Canada see Katherine McQuaid, "From Social Reform to Social Service. The Changing Role of Volunteers: the Anti-Tuberculosis Campaign 1900-30," *Canadian Historical Review* LXI (1980) 480-501.

14 See "An Esteemed Lady," in this chapter.

15 See "The Notorious Mrs. Chadwick," in this chapter.

1. WIDOWS AND THEIR PROBLEMS

"STRUGGLING AGAINST PENURY"

Poverty, vice, and crime were readily associated with each other in mid-nineteenth century Canada as many believed that the intemperate, immoral, or lazy swelled the poor classes. To redress this opinion, a Toronto *Globe* columnist in 1869 visited the homes of many poor widows and deserted women. The writer found, among these women, unexpected strengths, initiatives, respectability, and vision.

Toronto, 1869
"Poverty in Toronto", Globe, *26 January 1869.*

That a vast amount of honest poverty exists in the city at the present time, is a well known fact to every one who has paid any attention to the subject. Hundreds, if not thousands of men are out of employment, whose families are starving and the great cry of these men is for "work," but work they cannot get. Then how many hideous and deserted women have we in our midst, struggling against penury? There was nothing that struck us as much in the course of our visits as the sad case of many of these poor creatures.

We saw one old woman eighty-five years old, whose husband has been long dead, whose only son is a soldier, and whose only support is her daughter. From what we could gather, her daughter is an industrious and respectable woman, yet she can't get work. She goes out and does washing; but then, as the old lady explained, "washing is so scarce, so many are at it, and it is so difficult to get a full day's washing. For the people themselves get up in the morning; and fill the boiler and all my girl has to do is rub the clothes out and she is paid by the hour." The old creature herself tries various shifts to make a livelihood. In her window are a few bottles with a pound or two of concoctions inside of them; she does a little at stocking knitting, and sometimes thinly clad she goes out and peddles with her basket. Her whole appearance bespeaks respectability, and her whole conversation is tinged with religious feeling. In every sack of wood she receives; in every child that comes for a cent's worth of sweets; in every thing she recognizes the hand of Providence. And as we looked to her with her knitting in her hand and heard her speak so; and then thought of the thousands of men amongst us who are enjoying every luxury that the world can afford, and yet utterly ignore a beneficent Providence. Cowper's lines at once occurred to us.

> The cottager who weaves at the own door
> Pillows and bobbles, all her little store
> I knows this and knows no more—her bible true,
> A truth the brilliant Frenchman never knew.

It was a lamentable sight to look at the poor old lone one, with one foot in the grave, still forced to battle and strive and not for a morsel of bread, and her old soul distracted with the miserable question, "What shall I eat, and wherewithal shall I be clothed?"

We saw another widow about sixty. Her husband had once been a respectable farmer; but having gone into business, lost his all, and died leaving his wife penniless. She is in bad health, and endeavours to earn a subsistence by washing. In her case also, scarcity of labour is the misery, and a dollar a week is the utmost she has earned for many a long day. Still as she says, she strives to wrestle through somehow. She is a kind hearted mortal, too, as is illustrated by a little episode in history. Shortly after the death of her husband, her only sister died also, leaving a little boy, the only relative the poor widow had now left in the world. With a woman's affection: her heart clung to the little orphan; and though ignorant as to where tomorrow's breakfast was to come from she took him home and reared him, stuck to him in all her poverty, and he is now getting to be a manly little fellow, one day, it is to be hoped, to repay the old woman for all the affection she has shown to him. It is not true that when poverty comes in at the door, love flies out of the window.

Another widow is supported by her daughter, who provides food for both, by making pants at 15 cents a pair. Let the young gentlemen who adorn King street of an afternoon, and the old gentlemen who rattle their silver in their pockets, seriously reflect on that fact.

Another is forced to send her boy, nine years of age, away, weeks at a time, on peddling excursions. We saw another woman whose husband left her two years ago and went to the other side. She has two beautiful children, one about seven and the other about two years of age, and when she gets anything to do, the two forsaken little things have to pass the weary day alone. Several times this poor forlorn family have been found in literal starvation, and had not the missionary lighted upon them and relieved their wants it is more than probable, that a neglectful father and a neglectful country would, ere this, have had the lives of these three outcasts to answer for. We saw many more such cases, and all equally sad.

In every instance amongst the widows, we found what is perhaps the best test of a woman's respectability—thoroughly clean houses. And what was more striking still, was the care almost every one had taken to ornament her humble abode. The walls, in some cases, were literally covered with adornments of various sorts. Pictorial tracts—illustrated temperance pledges—numbers of the "Workman"—valentines—cloth marks and newspaper advertisements, all entered into the list of their fine art collections; and one old lady, seemingly less fortunate in her collective faculties aesthetic or the political, had papers of all sizes and all political creeds, spread over her walls.

Nor was there any whining or severe complaining on the part of these forlorn creatures, and when asked how they bore up so well, those who had children looked to the future; those who had no children, derived happiness from memories of the past, and one old widow betakes herself, when she feels a little discontented, to the Psalms, for as she said, David came through far more and greater trials than ever she had to endure, and it wonderfully relieves one's own troubles to pity some other body.

GEORGE-ETIENNE CARTIER'S WILL

On November 10, 1866, George-Etienne Cartier, the noted father of Confederation, made his will. The break-up of his marriage with Hortense Fabre had been a fact for several years. The will, however, was extremely hard on his wife, their children, and his wife's family and created a scandal when it was published in 1873 following his death. Relevant clauses from the will are translated below and reprinted with a commentary which appeared in the Montreal *Witness*.

Quebec, 1866 and 1873
Gérard Parizeau, La Chronique des Fabre *(Montreal, 1978) 300, 302-3, 305-6, 308-9.*

The year one thousand eight hundred and sixty-six, the tenth day of the month of November.

In the presence of Theod Doucet and of John Helder Isaacson, notaries public for this part of the Province of Canada called Lower Canada, residents of Montreal, in Lower Canada, undersigned. Appeared the Honourable George Etienne Cartier, lawyer of the City of Montreal....

7. I give and leave to Miss Luce Cuviller, of the City of Montreal, a female of full age..., to be used as she wants it and on the condition that she has twenty-five low masses said by the priest of the Saint Sulpice Seminary of Montreal for the rest of my soul, the sum of one hundred and fifty dollars, praying as much as she can that she give good advice to my two daughters named below or to my executors and trustees in the interest of my daughters, being myself convinced from what I know of her and because of her wisdom and carefulness which she has proved in the education of her niece, Miss Symes, who was committed to her care, that her advice concerning my daughters will be of great usefulness to them.

8. As to the rest of my property where it may be situated, and of whatever nature, value or description, I give and leave it in trust...and if the revenue is sufficient, to pay to each of my daughters, Josephine and Hortense Cartier, an

annual amount of one hundred and fifty dollars payable three times a year until my daughters reach the age of thirty at which age and after my said trustees and executors should pay to each of my said daughters, during their lives, one third of the revenue...

12. ...I provided by my marriage contract before Mr Girouard and his colleague notaries that allowed a division of property between my wife Hortense Fabre and myself, support for my said wife after my death, which is the reason why I have not made any legacy by this will....

I forbid and I prohibit either of my daughters to marry any member or kindred of the Fabre family whether of the maternal or paternal side, and if either of them do or both do they will lose the legacies I have made to them and their descendents by the present will....

Sir Geo. E. Cartier's Will.

(To the Editor of the Witness).

Sir,—A short synopsis of the late Sir Geo. Cartier's extraordinary will, published in a number of your paper this week, induces me to make a few remarks on some of its clauses. I trust that your usual love of fairplay and justice will secure their publication. Owing to the wide circulation of your paper, those strange clauses may cause unjust surmises and cast a slur on the character of Lady Cartier and her family. You may object that it is no business of the public; wills are seldom discussed in the Press; but when they are brought forward, they should be explained. Lady Cartier's life as a wife and a mother has ever been irreproachable. Married very young, she was entirely devoid of worldliness, and of remarkably frank and candid nature, and could not always join, I suppose, in the adulations and flattery to which the followers of the deceased had accustomed him. As to her family, on which such an unjust imputation is cast, it is equal in every respect to Sir George's— intellectually, socially and morally. If it was not a legal necessity, for the sake of the memory of the deceased, I am astonished at his executors having allowed those conditions of his will to become public.

It is neither just nor manly, because a man strays from the path of duty, that the odium should be thrown on the innocent, and that they should be branded before the world as if they were guilty, instead of victims.

Sir George had none of the elements of greatness in his character; he was active and energetic, devoted to his friends, and imperiously claiming from them the same unquestioning submission to his behests. I have nothing to do with his political career: it is as a husband and father I now view him. I feel for his wife and the daughters, who stood at his dying bedside, and for whom these invidious and cruel clauses in his will shall be a severe and undeserved shock. They will perhaps be forgotten in the extraordinary and uncalled for pageant that is to be displayed at his funeral—a continuation of the incense and adulation with which his followers have always surrounded him. I trust every true woman will give a thought to the absent and injured ones.

A Wife and a Mother.

Montreal, 7th June, 1873.

BENEDICTION

The loneliness and uncertainty faced by a widow are evident in Letitia Youmans' recollections of her husband's death. For that woman a strong religious belief provided some comfort. Also comforting must have been the knowledge that she need not be concerned about her economic future. Rather than take her ease in this security in her community, despite social conventions, Letitia Youmans pursued with even greater force her temperance cause.

Ontario, 1882
Letitia Youmans, Campaign Echoes, *(Toronto, 1893) 240-41.*

On inquiry of my friend, Mrs Yarwood (who stood at my husband's side when he passed away), if he left any message for me, she replied, "He went too suddenly to leave any message." My thoughts at once reverted to the letter he sent me a few days before, closing with this remark, "Do all you can, your reward will come in the great future. Your affectionate husband." I accepted that as his dying message, and none could have been better.

The thought came with overwhelming force, I can never go out alone, my journeying must cease. My mind was directed to the experience of Ezekiel, which I failed to remember that I had ever read before. "Son of man, behold, I take way the desire of thine eyes at a stroke; yet weep not, let not thine tears run down. Bind thy tire* on thine head, and thy shoes on they feet, and restrain not thy lips to speak to the people. And that night my wife died."

The next objection presented was, "your travelling alone will call forth unfriendly criticism." The words of Isaiah were given in response: "Every tongue that shall arise against thee in judgement, thou shalt condemn." I said, "It is enough, Lord, I will take Thee at Thy word." Accordingly I went on with my life-work, missing, oh, how sadly, the strong arm on which I had leaned; the tender sympathy that had always been mine; the gentle criticism of sentiment, style and manner which none but a bosom friend would bestow; but most of all, the earnest assurance, "I prayed for you all the time you were speaking." Thank God for those prayers.

*[a head-dress].

All through the weary journeyings of that long, cold winter through the State of Michigan and the Province of Quebec, I realized the presence of Him who said, "I will never leave thee, I will never forsake thee." And again, "Thy Maker is thy husband," and "underneath are the everlasting arms."

WORRYING AND WONDERING

Following the death of her husband, Madge Isabel Strong decided to return to her home in Canada with her young child, after twelve years in the United States. Accompanied by her mother, Strong and her child travelled to Alberta a half a year after her father and older brother had made the trip. The following excerpt from Madge Strong's reminiscences underlines the uncertainties which this widow faced as the result of her decision to move.

Lethbridge, Alberta, 1904
Madge Isabel Strong Papers, Acc. 68.93/1, Provincial Archives of Alberta.

Early in May 1904, we reached Lethbridge at seven in the evening, from Great Falls Montana, this being considered the easiest way, and found the small station floor completely covered by men in sheepskin coats fast asleep, or pretending to be, as they waited for transportation to the coal field. I approached the ticket agent, through a door on the platform, to ask if we would get a berth in the sleeping car going through to Fort McLeod on the eleven o'clock train and he said it was impossible. I then asked where we could wait; he took a look into the waiting room and shrugged his shoulders, so we settled for an old bench on the platform where I tried to make mother and my small child comfortable, while I spent most of the time walking back and forth, worrying and wondering why we had attempted such a crazy trip.

Finally, at eleven o'clock, the train from the east came in and standing at the steps of the sleeping car was the porter and one lone man.

I hurried to them and inquired of the porter if it were possible for him to find a place in his car where we could sit the distance to Fort McLeod; while he was shaking his head the man spoke up and offered his berth which was not made up. They helped us into the car, where my baby rewarded this gentleman by throwing up on him. However, in a few minutes he and the porter returned and he insisted we should leave the arrangements to him for a bedroom over the station, where we would rest until eight o'clock, when we would take the train to Calgary. How he accomplished it, I don't know, but we got the room where we could stretch out for the few remaining hours. I have never forgotten that man and his great kindness, although I forgot to ask his name in my gratitude....

Poverty was the most typical state for older women who were widowed, alone, or the sole support of a household during the period before the First World War. Few owned property either because of the economic circumstances of their lives or their legal disabilities. There were few places in the labour force for old women such as Mrs Soloman of Price's Lane in Toronto and although she would have been recognized as one of the deserving poor, urban relief systems were inadequate. Women like Mrs Soloman lived by their wits and from day to day.

Credit: Department of Health Collection, No. 440, City of Toronto Archives.

WIDOWS

The death of a husband deprived a late nineteenth-century woman not only of an emotional partner but often also of vital economic support for herself and her family. The widow's plight, as well as that of other women unsupported by men, prompted reformers to agitate for legal change. Most widows, however, were forced to rely on their own resourcefulness—in legal arrangements in the case of the author's grandmother in financial management and business development in his mother's case.

Ontario, 1916-21
A.W. Currie; Growing Up in Rural Ontario, *1885, 30,45-7, Queen's University Archives.*

My father was spared the strain of having to struggle up the agricultural ladder because his mother, after her husband's death, willed it [the farm] to him provided he looked after her in her old age. This was a common arrangement at the time and, in effect, was a kind of old age pension. Unfortunately a few sons, or their wives, treated the old person in a niggardly manner and in one case I learned of later, the mother had to threaten action in the courts to get something approaching justice—an approach because the widow got a pittance in money but little or no love....

When we moved to town after my father's death, our struggle to make a living was intensified. His estate was quite inadequate to support his widow and four children, ranging in age from 6 to 18. The situation was made worse because for all practical purposes our farm had been sold at the prices prevailing prior to 1914 and we had to live through the inflation which began about 1917 and lasted until 1921.

However, my father had very little insurance.... It was no disgrace for my father to have only $1,000. The real tragedy did not come until a few months after his death. On the advice of her parents and several trusted friends, mother invested the face value of the policy in the bonds of a mortgage and loan company. It failed and she was left, as she said between sobs, without a solitary thing to fall back on.

In fact, another calamity had already struck. I clearly remember going with my mother to a lawyer's office on a hot afternoon in August, 1916....

My mother gave the colonel the will which my father had drawn in his own hand a few weeks before his death. The lawyer sitting erect behind his desk read it with a concentration that surprised a spotlessly clean but poorly-dressed lad sitting ill at ease on a chair with his feet well off the floor. Finally, the colonel put down the document with the word, "I'm terribly, terribly sorry. This will is not valid. It has been witnessed by only one person not two as required by law." Mother burst into tears. Out of sympathy for her and perhaps out of fear of the unfamiliar surroundings and the dignified, white-haired man with a black patch over one eye, I cried too.

Mother was put to extra expense taking out letters of administration and, worse still, one-third of my father's small estate was held in trust by the Official Guardian for us four children until we individually reached the age of 21. The law was designed to protect infants against extravagant, selfish mothers but my mother was decidedly not in that class. Many a time over the next few months did I overhear her telling people that she needed the money then and there, not year ahead. Three or four years after this experience, mother casually mentioned the matter to a young lawyer who had recently come to town. Without charging her a cent, he took legal steps to have the Official Guardian release the trust fund. Small as it was, it came in handy.

With her two-thirds of the proceeds of the sale of the farm, stock and implements, mother was able to pay what lawyers call testamentary and funeral expenses, buy a smallish house in a nearby town, and pay her bills while searching round to discover how she could earn a living.... Children's allowances were non-existent and my mother rejected the widow's pension which the government had recently introduced. She thought she would irrevocably lose her self-respect if she applied for the allowance.

All things considered, mother was probably wise to start by using the skills she had learned on the farm. She kept the best milker in our small herd and arranged for a brother-in-law (one of my uncles) to feed her over the winter in return for the calf she produced. In the following spring, he brought the cow to town and we took over a milk route which a long-time friend was glad to get rid of for a few months. Every morning I would get up early, walk nearly half a mile to the pasture on the edge of town, lead the cow back on a halter, wait until my mother milked her, return the cow to pasture, and hustle off to school....

Meanwhile, in the goodness of God—that is how mother would have explained it—she was using her skill as a dress-maker to earn enough money to keep her family together. She had to work unbelievably long hours to do so. If she were not cutting out a dress on the dining room table, she was basting pieces together, doing a fitting for a customer, discussing suitable designs with the help of fashion magazines and mail order catalogues, or making the sewing machine hum as she drove it at full speed with her foot on the paddle. I also learned that while I could expect to be reasonably well fed, my bed would not be made more than once or twice a week unless I made it myself.

After mother had proven her ability to make a living in this way, she considered it safe to dip into her tragically small savings to improve our standard of living. We moved from our first house into a larger one which mother occupied for 46 years and then sold for not quite four times what it had cost her....

PLANS IN THE MORNING

The following is an excerpt from the reminiscences of May Appleyard Red-
maine who in 1911 left her upper middle-class home in England to settle down
as a bride on a homestead in western Canada.

Alberta, 1911-19
Bill McNeil, "Voice of the Pioneer," Early Canadian Life, *II (1978),*
Reprinted in Bill McNeil, Voice of the Pioneer *(Toronto, 1981) 42-47.*

My husband came out two years before I did...

The wedding was a glittering affair with lots of fine, but not very practical
gifts for a young couple preparing to leave for a home in the Canadian bush.
Things like a piano and a sterling silver tea service. However, the eve of sailing
day came along and both our families gathered for a final goodbye. I remember
we all sat around the fire in the drawing room. Everybody got lumps in their
throats, and of course my father was a real stickler for doing the right thing. No
tears allowed. I think I cried nearly all night in bed, but I'm not sure. We got on
this boat, and just came here, and that's all there was to it....

I was such a child really...just turned twenty....

I had lived a very sheltered life and my father was one of these Victorian
fathers, you know. I hadn't been into the business world, I didn't know
anything about it. When I left school...I was at boarding school...and when I
left school, my father's theory was...which of course is crazy now...that no
daughter of mine will ever go into the business world. She must learn to be
quite capable of taking care of a rich man's house or a poor man's house...and
doing it successfully. So there I was sitting on a train, rolling across the
Prairies, the white smoke from little houses going up into the sky. It was all
absolutely strange, but I think that I was so very much in love...with my
husband...and he with me...and the whole thought was just to be together. I
didn't care where I went. We were going together, and there was no thought of
money because money was something that I knew very little about. I mean,
everything was always looked after at home for me, and I knew that Norman
would do the same....

It took days on the train, but finally we got to Strathcona.... We came into
a clearing and there was my home...the little shack that Norman had built on
his first trip out. Norman had left a hired man to look after it when he went
back to England for me.

There was this man coming out of the shack door and throwing some
water. I imagine it was the washing-up water...he must have known we were
coming because of the bells on the horses. I was introduced to him, and he
barely acknowledged it. He was too shy. Then Norman took me into the house

or the shack...and I never saw anything like it in my life. The floor, I don't think it'd seen a broom for goodness knows how long. He had a bed made up...it wasn't even made...the pillowcases were dirty and the bed clothes were on it. It was the most terrible poverty-stricken place I've ever seen in my life. I couldn't believe it....

The next morning I got up with determination. I decided that this was my lot and I was going to make the best of it.

After two years of roughing it, the farm was gradually taking shape. And the house was starting to look like a home. The fences were built and the crops were in field...growing. A small stranger was added...just Norman and me and little Bobby, or "Bobbins" as we called him...made three....

Things were going well and we were very happy. It was early autumn, and we had special plans for the first real harvest from the farm. It was a load of grain and Norman was taking it to Clyde. It meant being away overnight. The money from it was to be the start of our baby's bank account.

I saw him off...I had Bob in my arms, and we waved and waved until he was out of sight. I thought after that...now, what can I do as a surprise for him when he comes back, you know.... We were quite pleased and happy about things. Just as I was thinking about getting dinner ready, a strange man drove up and he said that my husband had had an accident and thought I should go to him. So I pushed Bob over to Mrs Hill in the shack, and I told her where I was going....

Somebody, I don't know who, got an ambulance from Edmonton. I went in with him...and he died there. It just proves...how quickly our world can fall apart. In the morning, plans for the baby's bank account, at night, I'm a widow with a baby on a homestead in Northern Alberta, wondering what to do and whom to turn to....

I tried to get a passage to England. Well the government told me no. They weren't allowing women and children on the high seas, on account of the submarine business. The first World War was on. My friend, Mr Griesbah, was General Griesbah now and he was overseas in the 1914-18 war. Whether it was pull on his part I don't know, but I was phoned up from the CP saying that I was going to be allowed to go to England: someone would be up the next day to give me my tickets and instructions. They told me that I would have to hold myself in readiness for twenty-four hours. That was all they could tell me. So I was more or less packed all the time, you know, expecting to go....

Finally we left, and I knew we were on the last lap of our journey to St John. I said to Bob, to keep him quiet, soon we'll be going home to Grandma and Grandpa. But there was more to come. Delays in St John. The horror of a strange man who followed me wherever I went. A change of plans which sent me again by train to Halifax. But finally we got underway, and I felt sad. I felt the chain was broken. I had landed at Halifax; I left Halifax. And I felt I was just leaving my darling Norman and all his hopes and ambitions. I just felt, am I doing the right thing, and yet, what else could I do.... I certainly couldn't run the place alone....

When I got home, they had made two rooms at the top of their house for us. One was sort of a nursery, and the other was a bedroom for me and Bob. They made us very comfortable for the next four years, but I couldn't stop thinking about Canada. I couldn't adapt to the old life...the tea parties and the theatre. Not after the homestead and the dreams we had.

As soon as the war was over in 1919, I told mother and father I must go back, at least just to see it again. I came over and sold the farm, and visited around with the Hills and different people. Then I decided I couldn't go back, living the life in England.... So I stayed.

RELIEF TO WIDOWS

Although some workingmen's associations established benevolent funds, it is unlikely that many Canadian families had sufficient savings or insurance to rely on in the event of a husband's death. Even women who did receive a pension, like the widows of workers at Nova Scotia's Dominion Coal Company, were hard pressed to support their families without additional remuneration. It should be noted that the following figures represent total benefits payable over time, not the annual pension value.

Nova Scotia, 1913
"Dominion Coal Company Employees' Relief Fund," Royal Commission on Industrial Training and Technical Education, Report. (Ottawa, 1913) Part IV, 1732.

Under the Constitution the Company and the workmen contribute equally, and the Government contributes 3-10ths of a cent per ton on all coal sold.

Based on an average of 8,000 employees, the workmen, paying 50 cents per man, will contribute $48,000. Allowing for an output of 4,000,000 tons, the Government's contribution will amount to $12,000. This, with the Company's contribution of $48,000 will make $108,000 for the year....

It being almost impossible for a miner to get accident or life insurance, except at a rate almost prohibitory, a Society such as this provides the best means of support for his wife and family in case of disablement or death.

If a workman dies either from sickness or accident, his dependants receive a death claim $100, the widow receives $8 per month for five years, and each child receives $3 per month till the age of 14.

Examples of what families would receive in case of death:-

Wife with no children will receive .... $ 580
Wife and one child, age 1 1,048
Wife and two children, aged 1 and 3 1,444
Wife and four children, aged 1, 3, 4, & 7 2,020
Wife and six children aged, 1, 3, 5, 7, 9 & 11.................... 2,308
Wife and eight children, aged ½, 2, 3½, 5, 6½, 8, 9½, 11.......... 2,956

Besides this, the Government makes a special grant of $50 in the case of the death of any workman....

PENSIONS FOR MOTHERS

The legal and economic problems faced by widows, an object of British North American philanthropy, became by the late nineteenth and early twentieth century, the subject of social reform activity. For Mrs Rose Henderson, government-supported pensions for widowed mothers presented a solution for distressed widows and an opportunity to save the nation through the home.

1914
Mrs Rose Henderson, "Pensions for Mothers," Social Service Congress, *1914, 109-15.*

The Mother: The dependent widowed mother will form the topic of my address to-day.

There is no figure in society to-day more deserving of our earnest consideration than the widowed mother with her family dependent and penniless.

In discussing a pension for mothers, three considerations must guide us. First, the need; second, the financial aspect and what other countries have done; and lastly, its religious, moral and humane aspect.

First, its necessity. The proposal to endow mothers must have become necessary or else it would never have become law, and the arguments I have to bring forth in favor of mothers' pensions are advanced from the standpoint of our social and economic conditions....

The average wage of men in industry to-day is less than five hundred dollars a year. During the last twenty years prices have gone up forty-five per cent, while wages have only advanced about half. On this wage it is almost impossible to live. It means that the mother must leave her children to the care of an older child and also send the children of tender age into the factories and stores to try and eke out an existence. Under these conditions insurance is out of the question, and to suggest putting money away for a rainy day out of a salary not enough to clothe and feed a family, is not only farcical, but immoral and dangerous to the family and community. Men to-day do not earn enough to belong to their unions, much less to save money. The average worker's child cannot afford to stay out of the factory after it reaches the age of ten or twelve years.

Industrial accidents are also claiming a number of men in the prime of life. In nine cases out of ten, these men leave a wife and young family the oldest very often not older than eight or nine, and unable to assist in maintaining the family. In cases of this kind the suffering is very great; the mother must leave her home to earn a pittance to keep body and soul together, while the children run the streets half clothed, half fed and uneducated, and eventually are brought into the Juvenile Court, most of them in time finding their way to the reformatory, which many times is but the vestibule to the jail and penitentiary. We cannot blame either mother or children, society alone is responsible and must evolve a method dealing more humanely with the widow and orphan.

We must realize, no matter what our prejudices are, that home life for the masses has been almost destroyed by our modern industrial conditions. It is no use talking about the sacredness of home unless we consider shacks and overcrowded tenements sacred.

The Institution is a costly affair. The charges for superintendents, nurses, teachers, doctors, servants and all kinds of helpers are very great. All this extra expense is saved when you leave the child in its home with its mother. The mother asks nothing for her labor. Henry Neil, Chicago, says: "The facts I have gathered concerning the unhappy careers of children brought up in institutions sufficiently condemn them in the mind of any right-minded person." Judge Pinckny, Juvenile Court, Chicago, says: "I am an ardent supporter of mothers' pensions since the Act was passed giving pensions to mothers. Thousands of mothers and children are being made happy. It is helping us to do a great work!"

The Montreal Ladies' Benevolent Society's last report shows a deficit of $197.03, with an income of $15,166.35, for the maintenance of nine old women and forty-seven boys and forty-two girls. The cost for each head is $156.75 yearly, equal to $13 a month, to which you must add all the many monthly donations. Counting interest on the investment, the keep per annum for 89 children and 9 old women reaches about $19,000, of which only $7,216.43 went to the support of the 98 inmates. Is this not the most flagrant extravagance? The cost of other institutions is, in some cases, twice this amount, with no better results....

What do we who believe in mothers' pensions want? We desire that the money allowed by the tax payers for the care of fatherless and needy children should be given entirely to the mothers, on the grounds that institutional life is bad for the child, and uses up twice the amount of the tax payers' money that would be used if the mother was allowed to remain at home and keep her children with her. We believe that the child is the nation's greatest asset, and that patriotism, morality and good citizenship are born and nourished in the home, that the child to grow up to be normal, useful and self-respecting, must have his life and training in the home and the community, by his mother. We hold the just view "that if a woman bears and rears her children for the service of the state, she does her duty without earning their living as well, and we recognize the justice of the claim that if a mother risks her life for her children, she is entitled to the pleasures in which mother love finds its greatest compensation, namely, caring for her children at home. In granting mothers' pensions, the State will honour motherhood, and save money."...

The Mothers' Pension Act aims to protect the home as the center of human life and activity. We hold that the family ties, deeply embedded as they are in the laws of nature and life, are the greatest source of the strength, morality and stability of the social order, and should not be broken. We aim to direct the money now spent on matrons and institutions to the maintenance of the child in its proper environment, the home, to employ the mother to bring up her own children in her own home, instead of a matron in an institution. We aim to save tax payers and philanthropists half the money now paid by keeping children in their own home at half the expense. Nations have risen to power and eminence and have fallen, because the children, mothers and homes of the masses were not taken into account, and nations will again rise and fall until we recognize that no nation can be great until built on the stable foundation of good, strong men and women. That foundation must be built in the home; by the motherhood and childhood of the nation. Let out watchword be "save the nation through the home."...

---

2. THE WORK OF GRANDMOTHERS AND OLDER WOMEN

I AM OLD LYDIA CAMPBELL

When she wrote her diary life story in 1893, Lydia Campbell was seventy-five years old. The daughter of an Inuit mother and an English father, she lived and worked in Labrador. Despite her failing eyesight, Lydia Campbell shows herself to be a strong and capable woman.

Maligan River, Labrador, Newfoundland, 1893-94.
Lydia Campbell "Sketches of a Labrador Life," Canadian Women's Studies/les cahiers de la femme, *III (1981) 5-7.*

December 25, 1893; January 13 or 14, 1894

You must please excuse my writing and spelling, for I have never been to school, neither had I a spelling book in my young days—me, a native of this country, Labrador, Hamilton's Inlet, Esquimaux Bay. If you wish to know who I am, I am old Lydia Campbell, formerly Lydia Brooks, then Blake, after Blake, now Campbell. So you see, ups and downs has been my life all through, and now I am what I am.

Christmas Day. As this is a holy day for us, the Campbells and Blakes, my family, I think that it is a nice time to write a few lines, a beginning of this winter.

I have been very busy all this fall in particular, for I has a lot to do with three little motherless granddaughters to work for, beside their poor father and a big son, going off hunting and wood-chopping, and the weather so cold as to need all the warm clothing possible to warm them.

The weather thiry below zero often, and myself off to my rabbit snares about four miles going and coming, over ice and snow, with snow shoes and axe and game bag. Some days I has three rabbits in one day, caught in snares, for I has about twenty-four snares, made myself to set them up, and I gets pretty tired some days. Often the snow is deep and soft, just now about three feet deep in the woods, but it can't be expected otherwise with me to get tired, for I am last birthday seventy five years old, last month, first November.

I have seen many ups and downs, but the Good Lord has safely brought me through. I have been bereaved of my first husband and four of his children. One is left me, Thomas Blake. It is his little children that I has to look to now. The present husband that I has now is nearly as old as me. We has three children left by him out of eight—two boys and a girl. They all has a family to look to. We have a meeting some times, and when our large rivers freeze over hard enough to go on, then comes the time for trouting as we call it, then most of our granddaughters and grandsons gather together here to trout.

One family, John Campbell's children, comes along shore; about four miles he lives. My eldest son, Thomas Blake, my first husband's son, and his motherless children is near us, next door—none near us but them and our dear children's graves. We can see their headstones at a distance, over on the cranberry banks, so pretty it looks in the fall when we come home to our summer quarters above seventy milés from here.

When we are sailing up in our large boat, to see the ducks in our bay when we are nearing the river, and when we get ashore to the pretty river banks and walking up the path under our large trees, we often meet with a flock of partridges flying up to the trees. Before we get to the house, so pretty, then is the scramble among the young ones to see the first turnips and potatoes and, sure enough, all around the house is green with turnip tops and between them and the wall of the house is hanging red with moss-berries.

Then we are home to our winter house for ten months or more. We are home among ducks, partridges, trout, rabbits, berries, traps for snaring foxes, martins, wolverines, mountain cats, musk-rats, minks—and most of all them kinds of things have I caught in my lifetime.

Sometimes we have a visit from black bears and wolves; the former we often gets, but seldom the wolf. Some winters we have had the luck to get a deer or two. Some times, formerly, we have had as many as ten or more in one winter. I have myself been deer hunting and shot two but my sister, Hannah Meshlin, have killed three in one spring.

That was our happy days, with all our little children round us. That was about thirty years ago now. Ah, well, all works together for good, we are told. Now when I look back it seems not very long yet. When I look for my Susan, my eldest daughter, she has been married, left our home, went away with her husband, a clerk of the Hudson Bay Company and had three children. She died up to Seven Islands.

We are all scattered today. My husband, Dan Campbell, is not home yet from Labacatto, he went up there to see our brother-in-law, Mensie Meshlin. He is not able to work now but his wife Hannah, my old sister, she is over eighty years old and yet she can take her gun and axe and game bag and shoots a white partridge or two, now and then. I have known her fighting with a wolverine, a strong animal of the size of a good sized dog. She had neither gun nor axe but a little trout stick, yet she killed it after a long battle.

I wish there were more Hannahs in the world for braveness. She brought up her first family of little children when their father died, teached them all to read and write in the long winter nights and hunt with them in the day. She would take the little ones on the sled, haul them on over snow and ice to a large river, chop ice about three feet thick, catch about two or three hundred trout and haul them and the children home, perhaps in the night. The men of the Hudson Bay Company used to get her to make a lot of things—pants, shirts, flannel slips, draws, sealskin boots, deer skin shoes for the winter, socks, leggings, mitts made of duffel and deer skins, coats, caps, as well as washing, starching, ironing and what not. She had all the care of the children while a widow.

Dear friend, I have been a widow like her, and brought up children while a widow, but I had a brother-in-law and a mother-in-law and three sisters-in-law but I still worked pretty hard to bring them up. Ah, well, I am alive and well and able to work yet, with some few little motherless granddaughters and grandsons. And when I feel lonely I goes hunting, yes, and bring home some game. On my way I goes and sees the graves under the ground and deep snow. I oft sing a hymn or prayer, comes home light-hearted and think it won't be long my journey here, thank God—then to a better country, a better home for us to journey to, although I am only old Aunt Lydia Campbell now....

———————

Age did not necessarily bring with it retirement and increased leisure. Some of the documents show that women with adult children also had continuing responsibilities for the care of younger siblings or educational roles for their grandchildren. This was certainly the case for Madame Kenny, photographed in 1870, as she supervised the needlework of a girl and three younger women on the steps of her house.

Credit: Notman Photographic Archives 44, 776-BI, McCord Museum, McGill University.

A GRANDMOTHER'S LETTERS

Ellen Free Picton Osler wrote volumes of letters to her children, inlaws and grandchildren. As she grew older, she wrote more frequently and news of family health became increasingly important to her. She nursed her husband and daughter, Ellen, during long terminal illnesses, and outlived her sons Britton Bath and Edward Lake. Britton Bath, nicknamed Brick, had some kind of nervous and/or physical breakdown around 1897, the full extent of which was never told to Ellen; the reports on B.B.'s health were always "Better", but he died in 1901 at age 61. Ellen herself lived to be 100 years, 3 months and 4 days.

Toronto, Ontario, 1894-1900
Letters of Ellen Osler, Featherstone Lake Osler Papers, *Public Archives of Ontario.*

May 1, 1894

"My dear Herbert, [grandson]
...We send our best love and all the wishes we can think of for the future life before you. You have entered the service of a Good master "Be thou faithful unto death and I will give thee a crown of life." He is not a hard master. Be Strong in his Strength, and He will supply all your needs. Grandfather has laboured lone in the service of the King and many may think it is poor reward all these last years of helplessness, but he has that "peace which passeth all understanding," and the crown of righteousness laid up for him will make amends for all.

Ever your afftionate GMother,
Ellen Osler"

Dec 15, 1899

"My very dear Herbert,
I meant to have written yesterday but was a little tired after all the extra number of visitors that came on on the 14th—your letter was the first to greet me. Many thanks for all the kind wishes May you have as many loving friends around you at 93 as I have...I enclose you with my GMotherly love $5—odds and ends are always wanted at this time of year."

May 5 1900

"My dear Herbert
Just a word or two to wish you many happy turns of the day as the children often as the little ones often say, as well to let you know how Uncle B.B. is. Yesterday Dr Walker reported him better and expects him to improve greatly by taking some special Baths he has after which he will G.W. [God willing] go for a long rest to Kianvata. I do not think I have been told how thoroughly he

broke down, but when I last saw him a fortnight since I thought him so unlike himself that I felt quite uneasy then he had some imperative work that took him to Philadelphia and three nights on the Train and heavy brain work did its work too..."

83 Wellesley St. Toronto
August 27 1900

"My dear Chattie [daughter Charlotte]

Letter writing is all but over with me, but I want to send up the Boat Ticket, so must write half a scrap—these past hot days have made me more lazy than ever—My strength is to sit still. Perhaps we shall see you down one day this week to look in on the Poultry at the Exhibition, and to call on your new niece Mrs Hal Osler. We all take very kindly to her—there seems no lack of Common Sense which is a great matter...The report from BB [her son, Britton Bath] is as normal "Better" and we must hope on, but 'tis slow work and I get discouraged at times..."

A GRANDSON'S BIRTH

The late nineteenth-century childbirth experience on the prairies was primarily one of female kinship. Mothers, sisters, or even experienced neighbours attended the births and assisted in running the family after the confinement as did Mrs Deane-Freeman.

Mrs Deane-Freeman's attitude and concern for her daughter's safety during the birth of her first child are understandable. Her daughter faced the experience without the medical assistance of a nurse or doctor that Mrs Deane-Freeman felt necessary because she had come to believe the birth process to be an "illness".

Millarville, Alberta, 1896
Mrs H.O. Boyd Papers, M121, Glenbow-Alberta Institute Archives.

Monea Ranche
Millarville
November 21st 1896

Dear Mrs Boyd,—

We are much obliged for your kind congratulations upon my being a grandmother. Mr D.-F. is not at all proud of his new honours!! Thank god I had not time to be anxious about my dear child.—her father & I left her on the 20th looking so bright & well—we were going into Calgary for the event on the 23rd—At 3am on 21st Morrison came for me.—you may imagine my feelings having no nurse or Dr I never heard of such a quick confinement she was only ill 3 hours—everything right—no drawback—the wee grandson was extremely dark when born—much fairer now fine dark blue eyes & lots of brown hair —a small mouth—large nose with grand back & shoulders (W^h his father greatly admires). I remained 3 weeks—both very well; but for this extremely cold snap baby would have been christened last Sunday "Charles Deane Heger". Maud, Mr Douglas & Mr Marsack to be Godparents....

Yours affectionately
E.A. Deane-Freeman

A SUCCESSION OF FINE AND LOWERY* DAYS

Living alone with her husband Fred, both husband and wife in their sixties, Helen Sophia Perry in her diary provides a picture of work, daily life, and important events from the perspective of a rural Nova Scotia woman.

Nova Scotia, 1909
Lawrence Kent Sweeney, ed., "The Journal of Helen Sophia Perry, Winter of 1909-1910" Nova Scotia Historical Quarterly, *IV (1974) 345-53.*

1909
Tuesday, October 12th. Fine day, very hot. I labelled all my dahlias, baked several loaves of bread. Fred finished digging potatoes today. It rained all night. Friday, October 15th. Quiet this morning, is raining this afternoon. I have been putting a cloth on the parlour table and the ornaments on. This evening the wind blew a perfect gale for about 15 minutes. It frightened us very much. It seemed as if something fell with great force, I looked about the house to see if any pictures or dishes had fallen down, there was nothing in the parlour disturbed. Saturday, October 16th. Fine day but high wind. This morning when we went out of doors we saw what the wind had destroyed the evening before. Our old lilac tree was half broken down from the roots so there is only one piece of it. It must be a very old tree. The honeysuckle over the front door was down to the ground. Fred and I got a rope and ladder with blocks and hoisted it from the ground and tacked it up to the house again. Fred is shingling the side of the new stable.
Monday, October 18th. Lowery morning. I did a large washing this morning and preserved a peck of crab-apples. Fred is working in the cemetary today.

*[cloudy]

The dogwood trees in the cemetary are full of large bunches of berries, they look handsome.

Tuesday, October 19th. Cold lowery day. We gathered the most of our apples this afternoon and Fred has been shingling on the barn part of the day. I baked several loaves of bread. We bought a galvanized bucket today of Mr Porter.

Wednesday, October 20th. Lowery morning, quite cold. Fred went to town this morning with our team, I cleaned out the summer savory. He mailed a letter to Laurence, one to Jessie, one to Ella. Fred bought a pair of scissors today, something we have wanted for a long time. Got a peck of onions, or 13 pounds for 25 cents.

Monday, November 1st. Very fine day. Dug up my dahlias, are drying them today. Filled the under-bed with straw and the kitchen couch, baked several loaves of bread. Fred has been hauling carrots and turnips today.

Wednesday, November 10th. Very fine sunny day. Pig killed today, John Haley is here to dinner. This afternoon, Thomas Foulis, Harold Perry and Fred went across to Clement's Island and got our little heifer, "Clever," and 3 others. They swam across the river. Received a letter from Ernie Low and a postcard from Laurence. The sun set in red and gold colours.

Friday, November 12th. Lowery morning. Fred went to the Old Place for eel-grass with our horse. This evening Fred is cutting up the pork. We got 3 quarts of cranberries from the Old Place. Thomas Cook, brother of Tall Hannah Cook, was buried in Chebogue cemetary this afternoon.

Saturday, November 13th. Lowery day. Packed the pork and salted it, made head-cheese.

---

3. LAST ILLNESSES AND DEATH

SEVENTY-EIGHT IS RATHER OLD TO WORK

The lives of widows and old women in the late nineteenth century are frequently sketchy in the preserved record. We are fortunate that someone retained the following two letters from the 78-year-old Maria to Mr G. Alford in Montreal. We do not know a number of details about the relationship between these correspondents. Was Maria a relative or, perhaps, a former servant? How had their relationship changed? Despite these gaps in our knowledge, we can nevertheless discern a significant number of details about Maria's situation in life and about how she was actively responding to the circumstances in which she found herself. It is particularly clear that Maria was ill and confused and was finding the day-to-day details of life and survival extremely difficult to manage.

Ste Foye, Quebec, 1885
Maria to Mr G. Alford. G. Alford Papers, MG 55/29 No. 144, Public Archives
of Canada.

Mr. Alfred please to let me know this change which has come on you with me...78 is rather old to work. after I got in West was so grieved shed tears and it made me quite ill, I can't get over it yet. God help the Lone Widow's. I was boasting in Montreal how kind you had been telling John G. Georgian only this great affliction on them would have kept me sorry I am to been obliged to move in Town prefer the Country especially for the Cow. however lucky got other rooms & stable for the Cow. hard work to find it. thank God so far. would given anything to know what turned you so. can't imagine the Cause. time will tell the truth. _____ and then scolding me. it's a hard case. your mother never scolded me in that way. don't know what for never harmed a fly...

I do wonder at myself why I am so stupid. want of wisdom. Thank God free of craft & guilt if I had my poor brother George gone. However the hour of my departure can't be far off, may I depart in peace.

God grant

Rec'd November 7th/85

Mr. G Alford,

The purport of these few lines is to say I would like to know what a change as come over you of late & for what its a mystery to me...my time can't be long now 'ere below but trust to die *in peace*. great Dr of Montreal says my death will be sudden if the Cancer works near the heart & the swell breast is frightful going down near the heart. quite resigned...I must now say I left my poor little Cow at Ste Foye. they brought her in to me half starved & buying Hay by the bundle for her is very expensive...poor little Brute knew me when I went to the stable. I cannot bear to see any dumb animals half starved so may I request of you to be as usual to send me Hay to the Care of Mr Coveney grocer Scott St. to conclude George request your kindness in sending me the Hay as you have always done. Little money, little means and alone afflicted oblige to pay for every item no wood in, only could buy half a Cord of soft wood. I dread this winter. must I trust to your former kindness for I am sorrly afflicted. God only knows my position I can't bear the thought of parting the Cow its my principal food milk her milk is so rich buying milk lately found the difference. an answer at your earliest convenience. had to suffer many trials of late sick, sore & afflicted.

Maria

P.S. I am sometimes like my Grandfather Poyer staggering. fear if some saw me would think I am tipsy. the Montreal Dr ordered me to drink wine its little I get if I can get milk thank God. will be grateful for hay for my little Cow buying it by the bundle is expensive.

Address care
    Care of Mrs Coveney Scott St.
    Grocer

––––––––––

THE NOTORIOUS MRS CHADWICK

At the time of her death and in later biographies, Cassie Chadwick was immortalized as a forger, prostitute, clairvoyant, and society lady—a woman untypical of her times. Yet, the writers of her hometown obituary take care to point out those ideals of womanhood that can be uncovered in the life even of notorious women.

Woodstock, Ontario, 1908
"The Late Mrs Chadwick," Daily Sentinel-Review, *October 16, 1908.*

"Of the dead speak nothing but good", is an injunction that is sometimes abused, yet it has its uses and its justification. There are some people whose misfortune it is to figure prominently in a sensational way before the world that there is little opportunity for the presentation of an accurate portrait. There may be another side to their characters which the world would be interested in and perhaps benefited by knowing; but in the thirst for sensationalism everything else is forgotten. When such people find the kindly shelter of the grave, therefore, it is well that the old dictum should be remembered. Not that the saying of nothing but good of the dead is a sufficient compensation for the injustice done the living; but it is the only compensation that then remains to be rendered. Few women in these days have figured more prominently in the limelight than the late Mrs Chadwick, and there seems a disposition on the part of the sensational papers to follow her even beyond the grave. This is both unfair and unnecessary. "All that is left of her now is pure womanly." Even if there was no good to be told of her, she is entitled at least to the charity of silence. But fortunately for her reputation, the story of her life as told in the papers represents but one side of the shield. There is another side and one which in justice to herself and to humanity in general ought to be revealed. Of her exploits in the realm of "high finance" this much may be said, that her methods were scarcely better or worse than those of many men and women who have achieved honourable distinction, before their fellow citizens. The public is not too much given to the scrutiny of either methods or motives so long as the results loom up large and strong. Mrs Chadwick's calculations failed. She paid the penalty of failure. Had she been more fortunate in her calculations or more successful in covering up her tracks and evading her responsibility, she might have escaped much unenviable notoriety.

If there was nothing more to be said than that, it might not be worth the saying, but there is a good deal more. There was a side of Mrs Chadwick's life and character on which the light of publicity has never been turned. Those who knew her best know that she was richly endowed with many of the qualities that are held in highest esteem. She was a genuine friend to those she thought worthy of her friendship. There was much in her home life that told of womanly and motherly qualities. She was untiring in her solicitude for the welfare of her friends and relatives, and unsparing of her means when she had any. Her impulses were generous and those who knew her best have never had any reason to question the sincerity of her friendship. She was unevenly balanced but that is no reason why, if her portrait is to be presented at all, it should not be presented in entirety. One side of the woman has been painted before the world in colors sufficiently lurid. It is only fair now that the grave has closed over her, to do some justice to the other and less familiar side.

AN ESTEEMED LADY

Mrs Robert Dick came as a widow to the Ottawa Valley in 1856 with her three daughters and her son, Thomas Dick, to join her two brothers. No doubt her decision to emigrate from Ireland was based in part on her confidence in her family's assistance. Through perseverance Mrs Dick did very well, acquiring a farm that her son managed for her until her death. Moreover, this woman won the respect of her community, commanding a great many carriages at her funeral, as her son recorded in his diary.

Ottawa Valley, 1877-78
Thomas Dick Diary, Diaries Collection, Public Archives of Ontario.

1877
Dec. 31   Mother is very sick to night I dont think she will last long if there is not a change.
1878
Feb 19th   Mother died this morning about nine o'clock.
Feb 21   Mother had a large funeral there was 67 carriage [sic] it was a nice day

[Newspaper clippings pasted in Diary]

Died—   In Longeuil (Seignory) on the 19th inst., of Dropsy, after a long and painful illness, Mrs Robert Dick, sister of Samuel and Robert McAdam, a native of the village of Cullay backey, in the County Antrim, Ireland, aged 70 years, much respected during her life, and deeply regretted by all who knew her.

Death of an Esteemed Lady

On the 21st inst., one of the oldest and most esteemed inhabitants of this township, Mrs Robt. Dick, who died of dropsy, was escorted to the grave by one of the largest and most respectable concourses of the inhabitants of this section of the county which has ever taken place. Deceased was a native of the village of Culley backey, in the County Antrim, Ireland, and was a sister of our much respected township residents, Samuel and Robt. McAdam. The immense concourse of the surrounding inhabitants who attended to pay the last tribute of respect to the worthy departed, is a sufficient testimony to the respect in which she and the family were held. The deceased lady was mother of Mr Thos. Dick, of Longeuil.

SELECTED BIBLIOGRAPHY

PUBLISHED PRIMARY SOURCES

ABBOTT, MAUDE E.S., "Autobiographical Sketch," *McGill Medical Journal,* XXVII (1959), 127-52.

ALLEN, MARNEY, "Prairie Life: An Oral History of Greta Craig," *Atlantis,* VII (1982), 89-102.

ARCHER, S.A., comp., *A Heroine of the North: Memories of Charlotte Selina Bompas* (Toronto, 1929).

BAILEY, MARY C., "Reminiscences of a Pioneer," *Alberta Historical Review,* XV (1967), 17-25.

BERTON, LAURA B., *I Married the Klondike* (Toronto, 1954).

BINNIE-CLARK, GEORGINA, *A Summer on the Canadian Prairie* (London, 1910).

_____, *Wheat and Woman,* (London, 1914 and Toronto, 1914). Reprint edition with an introduction by S. Jackel. (Social History of Canada Series, 30, Toronto, 1979).

BLACK, MARTHA LOUISE, *My Ninety Years* (Anchorage, Alaska, 1976).

BRIGDEN, BEATRICE, "One Woman's Campaign for Social Purity and Social Reform," in Richard Allen, ed., *The Social Gospel in Canada* (Ottawa, 1975), 36-62.

CASWELL, MARYANNE, *Pioneer Girl* (Toronto, 1964).

CLINT, MABEL B., *Our Bit* (Montreal, 1934).

COOK, RAMSAY and MITCHINSON, WENDY, eds., *The Proper Sphere: Women's Place in Canadian Society* (Toronto, 1976).

DECHENE, LOUISE, ed., *Journal d'Henriette Dessaulles 1874/1880* (Montreal, 1971).

DUFFERIN, Marchioness of, *My Canadian Journal 1872-1878* (Toronto, 1971).

GOUDIE, ELIZABETH, *Woman of Labrador* (Toronto, 1973).

HOPKINS, MONICA, *Letters from a Lady Rancher* (Calgary, 1982).

MacBETH, MADGE, *Boulevard Career* (Toronto, 1957).

_____, *Over My Shoulder* (Toronto, 1953).

McCLUNG, NELLIE L., *Clearing in the West* (Toronto, 1935; reprint edition, 1976).

_____, *In Times Like These,* edited by Veronica Strong-Boag, (Toronto, 1972).

_____, *The Stream Runs Fast* (Toronto, 1945).

MITCHELL, ELIZABETH B., *In Western Canada Before the War,* introduction by Susan Jackel (Saskatoon, 1981).

MONTGOMERY, LUCY MAUD, *The Alpine Path: The Story of My Career* (Toronto, 1974).

NATIONAL COUNCIL OF WOMEN OF CANADA, *Women of Canada: Their Life and Work,* (1975).

ORMSBY, MARGARET A., ed., *A Pioneer Gentlewoman in British Columbia: The Recollections of Susan Allison* (Vancouver, 1976).

PURDY, HARRIET and GAGAN, DAVID, eds., "Pioneering in the North-West Territories: Harriet Johnson Neville," *Canada: An Historical Magazine,* II (1975), 1-64.

RASMUSSEN, LINDA, et al., *A Harvest Yet to Reap* (Toronto, 1976).

READ, DAPHNE, ed., *The Great War and Canadian Society: An Oral History* (Toronto, 1978).

ROBERTS, SARA ELLEN, *Alberta Homestead: Chronicle of a Pioneer Family* (Austin, Texas, 1971).

SALVERSON, LAURA, *Confessions of an Immigrant's Daughter* (London; 1939).

SAVAGE, CANDACE, *Our Nell: A Scrapbook Biography of Nellie L. McClung* (Saskatoon, 1979).

SAYWELL, JOHN T., ed., *The Canadian Journal of Lady Aberdeen, 1893-1898* (Toronto, 1960).

SMITH, ELIZABETH, *A Woman with a Purpose: The Diaries of Elizabeth Smith, 1872-1884,* edited and with an introduction by V. Strong-Boag (Toronto, 1980).

TIVY, LOUIS, *Your Loving Anna: Letters from the Ontario Frontier* (Toronto, 1972).

WILLIAMSON, N.J., ed., *The Diary of Mary Louise Pickering Thomson* (Altona, Manitoba, 1978).

WILSON, BARBARA M., ed., *Ontario and the First World War 1914-1918: A Collection of Documents* (Toronto, 1977).

YOUMANS, LETITIA, *Campaign Echoes* (Toronto, 1893).

SECONDARY SOURCES

GENERAL

ACTON, JANICE, et al, eds., *Women at Work, Ontario 1850-1930* (Toronto, 1974).

BACCHI, CAROL LEE, *Liberation Deferred? The Ideas of the English-Canadian Suffragists, 1877-1918* (Toronto, 1982).

BROWN, JENNIFER S.H., *Strangers in Blood: Fur Trade Company Families in Indian Country* (Vancouver, 1980).

CLEVERDON, CATHERINE LYLE, *The Woman Suffrage Movement in Canada,* introduction by Ramsay Cook (Toronto, 1970).

LE COLLECTIF CLIO, *L'Histoire des femmes au Québec depuis quatre siècles* (Montreal, 1982).

GAGAN, DAVID, *Hopeful Travellers: Families, Land and Social Change in Mid-Victorian Peel County, Canada West* (Toronto, 1981).

GILLETT, MARGARET, *We Walked Very Warily: A History of Women at McGill* (Montreal, 1981).

KEALEY, LINDA, ed., *A Not Unreasonable Claim: Women and Reform in Canada, 1880s-1920s* (Toronto, 1979).

LATHAM, BARBARA and KESS, CATHY, *In Her Own Right: Selected Essays On Women's History* (Victoria, 1980).

LAVIGNE, M. and PINARD, Y., *Les femmes dans la société québécoise* (Montreal, 1977).

L'ESPERANCE, JEANNE, *The Widening Sphere: Women in Canada, 1870-1940* (Ottawa, 1982).

MURRAY, HILDA C., *More than 50%* (St. John's, 1979).

PARR, JOY, ed., *Childhood and Family in Canadian History* (Toronto, 1982).

——————, *Labouring Children: British Immigrant Apprentices to Canada, 1869-1924* (London, 1980).

ROBERTS, WAYNE, *Honest Womanhood: Feminism, Femininity and Class Consciousness among Toronto Working Women, 1896-1914* (Toronto, 1977).

ROUILLARD, JACQUES, *Les Travailleurs du coton au Québec 1900-1915* (Montreal, 1974).

TROFIMENKOFF, SUSAN and PRENTICE, ALISON, eds., *The Neglected Majority: Essays in Canadian Women's History* (Toronto, 1977).

TROFIMENKOFF, SUSAN M., *Dream of Nation: A Social and Intellectual History of Quebec* (Toronto, 1982).

BIOGRAPHIES AND BIOGRAPHICAL SKETCHES

BOLGER, FRANCIS P., *The Years Before "Anne"* (Charlottetown, 1974).

BOIVIN, AURELIEN and LANDRY, KENNETH. "Françoise and Madeleine: Pionnières du journalisme féminin au Québec" *Atlantis,* IV, (Fall, 1978).

BUCK, RUTH MATHESON, *The Doctor Rode Side-Saddle* (Toronto, 1974).

CARPENTER, JOCK, *Fifty Dollar Bride: Marie Rose Smith* (Sidney, B.C., 1977).

COBB, MYRNA and MORGAN, SHER, *Eight Women Photographers of B.C. 1860-1968* (Victoria, 1979).

COOK, RAMSAY, "Francis Marion Beynon and the Crisis of Christian Reformism," in C. Berger and R. Cook, eds., *The West and the Nation* (Toronto, 1976), 187-208.

CORBETT, BEATRICE, "Susan Moulton Fraser McMaster" *Inland Seas,* XXXI (1975), 192-200.

FERGUSON, TED, *Kit Coleman: Queen of Hearts* (Toronto, 1978).

HAIG, KENNETHE M., *Brave Harvest: The Life Story of E. Cora Hind* (Toronto, 1945).

HAMEL, REGINALD, *Gaetane de Montreuil, journaliste québécoise 1867-1951* (Montreal, 1976).

KENNEDY, JOAN, E., "Jane Soley Hamilton, Midwife," *Nova Scotia Historical Review,* II (1982), 6-29.

ROBERTS, WAYNE, "Six New Women: A Guide to the Mental Map of Women Reformers in Toronto," *Atlantis,* III (1977), 145-64.

THOMPSON, JOANNE EMILY, "The Influence of Dr. Emily Howard Stowe on the Woman Suffrage Movement in Canada," *Ontario History,* LIV (1962), 253-66.

WOYWITKA, ANNA B., "Homesteader's Women," *Alberta History,* XXIV (1976), 20-24.

_____, "A Roumanian Pioneer," *Alberta Historical Review* (1973), 20-27.

ARTICLES

ANDERSON, ANN LEGER, "Saskatchewan Women, 1880-1920: A Field for Study," in H. Palmer and D. Smith, eds., *The New Provinces: Alberta and Saskatchewan, 1905-1980* (Vancouver, 1973), 65-90.

BACCHI, CAROL, "Race Regeneration and Social Purity: A Study of the Social Attitudes of Canada's English-Speaking Suffragists," *Histoire sociale/Social History* XI (1978), 460-74.

BARBER, MARILYN, "The Women Ontario Welcomed: Immigrant Domestics for Ontario Homes, 1870-1930," *Ontario History,* LXXII (1980), 148-172.

BAUDOIN, MARTHE, "The Religious of the Sacred Heart in Canada 1842-1980," Canadian Catholic Historical Association, *Study Sessions,* (1981), 43-60.

BEDFORD, JUDY, "Prostitution in Calgary, 1905-1914," *Alberta History,* XXIX, (1981), 1-11.

BLISS, MICHAEL, "Pure Books on Avoided Subjects: Pre-Freudian Sexual Ideas in Canada," in M. Horn and R. Sabourin, eds., *Studies in Canadian Social History* (Toronto, 1974) 326-46.

BRADBURY, BETTINA, "The Family Economy and Work in an Industrializing City: Montreal in the 1870s." Canadian Historical Association, *Historical Papers* (1979), 71-96.

BRANDT, GAIL CUTHBERT, "Weaving it Together: Life Cycle and the Industrial Experience of Female Cotton Workers in Quebec, 1910-1950," *Labour/le travailleur,* VII (1981), 113-126.

BUCKLEY, SUZANN, "British Female Emigration and Imperial Development: Experiments in Canada, 1885-1931," *Hecate,* III (1977), 26-40.

COOPER, JOY, "Red Lights in Winnipeg," *Manitoba Historical and Scientific Society Transactions* (16 February 1971), 61-74.

CROSS, D. SUZANNE, "The Neglected Majority: The Changing Role of Women in Nineteenth-Century Montreal," *Histoire sociale/Social History* (1973).

DANYLEWYCZ, MARTA, "Changing Relationships: Nuns and Feminists in Montreal, 1890-1925," *Histoire sociale/Social History,* XIV (1981), 413-34.

DUMONT-JOHNSON, MICHELINE, "Les communautés religieuses et la condition féminine," *Recherches sociographiques,* IX (1978), 79-102.

_____, "Des garderies au XIXe siècle: les salles d'asile des Soeurs Grises à Montréal," *Revue d'histoire de l'amérique française,* XXXIV (1980), 27-55.

GEE, ELLEN M.T., "Early Canadian Fertility Transition: A Comparative Analysis of Census Data," *Canadian Studies in Population* VI (1979), 23-32.

_____, "Female Marriage Patterns in Canada: Changes and Differentials," *Journal of Comparative Family Studies,* XI (1980), 457-73.

_____, "Marriage in Nineteenth Century Canada," *Canadian Review of Sociology and Anthropology,* XIX (1982), 311-25.

GODFREY, C.M., "The Origins of Medical Education of Women in Ontario," *Medical History,* XVII (January, 1973), 89-94.

GORHAM, DEBORAH, "English Militancy and the Canadian Suffrage Movement," *Atlantis,* I (1975), 83-112.

_____, "Singing up the Hill," *Canadian Dimension,* X (1975), 26-28.

HATHAWAY, DEBBIE, "The Political Equality League of Manitoba," *Manitoba History,* III (1982), 8-10.

HEADON, CHRISTOPHER, "Women and Organized Religion in Mid and Late 19th Century Canada," *Journal of the Canadian Church Historical Society,* XX (1978), 3-15.

INDRA, DOREEN MARIE, "The Invisible Mosaic: Women, Ethnicity and the Vancouver Press, 1900-1976," *Canadian Ethnic Studies,* XIII (1981), 63-74.

JAMESON, SHEILAGH S., "Women in the Southern Alberta Ranch Community: 1881-1914," in H.C. Klassen, ed., *The Canadian West: Social Change and Economic Development* (Calgary, 1977), 63-78.

JONES, DAVID C., "From Babies to Buttonholes: Women's Work at Agricultural Fairs," *Alberta History,* XXIX (1981), 26-32.

LACELLE, CLAUDETTE, "Les domestiques dans les villes Canadiennes au XIXe siècle: effectifs et conditions de vie," *Social History/histoire sociale.* XV (1982), 181-207.

LAVIGNE, MARIE and STODDART, JENNIFER, "Women's Work in Montreal at the Beginning of the Century," in Marylee Stephenson, ed., *Women in Canada* (Toronto, 1977), 129-47.

LEE, DANIELLE JUTEAU, "Les religieuses du Québec: leur influence sur la vie professionelle des femmes, 1908-1954," *Atlantis,* V, 2 (Spring, 1980) 22-23.

LEMIEUX, LUCIEN, "La Fondation de l'Ecole Ménagère St Pascal, 1905-1909," *Revue d'histoire de l'amérique française, XXX (1972),* 552-57.

LENSKYI, HELEN, "A 'Servant Problem' or a 'Servant-Mistress Problem?' Domestic Service in Canada, 1890-1930," *Atlantis,* VII (1981), 3-11.

LOWE, GRAHAM S., "Women, Work and the Office: The Feminization of Clerical Occupations in Canada, 1901-1930," *Canadian Journal of Sociology,* V (1980), 361-381.

McLAREN, ANGUS, "Birth Control and Abortion in Canada, 1870-1920," *Canadian Historical Review,* LIX (1978), 319-40.

_____, "What Has This to Do with Working Class Women? Birth Control and the Canadian Left, 1900-1939," *Histoire sociale/Social History,* XIV (1981), 435-454.

MITCHINSON, WENDY, "Canadian Women and Church Missionary Societies in the Nineteenth Century: A Step Towards Independence," *Atlantis,* II (1977), 57-75.

_____, "Gynecological Operations on Insane Women: London, Ontario 1895-1901," *Journal of Social History,* XV (1982), 467-84.

_____, "Gynecological Operations on the Insane," *Archivaria,* X (1980), 125-144.

_____, "Historical Attitudes Toward Women and Childbirth," *Atlantis,* IV (1979), 13-34.

_____, "The Woman's Christian Temperance Union: A Study in Organization," *International Journal of Women's Studies,* IV (1981), 143-56.

_____, "The YWCA and Reform in the Nineteenth Century," *Histoire sociale/ Social History,* XII (1979), 368-84.

MORRISON, W.R., "'Their Proper Sphere:' Feminism, the Family, and Child-Centred Social Reform in Ontario, 1875-1900," *Ontario History,* LXVIII (1976).

NEWTON, JANICE, "Women and the *Cotton's Weekly:* A Study of Women and Socialism in Canada, 1909," in *Women As Persons,* Special Publication 8, Resources for Feminist Research (Toronto, 1980), 58-61.

ROBERTS, BARBARA, "Sex, Politics and Religion: Controversies in Female Immigration Reform Work in Montreal, 1881-1919," *Atlantis,* VI (1980), 25-38.

RONISH, DONNA, "The Montreal Ladies' Educational Association, 1871-1885," *McGill Journal of Education,* VI (1971), 78-83.

ROOKE, PATRICIA T. and SCHNELL, R.L., "The Rise and Decline of British North American Protestant Orphan's Homes as Woman's Domain, 1850-1930," *Atlantis,* VII (1982), 21-35.

ROSENTHAL, STAR, "Union Maids: Organized Women Workers in Vancouver, 1900-1915," *B.C. Studies,* XLI (1979), 36-55.

SANGSTER, JOAN, "Finnish Women in Ontario, 1890-1930," *Polyphony* III, (1981), 46-54.

_____, "The 1907 Bell Telephone Strike: Organizing Women Workers," *Labour/ le travailleur,* III (1978), 109-30.

SCHULZ, PATRICIA V., "Day Care in Canada: 1850-1962." In Kathleen Gallagher Ross, ed., *Good Daycare* (Toronto, 1978), 137-158.

SHEEHAN, NANCY M., "Temperance, Education and the WCTU in Alberta 1905-1930," *Journal of Educational Thought,* XIV (1980), 108-124.

_____, "The WCTU on the Prairies, 1886-1930: An Alberta-Saskatchewan Comparison," *Prairie Forum,* VI (1981), 17-33.

SILVERMAN, ELIANE, "In Their Own Words: Mothers and Daughters on the Alberta Frontier, 1890-1929," *Frontiers,* II (1977), 37-44.

STAMP, R.M., "Teaching Girls Their 'God Given Place in Life:' The Introduction of Home Economics in the Schools," *Atlantis,* II (1977), 18-34.

STODDART, JENNIFER and STRONG-BOAG, VERONICA, "...And Things Were Going Wrong at Home," *Atlantis,* I (1975) 38-44.

STRONG-BOAG, VERONICA, "Working Women and the State: The Case of Canada, 1889-1945," *Atlantis,* VI (1981), 1-10.

TROFIMENKOFF, SUSAN M., "Henri Bourassa and 'The Women Question,'" *Journal of Canadian Studies,* X, (1975), 3-11.

_____, "One Hundred and Two Muffled Voices: Canada's Industrial Women in the 1880's," *Atlantis,* III (1977), 66-82.

INDEX